W9-DJE-691

Urban Myths about
LEARNING AND EDUCATION

Urban Myths about
LEARNING AND EDUCATION

PEDRO DE BRUYCKERE
Arteveldehogeschool, Gent and Antwerp University,
Antwerp, Belgium

PAUL A. KIRSCHNER
Open University of The Netherlands, Heerlen,
The Netherlands

CASPER D. HULSHOF
Utrecht University
Utrecht, The Netherlands

AMSTERDAM • BOSTON • HEIDELBERG • LONDON
NEW YORK • OXFORD • PARIS • SAN DIEGO
SAN FRANCISCO • SINGAPORE • SYDNEY • TOKYO
Academic Press is an imprint of Elsevier

Academic Press is an imprint of Elsevier
32 Jamestown Road, London NW1 7BY, UK
525 B Street, Suite 1800, San Diego, CA 92101-4495, USA
225 Wyman Street, Waltham, MA 02451, USA
The Boulevard, Langford Lane, Kidlington, Oxford OX5 1GB, UK

Copyright © 2015 Elsevier Inc. All rights reserved.

No part of this publication may be reproduced or transmitted in any form or by any means, electronic or mechanical, including photocopying, recording, or any information storage and retrieval system, without permission in writing from the publisher. Details on how to seek permission, further information about the Publisher's permissions policies and our arrangements with organizations such as the Copyright Clearance Center and the Copyright Licensing Agency, can be found at our website: www.elsevier.com/permissions.

This book and the individual contributions contained in it are protected under copyright by the Publisher (other than as may be noted herein).

Notices
Knowledge and best practice in this field are constantly changing. As new research and experience broaden our understanding, changes in research methods, professional practices, or medical treatment may become necessary.

Practitioners and researchers must always rely on their own experience and knowledge in evaluating and using any information, methods, compounds, or experiments described herein. In using such information or methods they should be mindful of their own safety and the safety of others, including parties for whom they have a professional responsibility.

To the fullest extent of the law, neither the Publisher nor the authors, contributors, or editors, assume any liability for any injury and/or damage to persons or property as a matter of products liability, negligence or otherwise, or from any use or operation of any methods, products, instructions, or ideas contained in the material herein.

ISBN: 978-0-12-801537-7

British Library Cataloguing-in-Publication Data
A catalogue record for this book is available from the British Library

Library of Congress Cataloging-in-Publication Data
A catalog record for this book is available from the Library of Congress

For information on all Academic Press publications
visit our website at http://store.elsevier.com/

Typeset by MPS Limited, Chennai, India
www.adi-mps.com

Printed and bound in the United States of America

Working together
to grow libraries in
developing countries

www.elsevier.com • www.bookaid.org

CONTENTS

PREFACE

In this book, the most common popular myths relating to learning and education are discussed with respect to whether there is any truth in the myth and what good educational and psychological research has to say about them. Examples of such myths range from learning styles to neuromyths such as left brain/right brain and brain-training programs, how large or small classes and schools should be, and explanations for why schools change. This book is written in a concise, humorous and accessible style, but at the same time based on an extensive scientific review of relevant empirical research. By the way, did you know that there are no pyramids in the work of Maslow and that the US National Training Laboratories (NTL) have no data to back up Dales' learning pyramid?

Not only does the book debunk most of these urban legends in education, it also discloses some interesting facts about learning and education that do have a proven effect. This book is neither progressive nor conservative; it only attempts to get the facts straight and present them in a way that those involved in teaching and education can understand and use.

The book consists of four main content-based sections (i.e. groups of chapters), with each chapter examining a particular genre of myth. The four content-based sections are: "Myths about learning", "Neuromyths", "Myths about technology and education" and "Myths about educational policy". A fifth and final section, "Myth persistence and myth busting", discusses why these myths are so persistent (i.e. nearly impossible to eradicate) and possible strategies to combat them.

Besides the basic "need to know" text, throughout the book, there are also "info-clouds" with "nice to know" information adding background material, additional facts and anecdotes.

Many teachers do good work, but all too often on the basis of incorrect theories.
Pedro De Bruyckere, Paul A. Kirschner & Casper Hulshof

Thus science must begin with myths, and with the criticism of myths; neither with the collection of observations, nor with the invention of experiments, but with the critical discussion of myths, and of magical techniques and practices.
Karl Popper, 2002, Conjectures and refutations:
The growth of scientific knowledge

"But the Emperor has nothing at all on!" said a little child.
"Listen to the voice of innocence!" exclaimed his father; and what the child had said was whispered from one to another.
"But he has nothing at all on!" at last cried out all the people.
Hans Christian Andersen, 1837, The emperor's new clothes

In religion and politics, people's beliefs and convictions are in almost every case gotten at second-hand, and without examination, from authorities who have not themselves examined the questions at issue, but have taken them at second-hand from other non-examiners, whose opinions about them were not worth a brass farthing.
Mark Twain/Samuel Langhorne Clemens, 1959,
Autobiography of Mark Twain

No amount of belief makes something a fact.
James Randi— retired stage magician and scientific skeptic

ACKNOWLEDGMENTS

This book — and its Dutch predecessor—could not have been written without the critical help of many people. For this reason, we would like to thank (in no particular order) Amber Walraven, Jeroen Janssen, Jeroen van Merriënboer, John Sweller, Dick Clark, Frederik Anseel, Stijn Dhert, Wouter Duyck, Bert Smits, Tommy Opgehaffen, Erwin Taets, Martin Valcke, Dimo Kavadias, Dirk Terryn, Elke Struyf, Fredo Fredonis and the GentM-mob, Patrick Vermeren, Daniel Willingham and Donald Clark.

Strangely enough, this book was a real "Twitter-work". Not only did the three authors first meet each other via this medium, but it was also later the channel for much of the input exchanged and received. If anyone still doubts that technology can assist knowledge creation, we are now in a position to assure them that it does!

We dedicate this book to the people who still help us to learn every day.

Pedro thanks Helena, Clement, Emile and Remi.

Paul thanks Catherine, Femke, Jesse, Mara and Aron for really appreciating why good education is so important.

Caspar thanks Petra, Myrthe, Benthe and Jesse for the much-needed distraction.

CHAPTER 1

The Big Clear-Out

Contents

We all like to believe and we all seem to hate uncertainty. We believe in many things and different people believe in different things. Many people, for example, believe in a god or an omniscient, omnipotent and all-powerful being who guides everything (the Dutch have the saying: "Believing is what you do in a church"), although this could be Yahweh, the holy trinity, Buddha, Mohammed or the flying spaghetti monster. Others – humanists – believe in and emphasize the value and agency of human beings, individually and collectively; a perspective that affirms some notion of a "human nature". Independent of this, we certainly seem to believe in education. We want our children to have the best, and nowhere more so than at school. This is why we are constantly looking for new insights and new possibilities, in the hope that they will improve on existing practice, so that our children and young people can learn even more effectively. But the problem is that just as in religion, different people have different beliefs and there are also different "religions", belief systems or ideologies within the field of education that sometimes simply disagree, but often fight with each other to the extent that one could speak of a holy war or crusade.

Imagine that tomorrow a new (and fictive) online tool is launched named Gomba. Gomba is a website where you can easily share simple handwritten notes. It sounds good and works well. As a result, it soon goes viral. Before you know it, everyone is Gomba crazy. Not quite the

Urban Myths about Learning and Education
DOI: http://dx.doi.org/10.1016/B978-0-12-801537-7.00001-9

© 2015 Elsevier Inc.
All rights reserved.

size of Snapchat or Instagram, but not bad for a start-up. What happens next? All of a sudden we start seeing blogs with titles like "16 ways to use Gomba in the classroom" or "How Gomba will change education".

We have to admit that we also like to get involved in this kind of thing; well, sometimes at least. But this is not always as positive as it looks. There seems to be an undercurrent to all this activity, almost a kind of panic (Bennett, Maton, & Kervin refer to it as an academic form of *moral panic*). In education, we have the feeling that we are finding it harder and harder to reach our public, our pupils. That is why we are so feverishly interested in anything new on the market that might help. Every new tool seems like a possible solution, although sometimes we really don't know what the problem is or even if there is one.

But this is not just about media and resources, as was the case in the past with school television and programmed learning. It is also about our educational and pedagogic approach. In fact, it goes to the very heart of our complete vision about education.

In the meantime, we have regrettably become saddled with a multiplicity of tools, methods, approaches, theories and pseudotheories, many of which have been shown by science to be wrong or, at best, only partially effective.

The purpose of this book is to initiate a big clear-out, a kind of "spring cleaning" for teachers, schools, parents, boards of education, educational policy-makers and politicians; in short, everyone involved in the educational process. We want to present an overview of the most important myths, the virtues of which have never been proven or which — in some cases — are just nonsense. These are pseudotheories (in other times we would have called them "snake oil") that we come across almost daily in books and newspapers, on radio and television, in popular "scientific" magazines for teachers and the general population, in training programs for teachers and — worst of all — in the classroom.

Sometimes the reality of the situation will be more nuanced. Not everything we discuss in the book is 100% a myth or completely wrong. When this is the case, we will attempt to put the theory into a proper perspective, so that you, the reader, can better understand how it works and know which elements to avoid and which to keep. For example, policy-makers like to argue that it has been scientifically proven that the size of the class has no effect on children's learning, while teachers argue the exact opposite. In relative terms, both viewpoints may be true, but there is enough research that suggest that both sides are right only in certain respects and in certain circumstances. It is above all noteworthy that you never hear much about the reasons why large class size seemingly makes so little or so much difference. And if you do, then they are always the same old hackneyed reasons, more often than not based upon anecdotes, one person's experiences, how it used to be, and so on. And why do you hear so little about these reasons? Probably because they would make clear why you might prefer not to have such large classes after all.

Some of the arguments put forward in this book will hurt. We speak from experience. We can well remember the moment when we came to the conclusion that learning styles are not fixed, usually not even measurable, and consequently that they have no added value in the class. To be honest, we felt pretty stupid when we realized not only that we believed in those things but also that we had been peddling the same false myths to our own students, often with great enthusiasm and commitment. It is painful to have to admit that you were wrong. So at this point we would like to express our apologies to the generations of students on whom we inflicted these faulty theories, and also to the teachers who will now have to learn this same bitter lesson. Let's just call it progressive insight.

The biggest problem with educational myths is that people who believe in them will often be able to find enough evidence in their day-to-day practice to support their beliefs. The reason for this is simple. It is like when you buy a new car: suddenly you see that same make of car everywhere you go, often in the same model and color. But these cars were all on the road before you bought yours; it is just that you did not notice them until now. In the same way, we are quick to recognize "indications" for the ideas we believe in. The experiences that don't support our case we simply ignore, unconsciously or not. Michael Shermer gives three reasons:

- *patternicity*: a tendency to find meaningful patterns in random noise
- *confirmation bias*: the seeking and finding of confirmatory evidence for what we already believe
- *hindsight bias*: tailoring after-the-fact explanations to what we already know happened.

As John Hattie so astutely noted when talking about people who had trouble with his epic work *Visible learning*,

The messages [from my book] have been questioned, labeled provocative, liked, and dismissed, among other more positive reactions. The typical comments are: "the results do not mirror my experience", "why have you not highlighted my pet method", "you are talking about averages and I'm not average", and "you are missing the nuances of what happens in classrooms". (Preface, p. viii)

This is why in the pages that follow we will systematically refer to scientific sources that are based on something more than anecdotal experience, which, almost by definition, is colored. We will also offer opinions based on metastudies, when these are available. These are the studies that bring together the results of different research projects in the same field.

Because in the past we have also believed in many of the theories that will be called into doubt in the following pages, we are the very last people to criticize teachers, principals, parents and even policy-makers for also believing and preaching the same things. However, there is one aspect of this situation for which we have much less understanding: some of these myths have reappeared in recent textbooks and sometimes even in research reports. These must be eliminated. We hope that this will be one of the contributions made by this book.

It is not easy to change things in education. But it is our conviction that these myths are one of the major factors standing in the way of innovation and renewal. If you introduce something new, it is often possible to achieve initial success. But initial success is, in itself, not enough. We know of three reasons why success can be and often is achieved, although actual implementation and use will be disappointing. The first is that there is a great difference between an innovation project and an implementation of the innovation for education (the project aimed the intervention's ultimate implementation). An innovation project is usually supported by a specific type of team leader (often the researcher), provides extra support and guidance for the teachers (in the form of training, time and money), often uses teachers who volunteer and thus are highly motivated, and so forth. An implementation usually does not have the benefit of these "extras", and thus success in the project often does not automatically generalize to success at the institutional level. Kirschner, Stoyanov, Wopereis, and Hendriks stated that extra care and resources are needed to make the jump to scalability, generalizability, temporal flexibility and financial sustainability.

The second reason is that much of the research that confirms that an innovation works is often poor. Those carrying out the project often make the mistakes of not presenting explicit and testable goals (i.e., what constitutes success, how will it be measured, etc.; see Willingham (2012) about how to tell good science from bad), involving respondents/teachers who are not random but are chosen by someone such as the principal or volunteer (a sure sign that they are not the "average" teacher and thus that the average teacher will not have the same mindset), and having no real control groups with which to compare the intervention (knowing that something led to learning does not ensure that it is more effective or efficient than "normal" good instruction). A good example of this last aspect is a study often cited to show that problem-based learning (PBL) works and that generation of prior knowledge is important (some go as far as citing it to show that PBL works better than instruction). One group (the intervention group) spent time generating all that they could remember about the topic to be learned while the other group (the so-called control group) generated prior knowledge about a completely different topic not relevant to what was to be learned. And ... Abracadabra! Hey-presto! ... the intervention achieved better learning. The real question, however, was whether the intervention group would have learned more than a group that had spent an equal amount of time listening to a good lecture on the relevant topic, or who had seen a good instructional video, and so on. Knowing that something may have worked is not the same as knowing that the intervention is an innovation that makes learning more effective, efficient or enjoyable.

The third reason is what is referred to as the Hawthorne effect, and it is the effect you experience because you are trying something new. You are more focused, possibly more enthusiastic; perhaps your pupils are curious or even surprised. These are all explanations for the temporary positive effect. But what happens once the shine has worn off the new idea? When its novelty value has disappeared? This is when disappointment sets in, so that you often return to the "old" ways, more frustrated than ever before, and determined not to try anything new ever again!

The Hawthorne Effect Actually Has the Wrong Name

The name of this phenomenon is derived from research carried out at the Hawthorne factory of the Western Electric Company in the 1950s (Figure 1). The researchers looked at the effect of rewards and working conditions on the functioning of the factory's employees; for example, whether they performed better in a particular kind of lighting. For many years it was assumed that the resulting positive effect came primarily from the fact that people were involved in an experiment, rather than as the result of a specific approach to environmental and other factors. Hence the effect was named after the place where this first experiment had taken

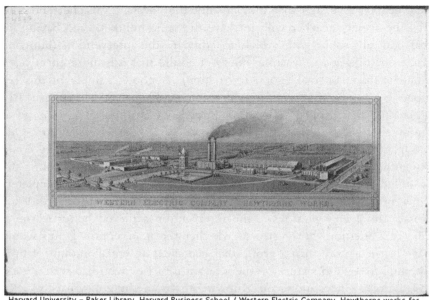

Harvard University – Baker Library, Harvard Business School / Western Electric Company. Hawthorne works for the manufacture of power apparatus. [Chicago, Ill.] : Western Electric Company, [19--]. Baker Library, Harvard Business School

Figure 1 An aerial view of the Hawthorne Works plant circa 1920, from their pamphlet "Hawthorne works for the manufacture of power apparatus" (1 January 1920). *Source: Western Electric Company, Chicago, IL. <http://pds.lib.harvard.edu/pds/view/7188058?n54> (No longer under copyright).*

place: Hawthorne. It was only years later, when the original Hawthorne data were reanalyzed, that it was realized that the effect did not come from the fact of the experiment itself and that the positive effects could actually be attributed to the manipulation of the independent variables.

Sources

Izawa, M. R., French, M. D., & Hedge, A. (2011). Shining new light on the Hawthorne illumination experiments. *Human Factors, 53*, 528−547.

Jones, S. R. G. (1992). Was there a Hawthorne effect? *American Journal of Sociology, 98*, 451−468.

In this book, we have tried to deal with a number of theories and applications that are not correct, need to be nuanced, are uncertain or have not had a positive effect. For example, some of the cognitive theory of Piaget about how the thinking of children develops is now largely obsolete (although his thoughts on assimilation and accommodation fit nicely with schema theory), but it still has a great influence on discovery learning. Moreover, it seems that taking account of the Piaget classification in the classroom does indeed result in a lasting learning effect. The reason for this is that we learn most effectively when we learn concretely. Most of what we remember is concrete and linked to the situation. That is why it is so difficult to apply insights that you have learned in one situation in a different situation. If you want to teach someone something new, it is therefore best to start with concrete examples, which you can gradually build up to a more abstract level as time passes. This works — and so Piaget will not have a chapter in our book.

But if Piaget is a good example of a theory that needs to be nuanced, some of the other theories we deal with in the book seem to us to be absolutely dangerous. Almost every time some new information and communications technology (ICT) application needs to be introduced into the education system, we are reminded by policy-makers and initiators that today's young people are "digital natives" and as such have developed certain knowledge, skills and attitudes that make the new application perfectly suited to them (we will discuss this later in the book, in Section 5.3). Unfortunately, this idea has been rejected by almost every serious study that has looked into the matter, including in an educational context. Basing a policy on an incorrect assumption means that many new initiatives have the potential to go wrong almost from the start.

SOMETIMES WE ARE LAZY

We human beings are creatures of habit. We don't like change; it seems so difficult. In reality, we are often just too lazy to change. This can sometimes apply to scientists as well. In our opinion, this is why some education myths are still perpetuated, even in scientific works. Here is a spectacular example, perhaps the most spectacular of all.

One of the most famous pyramids in science is the Maslow pyramid, first formulated in 1943 by Abraham Maslow. If you have ever read or heard about this pyramid, you will probably be familiar with a variant of the drawing shown in Figure 2.

Pop down to your local library and have a look in any of the many books and articles written by Maslow. What you will not find is . . . a pyramid! Maslow certainly described a hierarchy but he never framed it in the famous pyramid form. This may seem to be just a detail. Perhaps. But people continue to talk about a pyramid in five layers, even though in 1970 Maslow extended his hierarchy to seven elements, by adding "knowing and understanding" and "aesthetics".

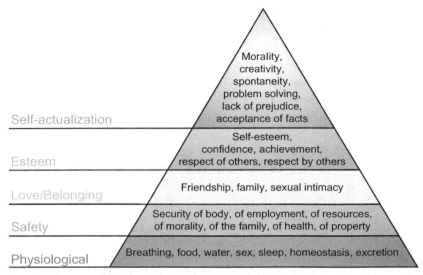

Figure 2 Diagram of Maslow's hierarchy of needs. *Source: <http://commons.wikimedia.org/wiki/File%3AMaslow's_hierarchy_of_needs.svg> (by J. Finkelstein, released under the terms of the GFDL).*

And is his pyramid actually right? In 1962 Maslow expressed his surprise that people had seemingly accepted his findings without question or criticism:

My motivation theory was published 20 years ago, and in all that time nobody repeated it, or tested it, or really analyzed or criticized it. They just used it, swallowed it whole, with only the most minor modifications.

To be honest, not much has changed during the past 50 years. You will still frequently come across the pyramid in educational literature, whether it is relevant or not — along with another pyramid that will be discussed later. But in the meantime, we have become wiser. And what transpires? The theory is flawed. For example, someone who has health problems can simultaneously feel the need for beauty and wisdom.

So why do we keep on using the pyramid? Because we like to keep things clear and neatly separated from each other, and the pyramid does this with its pleasingly transparent hierarchy. But in this way, the pyramid also implies that what is at the bottom is the most important, the basis, and that only very few people will ever reach the top.

The representation of the hierarchy as a pyramid is therefore a theory in itself, with its own assumptions and hypotheses. Maslow thought that people would use his findings to conduct further experiments of their own, but that did not happen before his death in 1970. Why? Because sometimes we are too lazy to check whether something is actually right — or not. This kind of laziness can be dangerous.

After Maslow's death in 1970, researchers did undertake a more detailed investigation, with attitude-based surveys and field studies testing out the hierarchy of needs, and what did they discover? As Gerard Hodgkinson states in an interview with the BBC on the topic, "The actual structure of motivation doesn't fit the theory. And that led to a lot of discussion and debate, and new theories evolved as a consequence". But still we keep on mentioning the non-existent and unproven pyramid.

THINKING IN BOXES

We are all against it but we all keep on doing it: putting people in pigeonholes. Numerous examples of this kind of "thinking in boxes" will be taken to task in the following pages. For instance, we have already mentioned learning styles, and sometimes we are quick to forget that there are both rational people with a left brain and creative spirits with a right brain, and that all of us have a whole brain!

The most fundamental of all the boxes into which we as educators put people is possibly the *gender box*. The available data make it easy to investigate the respective influence of boys and girls, but even here there are myths at play. For example, we will be looking at the question of whether boys and girls have different kinds of brains, and whether boys really are better at mathematics.

So what is the effect of thinking in boxes? Research by Cimpian, Mu, and Erickson suggests that it is not positive, for either boys or girls. They carried out two experiments on four- and seven-year-olds to see what the influence would be on the performance of a task, when the participating children were told that the successful completion of the task was dependent on being part of a particular social group; for example, "Boys usually do this task better than girls". What transpired? If you announce that one of the groups (boys) is better suited to a particular task, then both groups (boys *and* girls) actually perform worse. It is also possible that this applies for the social group "young people" as a whole.

OUR VISION OF EDUCATION?

Our intention is not to write a book that opposes or counteracts innovation. Quite the opposite! Although we are opposed to innovation for the sake of innovation, we are fervent supporters of finding ways to help learners to learn more quickly (i.e., making the learning process more efficient) and learn more things (i.e., making the learning process more effective), and to make learning more fun (i.e., making the learning process more enjoyable) as long as reaching any one of the three is not to the detriment of the other two. We call this our 3Es: effective, efficient and enjoyable. You could say that we want to make the 3Rs (reading, writing and 'rithmetic) and the other topics in school more 3E! And it is our conviction that achieving these 3Es for learning will also help to make the teaching process more effective, efficient and enjoyable for the teacher.

It is a waste of time to try and divide the educational world into "more progressive" and "more traditional" tendencies, although many gurus make a lot of money and get a lot of airtime doing this. Margaret Brown published an overview of research studies that had attempted to discover whether the progressive or the traditional approach is more beneficial. Her first problem was to define what exactly is meant by these terms. But leaving this to one side, Brown found no data to suggest that it is a good thing to opt for either an extremely progressive or an extremely traditional style of education. She concluded that the antagonism between these two extremes lives largely in the minds of educational thinkers at policy level, while the most important thing for teachers in the classroom is to find the right balance between the different methods of approach.

Nor is it our intention either to confirm or to undermine specific learning or knowledge theories.

The current paradigm in the educational policy of many countries, states and districts is what is called social constructivism. This paradigm is primarily concerned with the ways in which people construct knowledge themselves (constructivism) in collaboration with others (social). Central to this philosophy (the use of the word philosophy and not pedagogy is intentional; constructivism is a philosophy which states that we all construct our own realities based upon our prior experience and is not a pedagogy) is the belief that we must place children in a learning environment where they can actively acquire knowledge for themselves. Because we all have our own subjective perception of reality, it is also crucial that children should be able to work together, so that they can arrive at a shared truth. Group work, problem-directed education, the importance of authentic tasks and situations: these are all important elements of this social constructivist tendency.

Of course, there are other paradigms, of which behaviorism and cognitivism are probably the best known. In behaviorism, the influence of the importance of objectives is still strong. This influence is most noticeable in the use of punishments (in particular, ignoring children) and rewards. The theory is sometimes negatively associated with the so-called "drill-and-practice" method, which is still probably the best way to learn the alphabet, multiplication tables, and so on. Even so, the behaviorist approach — for example, for "maintaining order in the classroom" through a system of targeted rewards — can be very effective. Cognitive thinking has taught us the importance of differentiation, because it made us think about not only *what* people learn, but also *how* they learn it. Some of the earliest cognitive insights continue to be valid to this day, but others will be refuted later in the book.

You may already sense where we are coming from: we are fairly critical of all three of the above-mentioned theories. If we had to choose between them, we would probably align ourselves with the neocognitivists. Cognitive psychology, supported by new neuroscientific findings, is constantly providing new insights for education that can help us in concrete terms, although the neurosciences are often the spawning grounds of new myths.

Having said this, it is probable that every educational theory — either in whole or in part — will receive something of a pasting in pages that follow. People who know us will also know that we have invested much time and effort in recent years introducing new technologies and methods into the education system. That is why we are now so critical in our approach to this field.

If, when you have read the book, you want to accuse us of ill-will or vindictiveness, then honesty compels us to admit that you might have a point (here or there, at least). We must confess that occasionally during our writing we experienced the same devilish delight as the little boy who was able to shout to the entire crowd that the emperor was not wearing any clothes.

BRASS FARTHING

Mark Twain, speaking about religion and politics, lamented, "In religion and politics, people's beliefs and convictions are in almost every case gotten at second-hand, and without examination, from authorities who have not themselves examined the questions at issue, but have taken them at second-hand from other non-examiners, whose opinions about them were not worth a brass farthing".

If we replace "religion and politics" with "education and educational policy", we see the sorry state that we are in, and why. We hear many claims about what is wrong with education, what is needed to correct those wrongs, and why this is the case. Many of the claims, regrettably, are based on belief rather than science and have become tenacious urban legends used by instructional designers, curriculum reformers, politicians, school administrators and advisory groups, all vying for position to show how innovative and up-to-date they can be.

CREAM CAKES

The Woody Allen film *Sleeper* is set in the year 2173. In the film, scientists are amazed that people living at the end of the twentieth century thought that eating cream cakes was bad for your health, whereas twenty-second century technology saw only their exceptional nutritional value.

It is equally possible that someone who stumbles across this book at a virtual jumble sale in the year 2035 will smile and ask how the authors could have possibly been so naive. Since we do not have a crystal ball, we cannot predict which of our ideas will turn out to be true. But while we are all waiting to find out, it is probably advisable not to eat too many cream cakes!

DEAR EXPERTS...

This is a book for everyone involved in and concerned about education. It has not been written specifically for experts. We have deliberately chosen an easy and accessible style, with references to the professional literature being placed at the end of each section. We have done this to make the book as readable as possible. Having said that, a great deal has already been written about the different themes we explore. We do not pretend that our book is complete, but we have tried to offer readers the nuances we think are necessary to understand the important arguments that support our case, as outlined in the many books and articles we have read.

The book has been proofread by a number of researchers. Any inaccuracies or errors that remain are entirely our fault, not theirs. Naturally, we hope that the number of any such mistakes will be minimal and no worse, for example, than the absence of the full stop (period) at the end of this sentence

Myth :-\	Nuanced :-|	Unproven :-?
The statement is untrue or almost completely untrue or there is no proof.	The theme is still a subject of discussion and science has not yet provided conclusive evidence.	We — and we emphasize "we" — found no scientific evidence during the writing of this book.

A WHO'S WHO OF THE WORLD OF EDUCATION RESEARCH

When reading this book, you will probably come across the names of all different kinds of experts and specialists who you never knew were engaged in the field of educational research. For this reason, you may find the following summary useful. Be aware, however, that this summary is far from complete: in one way or another, we are all involved in education.

- **Educational theorists:** Educational theory is the science that seeks to describe the processes of learning, teaching and development in education and the world of business. These scientists therefore contribute towards the improvement of the education system and training programs. When you read about "learning effects" later in the book, the educational theorists will usually be involved in some way.

- **Pedagogues:** Pedagogy is the science and art of education; practitioners of pedagogy are called pedagogues (translated literally from the Greek meaning "to lead the child", originally used to denote someone who escorted a child to school). It studies how adults (parents, educators, teachers) bring up children and young people with a particular purpose in mind. More specifically for the world of education, pedagogics studies educational methods, including the objectives that are set and the manner in which those objectives can best be achieved. Pedagogues are generally more involved with the "why" of education than are the educational theorists (also see ethicists).

- Highly relevant, but also relatively rare, are the pedagogues who specialize in **comparative pedagogy**. They are experts in the comparison of educational systems in different countries or regions. At the present time, this is often done in the media, by organizations such as the Organization for Economic Cooperation and Development (OECD: Program for International Student Assessment — PISA) or International Association for the Evaluation of Educational Achievement

(IEA: Trends in International Mathematics and Science Study — TIMSS), or educational sociologists.

- **Instructional designers:** These are experts in designing and developing learning experiences. Instructional design is, as Merrill and colleagues (1996) state, the practice of creating "instructional experiences which make the acquisition of knowledge and skill more efficient, effective, and appealing".
- **Educational technologists:** These are experts who try to analyze, design, develop, implement and evaluate process and tools to enhance learning.

But we are not finished yet! There are also:

- **Educational sociologists** study the structures and processes that determine the educational opportunities of young people.
- **Economists** also have a voice in the discussion, since education inevitably has an economic impact. Also note that as an economic organization the Organisation for Economic Co-operation and Development (OECD) has a big influence on educational thinking through its Programme for International Student Assessment (PISA) studies.
- **Ethicists** and **moral scientists** belong to the branch of philosophy and engage in critical reflection about the rights and wrongs of particular courses of action. In general terms, ethics attempt to determine the criteria that will allow an assessment of right and wrong to be made, so that the motives and consequences of these actions can be evaluated.
- **Cognitive psychologists** are part of the wider branch of psychology and look at the way people learn. To do this, they focus on the physical processes involved in matters such as understanding, knowledge, memory, information recall, information processing and problem-solving. Their work plays an important role in this book.
- **Learning scientists** work in the interdisciplinary field of the learning sciences, investigating "fundamental inquiries on how people learn alone and in collaborative ways, as well as on how learning may be effectively facilitated by different social and organizational settings and new learning environment designs" (Mission Statement of the International Society of the Learning Sciences).
- **Neuroscientists** work in the field of neuroscience or any of its related subfields. Neuroscience, while very broad in nature, dealing with all aspects of the nervous system, is for education primarily limited to the study of the brain, the connections between different areas of the brain

and how these relate to learning. Techniques such as neuroimaging (magnetic resonance imaging), electroencephalography and deep brain stimulation are often used for this.

In discussions about education, it is unrealistic to expect that scientists will ever have the final say. In the Western world, it is the politicians who make the final decisions, based on the outcomes of research and social debate. Consequently, a whole variety of other people is also involved in this discussion process, including the different policy-makers (not only politicians and the political umbrella organizations, but also the heads of universities, university colleges and other academic groups), head teachers, teachers, teachers' representatives (including unions), publishers, parents, parent groups and — last but not least — the poor old pupils and students!

REFERENCES

Bennett, S., Maton, K., & Kervin, L. (2008). The "digital natives" debate: A critical review of the evidence. *British Journal of Educational Technology, 39,* 775–786.

Brown, M. (2012). Traditional versus progressive education. In P. Adey, & J. Dillon (Eds.), *Bad education* (pp. 95–110). Maidenhead, UK: Open University Press.

Cimpian, A., Mu, Y., & Erickson, L. C. (2012). Who is good at this game? Linking an activity to a social category undermines children's achievement. *Psychological Science, 23,* 533–541.

Clark, D. (2012, April 27). Maslow. Retrieved June 30, 2014, from <http://donaldclarkplanb.blogspot.be/2012/04/maslow-1908-1970-hierarchy-of-needs-5.html>.

Eaton, S. E. (2012). *Maslow's hierarchy of needs.* <http://drsaraheaton.wordpress.com/2012/08/04/maslows-hierarchy-of-needs>

Hattie, J. A. (2009). *Visible learning: A synthesis of over 800 meta-analyses relating to achievement.* London: Routledge, Taylor & Francis Group.

Johnson, S. (2005). *Everything bad is good for you: How today's popular culture is actually making us smarter.* Grand Rapids, MI: Riverhead Publishing.

Kirschner, P. A., Stoyanov, S., Wopereis, I., & Hendriks, M. (2005). *Determinants for failure and success of innovation projects: The road to sustainable educational innovation.* Heerlen, The Netherlands: Open Universiteit.

Kremer, W., & Hammond, C. (2013, August 31). The pretty pyramid that beguiled business. Retrieved June 8, 2014, from <http://www.bbc.com/news/magazine-23902918>.

Maslow, A. H. (1943). A theory of human motivation. *Psychological Review, 50,* 370–396.

Maslow, A. H. (1954). *Motivation and personality.* New York: Harper & Brothers.

Maslow, A. (1971). *The farther reaches of human nature.* New York: Viking Press.

Maslow, A. H., Lowry, R., & Maslow, B. G. (1979). *The journals of A. H. Maslow.* Monterey, CA: Brooks/Cole.

Merrill, M. D., Drake, L., Lacy, M. J., Pratt, J., & ID2 Research Group (1996). Reclaiming instructional design. *Educational Technology, 36*(5), 5–7.

Seels, B., & Richey, R. (1994). *Instructional technology: The definition and domains of the field.* Washington, DC: Association for Educational Communications and Technology.

Shermer, M. (2011). *The believing brain: From ghosts to gods to politics and conspiracies — How we construct beliefs and reinforce them as truths.* New York: Times Books.

Steinberg, L., & Morris, A. S. (2001). Adolescent development. *Annual Review of Psychology, 52,* 83—110.

Tay, L., & Diener, E. (2011). Needs and subjective well-being around the world. *Journal of Personality and Social Psychology, 101,* 354—365.

Twain, M. (2010). *Autobiography of Mark Twain, the authentic original version.* Lexington, KY: Seven Treasures (Original work published 1910).

Wahba, A., & Bridgewell, L. (1976). Maslow reconsidered: A review of research on the need hierarchy theory. *Organizational Behavior and Human Performance, 15,* 212—240.

Willingham, D. T. (2009). *Why don't students like school? A cognitive scientist answers questions about how the mind works and what it means for the classroom.* San Francisco, CA: Jossey-Bass.

Willingham, D. T. (2012). *When can you trust the experts? How to tell good science from bad in education.* San Francisco, CA: Jossey-Bass.

CHAPTER 2

Myths about Learning

Contents

© 2015 Elsevier Inc.
All rights reserved.

Introduction

We go to school to learn, but what exactly do we know about learning and how do we make use of what we know in daily practice? In this first series of myths we will look at a number of popular (in other words, stubborn and very persistent) thoughts about how we learn — or don't. Two different aspects come to light in this discussion. The first relates to "theories" surrounding learning. An example of this is all that has been written about learning styles, work forms, and knowledge versus problem solving. We will discuss questions such as: Are there different styles of learning? Are there different work forms that allow us to learn more or less? We will also look at what we need to learn: now that we can look everything up on the Internet, is all that knowledge really necessary? Is solving problems the best way to learn to solve problems? These different aspects will be discussed specifically in the first dozen myths or so.

The second relates to paradigms that people (researchers and teachers, but also politicians, administrators, advisers, etc.) use to justify their actions. The three most prevalent paradigms are the behaviorist paradigm, the cognitivist (also often called the instructivist) paradigm and the constructivist (and its off-shoots social-constructivist and constructionist) paradigm. We take the time to discuss this here, before going to the myths. There are three reasons why we oppose this approach.

The first reason is because this way of thinking tends to separate and compartmentalize people into camps where one is for or against and as such stimulates dogmas and academic wars. This is the last thing that education needs. The second reason is that, strangely enough, at least two of the three schools of thinking are so closely related to each other that differentiation is absurd. If we look at cognitivism and constructivism closely we see the following:

- Constructivism is a philosophy of the world which states that we all construct our own reality based on our own knowledge and experiences. A cognitivist — if such a thing actually existed — would say that each individual constructs her or his own schema based on prior knowledge and new learning experiences.
- Early constructivists couched their educational theories in terms of terminology and theorists such as situated cognition (Brown, Collins, & Duguid), cognitive apprenticeship (Collins) and cognitive flexibility (Spiro, Coulson, Feltovich, & Anderson).
- The "gurus" of constructivism such as Jean Piaget (i.e., assimilation and accommodation = accretion, tuning and restructuring) and Vygotsky (e.g., cognitive development results from an internalization of language) were originally seen as cognitive psychologists (see Vygotsky).

Finally, thinking that one paradigm is sufficient for effective, efficient and enjoyable learning is as absurd as thinking that there is one best way of cooking. A top chef makes use of a wide variety of techniques (e.g., baking, frying, freezing), tools (e.g., paring knife, steam oven, blender) and ingredients (e.g., vegetables, meats, herbs, spices) to create meals that fit both the eater and the occasion. An educational designer or teacher should, in our opinion, work as and be considered to be a top educational chef and should not be limited by artificial limits on her or his art and science.

In what you are about to read, those readers who are of bad faith (i.e., those who think that the word instruction is a curse) might find a reason or two that seems to argue against change or in favor of boring lessons, without taking due account of the differences between pupils. Nothing could be further from the truth. As stated, a good teacher works with a carefully considered mix of different work forms, based on a number of different elements. In part, this can be a matter of personal preference, but it is also important to take account of the initial starting point of the pupils. We will show that styles of learning do not exist, but this is not to say that pupils do not differ in terms of interests. We will also question the appropriateness of particular work forms, but this is not to say that they are not excellent in other situations and for other purposes. A real education professional knows that there is no such thing as a "one-size-fits-all" approach, not for learners and not for groups of learners.

REFERENCES

Anderson, R. C. (1977). The notion of schemata and the educational enterprise. In R. C. Anderson, R. J. Spiro, & W. E. Montague (Eds.), *Schooling and the acquisition of knowledge* (pp. 415–431). Hillsdale, NJ: Lawrence Erlbaum Associates.

Brown, J. S., Collins, A., & Duguid, P. (1989). Situated cognition and the culture of learning. *Educational Researcher, 18*(1), 32–42.

Collins, A. (1988). *Cognitive apprenticeship and instructional technology.* Cambridge, MA: BBN Labs (Technical Report No. 6899).

Rumelhart, D. E., & Norman, D. A. (1978). Accretion, tuning, and restructuring: Three modes of learning. In J. W. C. R. Klatzy (Ed.), *Semantic factors in cognition* (pp. 37–53). Hillsdale, NJ: Erlbaum.

Spiro, R. J., Coulson, R. L., Feltovich, P. J., & Anderson, D. K. (1988). *Cognitive flexibility theory: Advanced knowledge acquisition in ill-structured domains.* Champaign, IL: University of Illinois, Center for the Study of Reading (Technical Report No. 441).

Vygotsky, L. S. (1962). *Thought and language.* Cambridge, MA: MIT Press.

Vygotsky, L. S. (1978). *Mind in society: The development of higher psychological processes.* Cambridge, MA: Harvard University Press.

Vygotsky, L. S. (1987). Thinking and speech. In R. W. Rieber, & A. S. Carton (Eds.), *The collected works of L. S. Vygotsky, Volume 1: Problems of general psychology* (pp. 39–285). New York: Plenum Press (Original work published 1934).

MYTH 1

People Have Different Styles of Learning

People are all different and so we all learn differently. This is a truism that is hard to deny. Because of this, for many teachers it feels intuitively right to say that there are people who prefer to learn visually, while others prefer to learn auditively, and yet others kinesthetically. We all know the type of pupil who needs to have heard everything (i.e., auditive style), who works in stark contrast to the pupil who remembers things by linking them to a movement (i.e., kinesthetic style). Then there are those who prefer verbal methods, who again contrast strongly with those who prefer to think in images.

PROBLEMS?

Is there a problem here, then? The answer to this question is: Yes! And the problem is twofold. First, there is a great difference between the way that someone says he or she prefers to learn and that which actually leads to better learning. Let's go back to food. Nobody (we hope) would dispute, deny or confuse what someone prefers to eat and what is good for them to eat. If that were the case, then there would not be such a prevalence of overweight, obesity and morbid obesity and all of the health problems associated with this in the developed world. Most people prefer foods that are rich (i.e., fatty), sweet and/or salty, and in our society these things are readily available and relatively inexpensive. But fat, salt and sugar are not the best things for us to eat, and the same is true for learning.

In 1982, Clark found in a meta-analysis of studies using learner preference for selecting particular instructional methods that learner preference was typically uncorrelated or negatively correlated with learning and learning outcomes. That is, learners who reported preferring a particular instructional technique typically did not derive any instructional benefit from experiencing it. Frequently, as Clark later explained, so-called *mathemathantic* (from the Greek *mathema*, learning, and *thanatos*, death) effects are found; that is, teaching kills learning when instructional methods match a preferred but unproductive learning style. Giving children candy and soft drinks because they prefer them is an example of bad nutritional practice, just as catering to preferred but often unproductive "learning styles" is an example of bad educational practice.

The second problem deals with the concept of learning styles itself, as Kirschner and van Merriënboer noted. Most so-called learning styles are based on types; they classify people into distinct groups. The assumption that people cluster into distinct groups, however, receives very little support from objective studies (e.g., Druckman & Porter). There are at least three problems with this pigeonholing of learners: Most people do not fit one particular style (i.e., most differences, and especially differences in cognition, between people are gradual rather than nominal); the information used to assign people to styles is often inadequate (i.e., self-report measures are most often used, but the adequacy of such self-reports for assessing learning styles is questionable at best (e.g., Veenman, Prins, & Verheij); and there are so many different styles that it becomes cumbersome to link particular learners to particular styles (Coffield, Moseley, Hall, & Ecclestone described 71 different learning styles, which if dichotomous would produce 2^{71} combinations of learning styles — more combinations of styles than people on Earth).

And if we set all of the difficulties aside, the question would be how to tailor instruction to particular learning styles. This is where the learning styles hypothesis (Pashler, McDaniel, Rohrer, & Bjork) comes into play. For a true learning style, that is where there is a crossover interaction where type A learners learn better with instructional method A, whereas type B learners learn better with instructional method B. Here is an example: van Merriënboer compared a generation method for teaching programming which stresses writing programming code (i.e., impulsive learning style) with a completion method which stresses studying and completing a given code (i.e., reflective learning style). While reflective learners tended to profit more from completion than impulsive learners, completion was superior to generation for both types of learners. Thus, while studies might show interactions between supposed learning styles and specific instructional methods, they have no real practical educational implications since only crossover interactions provide acceptable evidence for learning styles.

A well-known and often used approach is to classify people as thinkers, doers, dreamers and deciders. This last system of categorization is known as the Kolb inventory, the basis of what is called *experiential learning*. Unfortunately, attempts to validate experiential learning and learning styles have not really been successful. In 1994, for example, in a meta-analysis of 101 quantitative studies using Kolb's Learning Style Inventory, Iliff reported low correlations (<0.5) and weak (0.2) to medium (0.5) effect sizes. The conclusion was, thus, that the sizes of these statistics do not meet standards of predictive validity to support using the inventory or experiential methods for teaching or training. Similarly, Ruble and Stout concluded that the Inventory has low test–retest reliability and that there is little or no correlation between factors that should correlate with the classification of learning styles. There are plenty of other such inventories, each invalid in its own different way, which form the basis on which schools, parents, teachers and companies continue to think that if we adapt our education to the style of learning that people use or say that they prefer to use, then they will learn better.

This is a particularly stubborn myth. Rohrer and Pashler summarize it as follows: "The contrast between the enormous popularity of the learning style approach in education and the lack of any credible scientific proof to support its use is both remarkable and disturbing" (p. 117). The question here is: Why?

First off, we like to identify ourselves and others and put ourselves and others into categories or groups. Kurt Vonnegut, in his 1963 book *Cat's cradle*, referred to this as a *granfalloon*; an association or society based on a shared but ultimately fabricated premise. Such categories are used by us to help bring order to our often chaotic environment and give us quick, though often unreliable, ways to understand each other.

Second, this pigeonholing appeals to us because it propagates the idea that each learner should be considered to be "unique", and that the differences between learners should be recognized and attended to. It is a comforting thought that by teaching to different learning styles, "all people have the potential to learn effectively and easily if only instruction is tailored to their individual learning styles" (Pashler et al., p. 107).

Third, and possibly a cynical reason, is that using the concept of learning styles allows both learners and parents to attribute any failure to learn not to themselves but rather to the mismatch of the industrial-age educational system with the specific qualities of the learner. The often heard claim sounds something like, "How can you expect me/my child to learn and score well when I am/(s)he is a holistic learner, visual learner, etc., but the lessons are atomistic, verbal, etc.?" In other words, it is a good way to blame a failure to learn on the teacher's, school's or pedagogy's failure to adopt and make use of teaching methods that do not match an individual's often self-diagnosed learning style.

Finally, according to Tanner, the wide acceptance of learning styles is because they look a lot like the concept of metacognition (i.e., how we think about our own thinking). In her research, Tanner prompted students to self-reflect on how they studied for an examination (and whether they succeeded or failed in their learning) as a way to help them to monitor their own learning and, eventually, learn more effectively for their next exam. She found that having students describe which strategies worked for them and which did not improved their learning for the next exam. Unfortunately, while integrating metacognitive activities into the classroom is supported by a wealth of research, using learning styles is not.

Furthermore, learning style theories are based on the premise that the way something is ordered or the way you think about something determines how quickly and easily you can learn that something. But Daniel Willingham has shown that this is not how the human brain works. Try to imagine the ears of a German Shepherd. There is a good chance that you are now thinking of the image of a dog. But if we now ask you to imagine the voice of your best friend, then there is an equally good chance that this time you will not see an image of your friend, but will hear his or her voice inside your head. And if we ask you to imagine something involving movement, then at your age you will probably no problem envisaging how to tie your shoelaces. In other words, we each think in different ways about different things all the time. But there are more serious lessons to be learned. Imagine that you have a visual learner and an auditory learner. You first read out a list of words and then you show a series of images. You would probably think that the auditory learner would remember the spoken words better than the visual images, and vice versa for the visual learner. But this is not the case. This does not mean that some people are not slightly better at remembering things in images, which may be useful if they need to remember, say, buildings or maps, but only a small minority will have any real problem with these things. Even auditory learners can work with maps without serious difficulties.

If you ask someone to memorize something, it is not really a question of what they see or hear; it is a question of meaning. And is this not what we primarily learn at school: meanings? If this were not so, a visual learner in a mathematics lesson would only remember the symbols and would not know what $(a + b)^2 = a^2 + 2ab + b^2$ really means.

So, should you adjust your lessons to the learning style of your pupils? There is almost no scientific evidence for the different learning style categorizations and no proof for their added value in the classroom. But does this mean that all learners are the same and should be treated and taught the same way? No! What it means is that learning styles is not a theory of instruction and should not be treated as such. Different learners react to different things in different ways and a good teacher, like a good chef, knows how to optimize this by playing to the learner's strong points and compensating for the weak ones.

As Pashler and colleagues stated, what actually is supported is "a thriving industry devoted to publishing learning-styles tests and guide-books" and "professional development workshops for teachers and educators" (p. 105). Thousands of articles and books have been written on learning styles and their application in education. Furthermore, as Kirschner and van Merriënboer note, there is an incredibly lucrative commercial industry for (1) selling measurement instruments meant to help teachers diagnose their students' learning styles and (2) holding workshops and conferences meant to provide information and training to teachers on how to align their teaching to the learning styles of their students.

Learning in Movement

A number of research projects have been conducted that show the positive link between movement and learning. Physical activity has been found to generate positive structural changes in the brain, such as development of nerves (neurogenesis), formation and differentiation of blood vessels (angiogenesis), and improved connectivity (Thomas, Dennis, Bandettini, & Johansen-Berg). These positive effects of physical activity on the brain are thought to consequently improve academic achievement. Many studies, for example, have indicated that children who spend more time in physical activities have better academic achievement than those who are less physically active (Fedewa & Ahn). These results appear to apply to all children, not just to those who have preference for a kinesthetic learning style. For example, developmental psychologist John Best carried out an experiment to investigate the influence of "exergames" on the brain (Figure 3). He asked 33 children to take part in games that differed in their levels of physical activity and cognitive engagement (the intellectual challenge of the game). He examined the effect of these games on the executive functions — the higher control functions — of the participants' brains. The results showed that the level of cognitive engagement had no effect, but that the level of physical activity did. Children were able to solve problems more quickly after playing a physical game than a cognitive game. He concluded that children "learn"

Figure 3 Movement and learning. *This image, which was originally posted to Flickr.com, was uploaded to Commons using Flickr upload bot on 09:24, 20 July 2008 (UTC) by Wowowwiki (talk). On that date it was licensed under the Creative Commons Attribution-Share Alike 2.0 Generic license. Original location: http://www.flickr.com/photos/13139702@N05/2038082937*

more (in the sense of using the higher part of their brain more effectively) from exergaming than from, say, watching an educational video. He explained this in terms of physiological excitement, which ensures that more attention is devoted by the brain to the coordination of the motor functions.

This is not only the case in children. Gao and Mandryk, for example, found acute cognitive benefits of even a casual exergame (10 minutes of light exercise) over the watching the same game bit not exercising on cognitive tests requiring focus and concentration. Maillot, Perrot, and Hartley found that exergaming significantly improved cognitive measures of executive control and processing speed functions in older adults. In our aging society this is an important finding!

We will see later in the book that you need to be very careful when making references to brain activity in this manner. Even so, the Best study is interesting. It not only demonstrates the positive effect of gaming, but also emphasizes how vitally important physical exercise is for children. It not only counteracts overweight and obesity, but can also improve people's learning.

Sources

Best, J. R. (2012). Exergaming immediately enhances children's executive functi. *Developmental Psychology, 48*(5), 1501–1510.

Fedewa, A. L., & Ahn, S. (2011). The effects of physical activity and physical fitness on children's achievement and cognitive outcomes: A meta-analysis. *Research Quarterly for Exercise and Sport, 82*, 521–535.

Gao, Y., & Mandryk, R. L. (2012). *The acute cognitive benefits of casual exergame play* (Austin, Texas, USA (pp. 1863–1872)). *CHI '12: Proceedings of the 30th international conference on human factors in computing systems.* New York: ACM Austin, Texas, USA (pp. 1863–1872).

Maillot, P., Perrot, A., & Hartley, A. (2012). Effects of interactive physical-activity videogame training on physical and cognitive function in older adults. *Psychology and Aging, 27*, 589–600.

Thomas, A. G., Dennis, A., Bandettini, P. A., & Johansen-Berg, H. (2012). The effects of aerobic activity on brain structure. *Frontiers in Psychology, 3*, 86.

:-\ Though appealing, no solid evidence exists showing that there is any benefit to adapting and designing education and instruction to these so-called styles. It may even be the case that in doing so, administrators, teachers, parents and even learners are negatively influencing the learning process and the products of education and instruction.

REFERENCES

Clark, R. E. (1982). Antagonism between achievement and enjoyment in ATI studies. *Educational Psychologist, 17*(2), 92–101.

Clark, R. E. (1989). When teaching kills learning: Research on mathemathantics. In H. N. Mandl, N. Bennett, E. de Corte, & H. F. Friedrich (Eds.), *Learning and instruction: European research in an international context* (Vol. 2, pp. 1–22). London: Pergamon.

Coffield, F., Moseley, D., Hall, E., & Ecclestone, K. (2004). *Learning styles and pedagogy in post-16 learning: A systematic and critical review.* London: Learning and Skills Research Centre.

Corbelis, M. C. (2012). Educational double-think. In S. Della Sala, & M. Anderson (Eds.), *Neuroscience in education* (pp. 222–229). Oxford: Oxford University Press.

Druckman, D., & Porter, L. W. (1991). Developing careers. In D. Druckman, & R. A. Bjork (Eds.), *In the mind's eye: Enhancing human performance* (pp. 80–103). Washington, DC: National Academy Press.

Geake, J. (2008). Neuromythologies in education. *Educational Research, 50*, 123–133.

Hattie, J. (2009). *Visible learning: A synthesis of over 800 meta-analyses relating to achievement.* London: Routledge.

Iliff, C. H. (1994). *Kolb's learning style inventory: A meta-analysis.* Unpublished doctoral dissertation, Boston University.

Kirschner, P. A., & van Merriënboer, J. J. G. (2013). Do learners really know best? Urban legends in education. *Educational Psychologist, 48*(3), 1–15.

Kirschner, P. A., Sweller, J., & Clark, R. E. (2006). Why minimal guidance during instruction does not work: An analysis of the failure of constructivist, discovery, problem-based, experiential, and inquiry-based teaching. *Educational Psychologist, 46*(2), 75–86.

Kolb, D. A. (1971). *Individual learning styles and the learning process.* Cambridge, MA: Sloan School of Management, Massachusetts Institute of Technology (Working Paper No. 535–71).

Kolb, D. A. (1984). *Experiential learning: Experience as the source of learning and development.* Englewood Cliffs, NJ: Prentice-Hall.

Lilienfeld, S. O. (2010). *50 great myths of popular psychology: Shattering widespread misconceptions about human behavior.* Chichester, UK: Wiley-Blackwell.

Pashler, H., McDaniel, M., Rohrer, D., & Bjork, R. (2008). Learning styles: Concepts and evidence. *Psychological Science in the Public Interest, 9*(3), 105–119.

Rohrer, D., & Pashler, H. (2012). Learning styles: Where's the evidence? *Medical Education, 46,* 630–635.

Ruble, T. L., & Stout, D. E. (1993). Learning styles and end-user training: An unwarranted leap of faith. *MIS Quarterly, March 1993,* 115–117.

Tanner, K. D. (2012). Promoting student metacognition. *CBE-Life Sciences Education, 11,* 113–120.

van Merriënboer, J. J. G. (1990). Instructional strategies for teaching computer programming: Interactions with the cognitive style reflection – impulsivity. *Journal of Research on Computing in Education, 23,* 45–53.

Veenman, M. V. J., Prins, F. J., & Verheij, J. (2003). Learning styles: Self-reports versus thinking-aloud measures. *British Journal of Educational Psychology, 73,* 357–372.

Willingham, D. (2008, August 21). Learning styles don't exist. Retrieved June 19, 2012, from <http://www.youtube.com/watch?v=sIv9rz2NTUk>.

MYTH 2

The Effectiveness of Learning Can Be Shown in a Pyramid

Have you ever heard the Zen saying, "Give a man a fish and you feed him for a day; teach a man to fish and you feed him for a lifetime?" This seems to lie at the basis of this second myth about learning, namely the learning pyramid. In 1946, Edgar Dale authored possibly the first book on the use of media in education. In that book, which was revised in 1954 and 1969, he presented what he called the "cone of experience" (Figure 4). That cone is a visual device which summarized his classification system for different types of mediated learning experiences. This classification system went from very concrete experiences (at the bottom of the cone) to very abstract (at the top). Texts, composed of verbal symbols, are very abstract. The way in which letters are written and the sounds associated with them are arbitrary and abstract (although this differs between languages; for instance, Chinese has an ideographic character set depicting concrete and abstract objects) whereas direct purposeful experience (first hand experience) is concrete.

The cone of experience was a simple and efficient intuitive model of the concreteness of various audiovisual media. Dale used no numbers or teaching pedagogies and even went as far as to warn readers not to regard the bands on the cone as rigid, inflexible divisions. He said, "The cone device is a visual metaphor of learning experiences, in which the various types of audio-visual materials are arranged in the order of increasing abstractness as one proceeds from direct experiences". In the 1969 edition of his book, Dale tells us:

> In addition, we have suggested the narrowing upward shape of the cone does not imply an increasing difficulty of learning. Both verbal and visual symbols are used by little children. Demonstrations may be complex and quite involved — much more so than a map (a visual symbol) of Alaska. The basis of the classification is not difficulty but degree of abstraction — the amount of immediate sensory participation that is involved. Thus, a still photograph of a tree is not more difficult to understand than the dramatization of Hamlet. It is simply in itself a less concrete teaching material than the dramatization. (p. 110)

Through the years, this metaphor transitioned to a what is now alternatively called the *cone of learning* or, more often, the *learning pyramid*, with

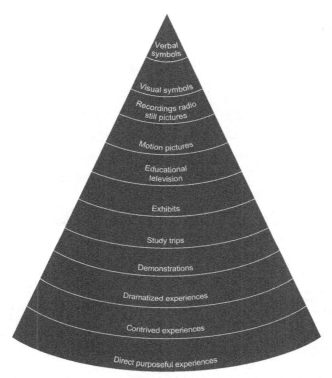

Figure 4 Dale's cone of experience. *Taken from Dale, E. (1969).* Audiovisual methods in teaching *(3rd ed.). New York: Dryden Press; Holt, Rinehart and Winston. Reprinted within the STM Permissions Guidelines (see http://www.stm-assoc.org/permissions-guidelines/ and http://www.stm-assoc.org/2014_06_24_STM_Permissions_Guidelines_2012.pdf).*

various pedagogic labels and numbers/percentages (none of which was in the original cone). You have probably seen this pyramid in different colors, shapes and forms with varying percentages and different attributions somewhere in a textbook or during a presentation (Figures 5 and 6).

Most people attribute the learning pyramid, as it is now known, to the National Training Laboratories (NTL) in Bethel, Maine, USA. The laboratory, when asked, sends the following standard e-mail:

> [The research was carried out] at our Bethel, Maine campus in the early sixties, when we were still part of the National Education Association's Adult Education Division. Yes, we believe it to be accurate, but no, we no longer have — nor can we find — the original research that supports the numbers. We get many enquiries about this every month — and many, many people have searched for the original research and have come up empty handed. We know that in 1954

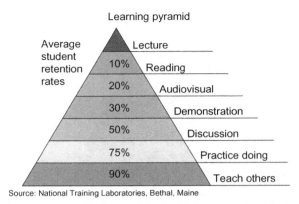

Source: National Training Laboratories, Bethal, Maine

Figure 5 The learning pyramid. *Credited to NTL but as explained in the text the real source could be in the public domain (if considered a "work of the US government"), so no written permission is needed as it is uncopyrightable.*

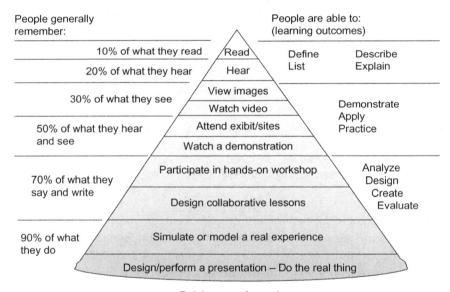

Dale's cone of experience

Figure 6 The learning pyramid 2. *Credited to NTL but as explained in the text the real source could be in the public domain (if considered a "work of the US government"), so no written permission is needed as it is uncopyrightable.*

a similar pyramid with slightly different numbers appeared on page 43 of a book called Audio-Visual Methods in Teaching, *published by the Edgar Dale Dryden Press in New York. Yet the Learning Pyramid as such seems to have been modified and has always been attributed to the NTL Institute.*

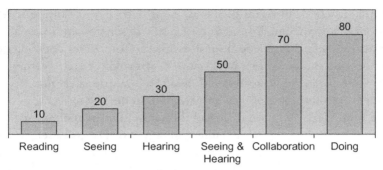

Figure 7 Another representation of the learning pyramid. *Image falsely credited to Chi, M. T., Bassok, M., Lewis, M. W., Reimann, P., & Glaser, R. (1989). Self-explanations: How students study and use examples in learning to solve problems.* Cognitive Science, *13(2), 145−182.*

Another representation we have found is shown in Figure 7. And while the pyramid is a derivative, adaptation or degeneration (take your pick) of Dale's original cone, the graph appears to be an outright fraud. Michelene Chi (Director of the Learning Sciences Institute at Arizona State University) debunked the graph in one sentence: "I don't recognize this graph at all. So the citation is definitely wrong; since it's not my graph".

Michael Molenda traced the figures back to the Second World War, making them older than Dale's cone of experience. Molenda found evidence in a letter by Charles Cyrus, a training specialist at the University of Texas, that the figures were first noted by Paul John Philips, who brought the data with him after serving as head of the Training Methods branch of the US Army's Ordnance School at the Aberdeen (Maryland) Proving Grounds. During the period 1940−1943 his unit conducted research on training that supported the findings now seen in the learning pyramid. However, no documentation of the research is available. Dwyer traced back probably the first combination of the figures and the cone of experience to the Socony-Vacuum Oil Company, who probably found the data via the Division of Extension, University of Texas, who found it via Paul John Philips. But is this the oldest source? Probably not. In four articles Subramony, Molenda, Betrus and Thalmeier traced the statistics in the chart back to 1912 and they even suspect that the statistics are probably older still.

What does this pyramid tell us? It tells us that if you are a teacher who just "teaches" the material that needs to be learned, your pupils won't remember very much. The traditional teaching methods — reading, audiovisual, and so on — all have low retention scores. As a teacher, you will be most successful (in terms of retention, at least) if you can create lesson situations where the pupils have to explain the lesson content to each other. Noteworthy here is how educational myths can sometimes contradict each other, because this pyramid is totally at odds with almost every learning style theory (see above). So is the pyramid right? No, unfortunately not.

There are two problems with the pyramid. In the first instance, its origins are far from clear. We have discussed this above, but in addition success — even in mythdom — has many fathers. Along with Dale, Glasser, the NTL and others, the real father may be John Adams who, in *Exposition and illustration in teaching* (1910), included the following order of concreteness: "(1) the real object, for which anything else is a more or less inefficient substitute; (2) a model of the real object; (3) a diagram dealing with some of the aspects of the object; and (4) a mere verbal description of the object" (p. 140). Hoban, Hoban, and Zissman, in their 1937 book *Visualizing the curriculum,* posited that the value of audiovisual material was a function of its degree of realism with the categories: total situation, objects, models, films, stereographs, slides, flat pictures, maps, diagrams, and words (Figure 8). Again, none of these theories was backed by any research whatsoever.

Secondly, the percentages are too nicely rounded off, which is almost impossible in scientific research. As Dwyer points out, the reported percentages are impossible to interpret or verify without specifying at least the method of measurement, the age of the learners, the type of learning task and the content being remembered (p. 10). Also, all of the percentages and even the order of the different approaches are

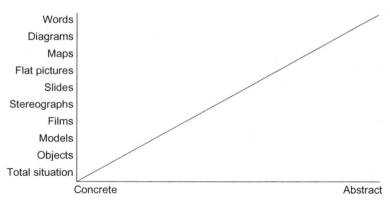

Figure 8 Value of audiovisual material. *From Hoban, C., Sr., Hoban, C., Jr., & Zissman, S. (1937). Visualizing the curriculum. New York: Dryden Press.*

affected by things such as what is to be recalled or learned (while the determining characteristics of a mammal can be summed up in five simple characteristics, one would have to concretely interact with possibly hundreds of mammals to discern them), delay between study and test (while the percentage of what is retained usually drops with delay, some approaches actually improve with delay, such as using testing as a pedagogical technique), expertise or prior knowledge of the learner (if you know a lot about distillation, a picture of a set-up is very concrete; if you know nothing about the topic, it makes no sense), activities employed during the lecture, while reading, during the hands-on experience, and so on.

Possibly the best treatment of this myth is an article by Lalley and Miller from 2007, which covers most of the problems with the learning pyramid, ranging from what was discussed above through the pyramid's overlapping of media/pedagogies to the lack of research and non-rigor of the research that has been carried out. For example, they note that "one might encounter visual and verbal symbols when watching television, on a field trip, or observing a demonstration" (p. 70). Has the learner then learned from text, lecture, pictures, film …? In addition, they note a number of empirical issues for the pyramid to have any instructional value, such as: (1) the methods should be of the same duration (i.e., equal time on task), (2) the same teacher should carry out the experiment (hoping that there was no crossover effect) or multiple teachers carry out the interventions, matched for education, experience, domain of instruction, and so forth; (3) the content to be learned with each method should be the same; and (4) the outcome measures should actually measure retention, recall or whatever after a time delay. This is very similar to the criticism that Richard Clark discussed in his 1983 meta-analysis of research comparing the value of different media for learning.

They concluded that no significant difference between the efficacy of the different approaches could be established. In fact, the pyramid should be more square shaped, not triangular, with all the percentages distributed equally. But then it would probably not be quite so easy to persuade people that the lowest step of the pyramid is the most important.

We would like to rename this pyramid the Loch Ness Monster of educational theory. It keeps cropping up, whether appropriate or not. No, wait: scrap the "or not". It is always inappropriate, because the pyramid — like Nessie — is a fake!

Micro-Teaching Works Well — for Teachers in Training

In research conducted to find out which learning techniques work well in education, micro-teaching scores consistently high. But what exactly is micro-teaching? In his book *Visible learning*, John Hattie describes micro-teaching as a practice that is often used in laboratory settings that "typically involves student-teachers conducting (mini-) lessons to a small group of students, and then engaging in a post-discussion about the lessons" (p. 112). In his meta-analysis of more than 800 meta-analyses, micro-teaching was ranked number 4 of 130 teaching/educational interventions based on 402 studies with an effect size of 0.88! You might think that this is evidence to show that the lowest step in the learning pyramid is indeed more important than all the rest, since an important part of micro-teaching is either actual or simulated (i.e., watching a demonstration) laboratory experience. But it is not that simple, as a crucial element of micro-teaching is a debriefing where the lesson is reviewed so as to improve the teaching and learning experience. Immediate feedback and support, along with new chances to practice based on the feedback and support, lie at the basis of micro-teaching. In other words, the crucial element in this approach is the discussion and the personalized feedback it generates. It seem that this method is above all effective for teaching people how to give lessons, rather than acquiring and remembering content (which, one hopes, the students will have already done before they engage in micro-training!). As such, it is a long-used technique for the training of both pre-service and in-service teachers which has been used since its inception in the early 1960s as a way to train teachers and prospective teachers.

Indeed, one of the authors introduced this as one of the best techniques to be used in normal science classroom work as an alternative to traditional laboratory practicals, namely *experimental seminars* (Kirschner, 1992).

Sources

Hattie, J. (2009). *Visible learning: A synthesis of over 800 meta-analyses relating to achievement*. New York: Routledge.
Kirschner, P. A. (1992). Epistemology, practical work and academic skills in science education. *Science and Education*, 1, 273–299.

:-\ The origin of the Adams, Hoban, Glasser, Dale, NTL pyramid is unclear and the percentages are wholly inaccurate. Part of its power may lie in its Zen-like message and part in what Newman, Garry, Bernstein, Kantner, and Lindsay (2012) have shown, namely that we are more inclined to believe something if it is accompanied by an image, even if it is purely decorative ("truthiness" — the feeling that something is true). We have no hard evidence, but it seems that pyramids are particularly good at this. Whenever we see a pyramid in an educational context, the information it contains somehow seems more believable!

REFERENCES

Adams, J. (1910). *Exposition and illustration in teaching.* New York: MacMillan Company.

Clark, R. E. (1983). Reconsidering research on learning from media. *Review of Educational Research, 43*, 445–459.

Dale, E. (1946). *Audio-visual methods in teaching.* New York: Dryden Press, 1954, 1969.

Dwyer, F. M. (1978). *Strategies for improving visual learning.* State College, PA: Learning Services.

Hoban, C., Sr., Hoban, C., Jr., & Zissman, S. (1937). *Visualizing the curriculum.* New York: Dryden Press.

Lalley, J. P., & Miller, R. H. (2007). The learning pyramid: Does it point teachers in the right direction? *Education, 128*(1), 64–80.

Molenda, M. (2004). Cone of experience. In A. Kovalchick, & K. Dawson (Eds.), *Education and technology: An encyclopedia* (pp. 161–164). Santa Barbara, CA: ABC-CLIO.

Newman, E. J., Garry, M., Bernstein, D. M., Kantner, J., & Lindsay, S. D. (2012). Nonprobative photographs (or words) inflate truthiness. *Psychonomic Bulletin & Review, 19*, 969–974.

Subramony, D., Molenda, M., Betrus, A., & Thalheimer, W. (2014). The mythical retention chart and the corruption of dale's cone of experience. *Educational Technology, 54*(6), 6–16.

Subramony, D., Molenda, M., Betrus, A., & Thalheimer, W. (2014). Previous attempts to debunk the mythical retention chart and corrupted dale's Cone. *Educational Technology, 54*(6), 17–21.

Subramony, D., Molenda, M., Betrus, A., & Thalheimer, W. (2014). The good, the bad, and the ugly: A bibliographic essay on the corrupted cone. *Educational Technology, 54*(6), 22–31.

Subramony, D., Molenda, M., Betrus, A., & Thalheimer, W. (2014). Timeline of the mythical retention chart and corrupted dale's cone. *Educational Technology, 54*(6), 31–24.

MYTH 3

You Learn 70% Informally, 20% from Others and Just 10% through Formal Education

In occupational training and in other texts about learning in the workplace, increasing reference is being made to the 70−20−10 rule. This rule posits that learning based on experience (70%) is significantly higher than learning acquired through interaction with others (20%). The impact of classic, traditional workshops and training courses accounts for just 10%. This model is gaining popularity, with promotion by people such as Charles Jennings, and is often associated with the work of Morgan McCall, Robert W. Eichinger and Michael M. Lombardo.

If we look at the list of companies that apply this rule (according to Jay Cross), it contains some very impressive names, including Reuters, Goldman Sachs, Nike, Mars, Nokia, PricewaterhouseCoopers, Ernst & Young, L'Oréal, Adecco, Boston Scientific, American Express, HP, Caterpillar, Sony Ericsson, BT, Westfield, Wal-Mart and Coca-Cola.

However, in a blog post, Doug Lynch argued that this "rule" is actually a myth based on a metaphor that dates back to the days of Archimedes! During the 1960s, Allan Tough was the first educationalist to make use of the iceberg as a metaphor. But it was Archimedes (287−212 BC) who first showed that the largest part of an iceberg is hidden under water, resulting in the 70−20−10 ratio.

This all sounds very good, but a blog post is not (yet) real science. And so we decided to investigate further. The rule is most frequently cited in association with McCall, Eichinger and Lombardo. But when you check this source, two things are immediately noticeable:

- Their chapter on the 70−20−10 rule relates exclusively to training *in leadership of executives.*
- The authors are very careful when proposing the rule; the phraseology is guarded: "the odds are that development will be . . ." or "there is a good chance that . . .", etc.

Of course, it is not unusual for scientists to be cautious when making claims for their evidence. All knowledge is provisional. But while this particular aspect is open to interpretation, one thing is certain: they talk about the rule specifically within the context of acquiring leadership skills:

The 70–20–10 rule emerged from 30 years of CCL's Lessons of Experience research, which explores how executives learn, grow and change over the course of their careers. The underlying assumption is that leadership is learned. We believe that today, even more than before, a manager's ability and willingness to learn from experience is the foundation for leading with impact.

This is an important indicator. Can we automatically transfer these insights and use them for other purposes? Or does the rule only apply to our future leaders?

The biggest problem in answering these questions is the fact that we can find no evidence to support the 70–20–10 proportional split in the professional literature. In most cases, it is "assumed" that the rule "would apply" by referring again to the work of McCall et al.

We made appeals through various channels to try and find more conclusive supporting evidence. To our amazement, in response a number of people tried to defend the rule by downplaying the importance of empirical science and arguing that the figures mentioned in the rule do not need to be taken with such academic seriousness. This is one point of view, of course, and nobody doubts the importance of informal learning. Even so, our investigations suggest that we need to be careful about accepting the 70–20–10 ratio at face value. One of the few studies that came close to investigating this figure, also looking at executives, by Enos, Kehrhahn, and Bell, actually shows a totally different ratio, more precisely 16–44–30, with only 16% learning from experience, 44 learning by talking to others and 30% from formal training. A quick addition teaches us that 10% is missing, but this was for influences on the learning that were not mapped by the researchers. It is also important to note that for this study only a small sample size was used, 84 executives from the same company. Another important limitation of the study was that the executives were asked for perceptions of the ways that they had learned, rather than looking how they actually learned. Therefore, this split ratio also has many flaws.

We found this study via Patrick Vermeren who interviewed many of the people involved in this story on the magic numbers, including both Jennings and McCall. McCall calls the rule that Jennings is promoting "folklore".

We see a basic assumption underlying this rule of thumb as being problematic by nature, namely that we learn best by discovering things ourselves. See Section 3.6 on discovery learning.

:-? Informal learning is certainly very important, but we could find no evidence in the scientific literature to support the ratio of 70% informal learning, 20% learning from others and 10% formal learning.

REFERENCES

Cross, J. (2013, April 6). *50 suggestions for implementing 70–20–10*. Retrieved from < http://internettime.com/2013/04-50-suggestions-for-implementing-70-20-10-6/ >.

De Bruyckere, P. (2012, September 3). *Never trust neat percentages? 70–20–10 rule. From experience to meaning ....* Retrieved September 3, 2012, from <http://theeconomyof meaning.com/2012/09/03/never-trust-neat-percentages-70-20-10-rule/>.

Dillon, J. (2012). Is informal education better than formal education? In P. Adey, & J. Dillon (Eds.), *Bad education* (pp. 129–142). Maidenhead, UK: Open University Press.

Enos, M. D., Kehrhahn, M. T., & Bell, A. (2003). Informal learning and the transfer of learning: How managers develop proficiency. *Human Resource Development Quarterly, 14*, 369–387.

Jennings, C. (2013). *70:20:10 framework explained: Creating high performance cultures*. Surrey Hills, Australia: 70:20:10 Forum.

Kajewski, K., & Madsen, V. (2012). *Demystifying 70:20:10*. Melbourne: Deakin Prime (Report).

Lombardo, M. M., & Eichinger, R. W. (1996). *The career architect development planner* (1st ed.). Minneapolis: Lominger.

Lynch, D. (2012, February 16). Busted learning myths. Chief Learning Officer. Retrieved September 18, 2012, from <http://clomedia.com/articles/view/busted-learning-myths/1>.

Vermeren, P. (2014, September 6). *Jennings' 70–20–10 framework*. Retrieved from <http://evidencebasedhrm.be/702010-framework-jennings/>.

Wilson, M., Van Velsor, E., Chandrasekar, A., & Criswell, C. (2011, September). Grooming top leaders. Center for Creative Leadership. Retrieved September 16, 2012, from <http://www.ccl.org/leadership/pdf/research/GroomingTopLeaders.pdf>.

MYTH 4

If You Can Look Everything Up, Is Knowledge so Important?

We live in a knowledge society in which all knowledge seems to be within easy reach of everybody. Why should you bother learning how high Mount Everest is if you have the answer on the smartphone in your pocket? It is indisputable that the ability and the opportunity to look up knowledge in this manner is important. In other words, all that one really needs to know and learn is "out there on the Web" and, thus, it is now irrelevant and actually a waste of time (this will be discussed later, in Section 3.5, when we discuss the myth that knowledge is as perishable as fresh fish) for teachers to teach and/or learners to acquire knowledge. Teachers have been demoted from experts whose job it is to combine their domain knowledge with their pedagogical content knowledge to teach those lacking this knowledge to being coaches who stand on the sidelines to guide and/or coax a new breed of self-educators (which too will be discussed later, in Section 5.3 on digital natives).

This probably sounds familiar to you: surely it can't be a myth! Do we really need to teach any more? Do learners really need to acquire factual knowledge? Doesn't the present generation of digital natives already possess these skills? The answers to these questions are: Yes, Yes, and No.

Indeed, much, if not all of the "knowledge" that we want children and young adults to learn in school is to be found on the Web; along with a great deal more non–information from disreputable sources. However, as Kirschner wrote, what we already know determines what we see and understand, and not the other way around. This is actually at the basis of constructivism, which we discussed earlier (although, strangely enough, convinced and confirmed constructivists often argue against teaching for the acquisition of knowledge). It is our prior knowledge and experiences that determine how we see and interpret the world around us (an avid road cyclist will see a mountain in terms of climbing percentages and gear ratios that should be used while a geologist will see that same mountain in terms of geological time periods, fossils and rock formations). It is also our prior knowledge and experiences that determine how successfully we are able to search for, find, select and process (i.e., evaluate) the information available on the World Wide Web. Learners are often given learning tasks or assignments that contain an information problem where they are expected to identify the information needs, locate corresponding information sources, extract and organize the relevant information contained in each source, and synthesize the information from those relevant sources in a cogent, productive way (Brand-Gruwel, Wopereis, & Walraven; Moore).

Unfortunately, in most cases students' prior knowledge of the subject matter is at best minimal (this is not strange since, in essence, this is the definition of a learner; if they had the knowledge they would be experts and wouldn't need to learn it). And research has shown that low prior knowledge negatively influences the search process (Fidel et al.,; Hirsch). This is not only true at the elementary and/or secondary school level. (Nievelstein; Nievelstein, van Gog, Boshuizen, & Prins), studying first and third year law students, found that they experienced a great deal of difficulty using sources such as law books and court judgments owing to a lack of the conceptual and epistemic knowledge necessary to interpret the information found in the source. Students with more prior knowledge have an advantage because they can easily link that knowledge to the task requirements and to information found on the Web.

"What You Talking About, Willis?"

To make this clear, we are going to borrow an idea from the excellent book by Daniel Willingham (2009). First, read the following text:

> *The procedure is actually quite simple. First arrange the items in different groups. Of course, in some cases a single pile may be enough, depending on how much you have to do. If you need to move because the required facilities are not available where you are, this is the next step. Otherwise, you can begin. It is important not to do too much. It is better just to do a couple of things at the same time, rather than trying to do everything at once.*

You are probably thinking: "What on earth is all that about?" Yes, it does sound rather vague, even though you doubtless know what all the words mean. But if we tell you that it is actually about washing clothes, then suddenly everything becomes clear. Furthermore, the likelihood that you would ever remember the fragment of text without the knowledge that it is about washing clothes is minimal. Why? Because to understand what you just read and then remember it, you need prior knowledge. There are mental "tricks" that allow us to memorize pure facts, but if you really want to learn and understand something with full insight, then you need knowledge — whether you like it or not!

Source

Willingham, D. T. (2009). *Why don't students like school? A cognitive scientist answers questions about how the mind works and what it means for the classroom.* San Francisco, CA: Jossey-Bass.

We are now more than a decade into the twenty-first century. Consequently, it is high time to introduce the so-called twenty-first century skills about which we hear so much. These will be necessary to deal with the demands of contemporary and future society. There are various lists itemizing these twenty-first century skills (Anderman, Sinatra, & Gray; Dede), but they nearly all contain the same elements: collaboration, communication, information and communications technology (ICT) literacy, social and/or cultural skills (including citizenship), creativity, critical thinking and problem solving.

The set of activities and/or skills for adequately dealing with the explosion of information on the Web is known as *information literacy* or *digital literacy*, one of the core twenty-first century skills propagated in much school policy. Although many educational gurus and policy-makers believe and propagate the thought that modern-day learners are competent or even expert in information problem solving (i.e., they are information and digitally literate) because these learners are seen searching the Web daily, much research has shown that effectively solving information problems is, for most students, a real problem. According to Miller and Bartlett, effective Internet use requires distinguishing good information from bad. They noted that learners not only have problems finding the information that they are actually seeking, but also often trust the first thing they see, making them prone to "the pitfalls of ignorance, falsehoods, cons and scams" (p. 35). Many researchers (e.g., Bilal; Large & Beheshti; MaKinster, Beghetto, & Plucker; Wallace, Kupperman, Krajcik, & Soloway) have demonstrated that learners of all ages, ranging from young children and teenagers to adults cannot effectively choose good search terms, combine them properly, select relevant websites, and question and test the validity of the sources retrieved. Taking all of this into account, we can conclude that learners cannot effectively and efficiently solve information problems by themselves, but rather that they must learn to solve such information-based problems.

In other words, "the fact that students make use of many electronic devices and are called digital natives, does not make them good users of the media that they have at their disposal. They can Google® but lack the information skills to effectively find the information they need, and they also do not have the knowledge to adequately determine the relevance or truth of what they have found" (Kirschner & van Merriënboer). The mistaken beliefs that (1) the teaching/acquisition of knowledge is no longer necessary, and (2) learners are digitally literate and capable of solving information problems lead to them writing essays on Baconian science with texts about the twentieth century British artist Francis Bacon and on the problems that Martin Luther King had with Pope Leo X and Holy Roman Emperor Charles V. It also leads to prospective presidential candidates (i.e., Michelle Bachmann) painfully yet ignorantly confusing the birthplace of John Wayne (the actor) with that of John Wayne Gacy (the murderer convicted of killing more than 30 young men in the 1970s)!

:-\ We actually need more knowledge to learn and apply the skills we need in our knowledge society. And the skills that we need also need to be learned!

REFERENCES

Anderman, E. M., Sinatra, G., & Gray, D. (2012). The challenges of teaching and learning about science in the 21st century: Exploring the abilities and constraints of adolescent learners. *Studies in Science Education, 48*(1), 89−117.

Bilal, D. (2000). Children's use of the Yahooligans! Web search engine: I. Cognitive, physical, and affective behaviors on fact-based search tasks. *Journal of the American Society of Information Science, 51*, 646−665.

Brand-Gruwel, S., & Gerjets, P. (2008). Instructional support for enhancing students' information problem solving ability. *Computers in Human Behavior, 24*, 615−622.

Brand-Gruwel, S., Wopereis, I., & Walraven, A. (2009). A descriptive model of information problem solving while using internet. *Computers & Education, 52*, 1207−1217.

Dede, C. (2010). Comparing frameworks for 21st century skills. In J. Bellanca, & R. Brandt (Eds.), *21st century skills* (pp. 51−76). Bloomington, IN: Solution Tree Press.

Fidel, R., Davies, R. K., Douglass, M. H., Holder, J. K., Hopkins, C. J., Kushner, E. J., et al. (1999). A visit to the information mall: Web searching behavior of high school students. *Journal of the American Society of Information Science, 50*(1), 24−37.

Hirsch, S. G. (1999). Children's relevance criteria and information seeking on electronic resources. *Journal of the American Society for Information Science, 50*, 1265−1283.

Kirschner, P. A. (1992). Epistemology, practical work, and academic skills in science education. *Science and Education, 1*, 273−299.

Kirschner, P. A. (2009). Epistemology or pedagogy, that is the question. In S. Tobias, & T. M. Duffy (Eds.), *Constructivist instruction: Success or failure?* (pp. 144−157). New York: Routledge.

Kirschner, P. A., & van Merriënboer, J. J. G. (2013). Do learners really know best? Urban legends in education. *Educational Psychologist, 48*(3), 1−15.

Kolb, D. A. (1971). *Individual learning styles and the learning process.* Cambridge, MA: Sloan School of Management, Massachusetts Institute of Technology (Working Paper No. 535−71).

Large, A., & Beheshti, J. (2000). The web as a classroom resource: Reaction from the users. *Journal of the American Society of Information Science, 51*, 1069−1080.

MaKinster, J. G., Beghetto, R. A., & Plucker, J. A. (2002). Why can't I find Newton's third law? Case studies of students' use of the web as a science resource. *Journal of Science Education and Technology, 11*, 155−172.

Miller, C., & Bartlett, J. (2012). "Digital fluency": Towards young people's critical use of the internet. *Journal of Information Literacy, 6*(2), 35−55.

Moore, P. (1995). Information problem solving: A wider view of library skills. *Contemporary Educational Psychology, 20*, 1−31.

Nievelstein, F. (2009). *Learning law* Heerlen, The Netherlands: Open University of the Netherlands Unpublished doctoral dissertation.

Nievelstein, F., van Gog, T., Boshuizen, H. P. A., & Prins, F. J. (2008). Expertise-related differences in conceptual and ontological knowledge in the legal domain. *European Journal of Cognitive Psychology, 20*, 1043−1064.

Wallace, R. M., Kupperman, J., Krajcik, J., & Soloway, E. (2000). Science on the Web: Students online in a sixth-grade classroom. *Journal of the Learning Sciences, 9*, 75−104.

MYTH 5

Knowledge Is as Perishable as Fresh Fish

A major, often heard premise underlying the idea of substituting information seeking for teaching and learning of that information is that the half-life of information is getting smaller every day, making knowledge rapidly obsolete. This led a Dutch professor of government policy and one time Undersecretary of Education to state that "Knowledge is as perishable as fresh fish". This, among other things, has played an important role in the "Googlification" of education, which Hill and Hannafin describe as a watered-down version of resource-based learning. (Marcum, p. 28), for example, wrote:

> ... the "half life" of information usefulness has shrunk from a century or a generation to perhaps no more than days or even hours in some fields, where anything in print is automatically deemed obsolete. Today the information underlying the first year of a certain technical degree can be half useless by graduation day. Currency now prevails.

The problem is that the idea that the present body of knowledge is rapidly becoming out of date or obsolete is far from true. There are two problems with this idea. The first is that we need to make a distinction with respect to the difference between knowledge obsolescence on the one hand and information growth on the other. It is incontrovertible that the two decades since the introduction of the World Wide Web have seen an enormous — exponential — growth in the amount of information available. Ex-Google CEO Eric Schmidt reportedly stated: "Between the birth of the world and 2003, there were five exabytes [10^{18} bytes = 1 billion gigabytes = 1 million terabytes] of information created. We [now] create five exabytes every two days. See why it's so painful to operate in information markets?"[1] Robert J. Moore, CEO of RJMetrics, states that "a more honest quote would have been '23 Exabytes of information was recorded and replicated in 2002. We now record and transfer that much information every 7 days'", and according to the International Data Corporation (Gantz), "the digital universe — information that is either created, captured, or replicated in digital form — was 281 exabytes in

---

[1] http://www.huffingtonpost.com/brett-king/too-much-content-a-world-_b_809677.html.

2007. In 2011, the amount of digital information produced in the year should equal nearly 1800 exabytes [1.8 zetabytes], or 10 times that produced in 2006". It really is not important who is right here and how rapidly our information universe is expanding. What is important is that while no one really knows how much information there is out there or how quickly the information is being produced or replicated, nobody really doubts that the amount of information that we have at our fingertips — some of it trustworthy, some not — is enormous and that this amount is increasingly very quickly, mostly because of the simple and low cost of publishing on the World Wide Web.

This brings us to the second problem, namely that this does not mean that the knowledge that existed before the Internet revolution is obsolete, irrelevant, or no longer holds. To name just a few things that we learned when we were children: the Pythagorean theorem still holds true (in a right triangle, the sum of the squares of the two other sides is equal to the square of the hypotenuse; $a^2 + b^2 = c^2$), as does the gravitational constant and the acceleration of a falling body on Earth ($G = 6.67 \times 10^{-11}$ N • $(m/kg)^2$ and in a vacuum, an object falls at a rate of $9.80665 \, m/s^2$), there are still seven continents (Asia, Africa, North America, South America, Antarctica, Europe and Australia), the Norman conquest of England took place in 1066, a limerick has five lines and a sonnet fourteen. The fact is that much or most of what has passed for knowledge in previous generations is still valid and useful. To adequately deal with the stream of new information that increases in size and tempo daily, we — as stated in Myth 4 — must be able to search, find, select, process, evaluate and organize that information, turning it into knowledge. However, as (Hannafin and Hill, p. 526) warned, "... while technology has been lauded for potentially democratizing access to information, educational use remains fraught with issues of literacy, misinterpretation, and propagandizing".

An interesting anomaly here, but anomalies are very often the case when dealing with myths, is that many of those who are of the mistaken opinion that knowledge is as perishable as fresh fish propagate problem-based learning as one of the pedagogies that should be applied. And what, you may ask, is the anomaly here? One of the basic tenets of problem-based learning is that the learner should make use of prior knowledge, knowledge gained anywhere from yesterday to a decade or more ago in the case of university students and even longer in continuing education. The first principle of problem-based learning, according to

Schmidt, is the activation of prior knowledge. He states, "Learning, by its nature, has a restructuring character. It presupposes earlier knowledge that is used in understanding new information ... This prior knowledge and the kind of structure in which it is available in long-term memory, will determine what is understood" (Schmidt, p. 12). In a more recent article, Schmidt and colleagues stated that "prior knowledge seems to guide what students recall from new information ... improved achievement on learning tasks that were related to the activated prior knowledge ... [and] has also been shown to moderate the positive effect of elaboration on the learning of facts" (Van Blankenstein, Dolmans, van der Vleuten, & Schmidt, p. 731). In problem-based learning, students are asked to construct one or more explanatory models using their own prior knowledge which has been activated by the problem (see also Barrows & Tamblyn; Schmidt, De Volder, De Grave, Moust, & Patel). Finally, according to Boekaerts, prior knowledge is a prerequisite for self-regulated learning because without prior knowledge learners would be unable to plan a learning goal and monitor the learning process. Thus, without this prior knowledge, the floor would fall out from under problem-based learning. Apparently, it does not matter for proponents of this twenty-first century approach to knowledge and learning that the knowledge that is being used to understand texts, construct models and even regulate the learning process itself is no longer relevant or true since it is as perishable as fresh fish! And, by the way, the article by Barrows and Tamblyn is more than 35 years old at the time of publishing; we wonder if we can use it.

> :-\ The amount of information coming at us daily is increasing at an ever faster rate. But the knowledge that we need to understand and interpret that information is still fairly stable. Although the knowledge in certain domains does increase and change, it is more important to teach students to deal with these changes than to view knowledge as being unimportant!

REFERENCES

Barrows, H. S., & Tamblyn, R. M. (1980). *Problem-based learning: An approach to medical education*. New York: Springer.

Boekaerts, M. (1997). Self-regulated learning: A new concept embraced by researchers, policy makers, educators, teachers and students. *Learning and Instruction, 7*, 161–186.

Gantz, J. F. (2008). *The diverse and exploding digital universe. An updated forecast of worldwide information growth through 2011*. IDC (International Data Corporation) White Paper, available at: <https://www.emc.com/collateral/analyst-reports/expanding-digital-idc-white-paper.pdf>.

Hannafin, M. J., & Hill, J. (2007). Resource-based learning. In M. Spector, M. D. Merrill, J. van Merrienboer, & M. P. Driscoll (Eds.), *Handbook of research on educational communications and technology* (3rd ed., pp. 525–536). Mahwah, NJ: Erlbaum.

Hill, J. R., & Hannafin, M. J. (2001). Teaching and learning in digital environments: The resurgence of resource-based learning. *Educational Technology, Research and Development, 49*(3), 37–52.

Marcum, J. (2003). The 21st century library. *FDU Magazine, 11*(2), 26–29.

Schmidt, H. G. (1983). Problem based learning: Rationale and description. *Medical Education, 17,* 11–16.

Schmidt, H. G., De Volder, M. L., De Grave, W. S., Moust, J. H. C., & Patel, V. L. (1989). Explanatory models in processing of science text: The role of prior knowledge activation through small-group discussion. *Journal of Educational Psychology, 81,* 610–619.

Van Blankenstein, F. M., Dolmans, D. H. J. M., van der Vleuten, C. P. M., & Schmidt, H. G. (2013). Relevant prior knowledge moderates the effect of elaboration during small group discussion on academic achievement. *Instructional Science, 41,* 729–744.

MYTH 6

You Learn Better if You Discover Things for Yourself rather than Having Them Explained to You by Others

There is a good chance that many educational researchers, having read the contents table at the front of the book, will immediately have flicked through to this page. It is a very popular theme. Type the search term "discovery learning" in Google, and you will get page after page of references and publications. But in contrast to learning styles, the scientific consensus on this issue is not so uniform. Before we go any further, what exactly do we mean by "discovery learning"? The concept, which is sometimes also referred to as self-discovery or active learning, was launched by Jerome Bruner in the 1960s. According to Bruner, education needs to be organized in such a way that the learner interacts with the material to be learned in an active and self-investigatory manner. It is intended that the child should learn to think and solve problems independently. This corresponds closely with the arguments of Piaget, who stated:

Each time one prematurely teaches a child something he could have discovered for himself, that child is kept from inventing it and consequently from understanding it completely. (Piaget, p. 715)

The following positive effects are often associated with discovery learning:
* Concepts and rules are more fully remembered.
* Intrinsic motivation replaces extrinsic motivation.
* By discovering the rules for him- or herself, the learner will be more easily able to find solutions in new problem situations.

But what of this is actually true? All too often, the discussions relating to discovery learning are reduced to a polarization between two extreme positions: direct instruction and active learning. According to this reasoning, there is no instruction of any kind involved in active learning and no active processing of information in direct instruction. This leads to the faulty perception of both schools of thought.

If we look at the metastudies on this subject, then we can see that discovery learning does have a clear positive learning effect. The problem is that it is difficult to pin down exactly where its added value comes from. Opinions differ on this matter. Some research has shown that knowledge acquisition is not always optimal with discovery learning and that the focus tends to be more on processes. This is not illogical, in view of the new insights we now possess about how people learn. You need lots of knowledge to solve problems and you need a frame of reference to acquire knowledge through self-tuition.

While some studies praise the added value of discovery learning in the field of critical thinking skills, other studies argue that it is precisely in this domain that discovery learning falls down. And so it continues.

Sometimes this myth appears in the form of "the child as the little scientist", an idea that is inherent in the concept of discovery learning. The question of whether children are actually able to behave in this manner is, however, yet another gray area, with no conclusive arguments on either side of the debate. However, it does seem clear that if you organize your learning environment with this in mind, you can be sure that your pupils will not recognize it as such and will therefore not start working in a self-discovering way.

This is all based on the premise that since the discovery of new facts and relationships through exploration and experimentation is of utmost importance in science, in order to educate scientific thinkers we must also use discovery learning as an instructional method in schools. Bruner put forth discovery learning as a form of inquiry-based instruction, assuming that it is best for learners to discover facts and relationships for themselves rather than being taught. Here a note is needed: some years after launching "discovery learning", Bruner put forward a new concept which he this time called "guided discovery". This new concept, as the name implied, recognized the importance of a degree of external guidance and instruction for the child. It is now generally understood that many pupils are not capable or are insufficiently capable of constructing and processing knowledge without some form of assistance. For example, a report published by the Royal Netherlands Academy of Arts and Sciences (KNAW) on the subject of arithmetic education at primary school level concluded that the less bright pupils benefited from direct instruction.

But as described for problem solving, the use of discovery as an instructional method for novice learners ignores the limitations of human working memory. It requires the learner to search a domain (either in the real world or in a computer-simulated microworld) for relationships between two or more variables; that is, for the principles that apply in the domain. If learners have no or little knowledge about the domain to begin with and also lack a systematic approach to exploration and experimentation, this discovery process makes extremely heavy demands on working memory because for the novice learner, each element in the domain might possibly be related to each other element. The learner is facing a combinatorial explosion without having the knowledge to control it. Furthermore, the resulting working memory load does not contribute to the accumulation of knowledge in long-term memory because while working memory is being used to search for meaningful relationships, it is not available and cannot be used to learn. Indeed, it is possible to "learn" by discovery for extended periods with minimal alterations to long-term memory; that is, without learning anything (Sweller, Mawer, & Howe).

There are two more problems with discovery learning resulting from the substitution of the pedagogy of a domain with the epistemology of that domain, especially in the domain of the natural sciences. The first problem is especially relevant to children. Piaget long ago made clear that children and adolescents are not miniature adults: "Intelligence progresses from a state in which accommodation to the environment is undifferentiated from the assimilation of things in the subject's schemata to a state in which the accommodation of multiple schemata is distinguished from their respective and reciprocal assimilation" (np). This process proceeds through a series of cognitive stages, each characterized by a general cognitive structure that affects all thinking. Each stage represents how reality is understood during that stage, and each stage, except the last one, is an inadequate approximation of reality. In other words, learners in initial education see the world differently from adults (let alone scientists), interpret and understand it differently, and are not capable of carrying out the abstract cognitive transformations necessary for fruitful knowledge construction as it occurs in the sciences.

Hattie and Yates added a last important problem, closely related to the importance of prior knowledge:

> ... several studies have found that low ability students will prefer discovery learning lessons to direct-instruction-based lessons, but learn less from them. Under conditions of low guidance, the knowledge gap between low and high ability students tend to increase. The lack of direct guidance has greater damaging effects on learning in low ability students especially when procedures are unclear, feedback is reduced, and misconceptions remain as problems to be resolved rather than errors to be corrected. (p. 78)

Even if we concentrate on teaching for and learning by adults who might be able to think abstractly and carry out the necessary cognitive transformations to think inductively and construct theories, we are confronted with a second problem when using epistemology as pedagogy, namely that novice learners are not miniature experts. As explained before, experts possess sophisticated schemas in long-term memory, allowing them to deal differently with problems and solve them in different ways from novices. For example, De Groot determined that chess grandmasters determining what the next move should be do not consider more moves than less highly ranked expert chess-players, but "zoom in" on potentially good moves earlier in their search than "weaker" players. Thanks to available schemas, they have a greater ability to recognize significant features, as Gobet and Simon noted. As another example, Cuthbert et al. found that experts in medical diagnosis produce fewer but more general hypotheses at an earlier stage of problem solving than novices, use forward reasoning (working from findings to hypotheses) rather than backward reasoning, use a breadth-first approach (considering and evaluating several hypotheses at once) rather than depth-first approach, and demonstrate superior hypothesis evaluation skills. In other words, the differences between experts and novices manifest themselves not only at the conceptual level, but also at the level of epistemology and ontology (Jacobson). A novice sees, experiences and learns differently from an expert.

So where does this leave us? Is discovery learning a myth? The conclusion is not yes or no. Our opinion, for what it is worth, is that the value of discovery learning, like many other educational visions, is dependent on the target group, the objectives and the subjects. Just as education based exclusively on direct instruction is not necessarily the best option for all groups and all objectives, so education based exclusively on discovery learning is also not a one-size-fits-all solution. For novice learners discovery learning could never be the method, although it may be a goal. Effective educational methods should carefully and gradually help learners to move towards this goal. Van Merriënboer and Kirschner sum it up in their 2013 article as follows: First, such methods should help learners to gain some knowledge about the learning domain, because new relationships can only be discovered thanks to things you already know (what you know determines what you see, not the other way round). Second, such methods should help learners develop skills and cognitive strategies for systematically exploring and experimenting in the domain, using the rules of thumb that are useful in the domain. And third, such methods should provide support and guidance during the discovery process, and only decrease support and guidance as learners gain more expertise. However, for experts in a domain, it might be really effective.

In conclusion, in the educational world there is no longer any real support for "pure" discovery learning and nobody really expects it to make a comeback. For this reason, it is now more common to speak of investigative learning rather than discovery learning.

:-| There are many fervent supporters of discovery learning and there are just as many other researchers who have shown it to be a myth. Both are right to a certain extent. Pure discovery learning does not work, but inquiry can still be effective with the right guidance and support. And the more novice the learner is, the more important support and guidance are, to the point where discovery learning actually becomes good case-based instruction.

REFERENCES

Bangert-Drowns, R. L., & Bankert, E. (1990). *Meta-analysis of effects of explicit instruction for critical thinking*. Paper presented at the Annual Meeting of the American Educational Research Association, Boston, MA.

Bruner, J. S. (1967). *On knowing: Essays for the left hand*. New York: Atheneum.

Cuthbert, L., du Boulay, B., Teather, D., Teather, B., Sharples, M., & du Boulay, G. (1999). *Expert/novice differences in diagnostic medical cognition: A review of the literature*. Sussex: University of Sussex (Cognitive Sciences Research Paper 508).

De Groot, A. D. (1946). *Het denken van den schaker*. Amsterdam: Noord Hollandsche [Thinking processes in chess players].

De Groot, A. D. (1978). *Thought and choice in chess* (2nd ed., Revised translation of De Groot, 1946). The Hague: Mouton Publishers Revised translation of De Groot, 1946.

Gelderblom, G. (2007). *Effectief omgaan met verschillen in het rekenonderwijs*. Amersfoort: CPS [Effectively dealing with differences in mathematics education].

Gobet, F., & Simon, H. A. (1996). The roles of recognition processes and look-ahead search in time-constrained expert problem solving: Evidence from grandmaster level chess. *Psychological Science*, 7, 52–55.

Hattie, J., & Yates, G. C. (2013). *Visible learning and the science of how we learn*. New York: Routledge.

Jacobson, M. J. (2001). Problem solving, cognition, and complex systems: Differences between experts and novices. *Complexity*, 6(3), 41–49.

Kirschner, P. A. (2009). Epistemology or pedagogy, that is the question. In S. Tobias, & T. M. Duffy (Eds.), *Constructivist instruction: Success or failure?* (pp. 144–157). New York: Routledge.

Kirschner, P., Sweller, J., & Clark, R. (2006). Why minimal guidance during instruction does not work: An analysis of the failure of constructivist, discovery, problem-based, experiential, and inquiry-based teaching. *Educational Psychologist, 41*(2), 75—86.

Koninklijke Nederlandse Academie van Wetenschappen (2009). *Rekenonderwijs op de basisschool. Analyse en sleutels tot verbetering.* Amsterdam: KNAW [Mathematics education in elementary school: Analysis and keys to improvement].

Mayer, R. E. (2004). Should there be a three-strikes rule against pure discovery learning? *American Psychologist, 59*(1), 14—19.

Piaget, J. (1955). *The construction of reality in the child* (M. Cook, Trans.). London: Routledge and Kegan Paul <http://www.marxists.org/reference/subject/philosophy/works/fr/piaget2.htm>.

Piaget, J. (1970). Piaget's theory. In P. Mussen (Ed.), *Carmichael's manual of child psychology* (Vol. 1, pp. 703—772). New York: John Wiley & Sons.

Shymansky, J. A., Hedges, L. V., & Woodworth, G. (1990). A reassessment of the effects of inquiry-based science curricula of the 60s on student performance. *Journal of Research in Science Teaching, 27*, 127—144.

Sweller, J., Kirschner, P. A., & Clark, R. E. (2007). Why minimal guidance during instruction does not work: A reply to commentaries. *Educational Psychologist, 47*(1), 115—121.

Sweller, J., Mawer, R. F., & Howe, W. (1982). Consequences of history-cued and means-end strategies in problem solving. *The American Journal of Psychology*, 455—483.

Taraban, R., Box, C., Myers, R., Pollard, R., & Bowen, C. W. (2007). Effects of active-learning experiences on achievement, attitudes, and behaviors in high school biology. *Journal of Research in Science Teaching, 44*, 960—979.

van Merriënboer, J. J. G., & Kirschner, P. A. (2013). *Ten steps to complex learning* (2nd ed.). Hillsdale, NJ: Erlbaum/Taylor and Francis.

MYTH 7

You Can Learn Effectively through Problem-Based Education

A popular premise is that learning to solve problems is of utmost importance (Popper) and that to achieve this goal we must use problem solving as an instructional method in schools. This has led to the evolution of problem–based education as the teaching/learning approach of choice by many educational systems. The University of Maastricht, for example, has been working with problem–based learning for the past 35 years. The university summarizes its philosophy as follows:

> In problem-based learning, the students work together in small groups of about ten students with the aim of solving problems or completing a learning task under the guidance of a teacher. The students discuss the problem or learning task, which is often related to their ultimate professional context. In the first instance, at this stage the students activate their existing knowledge.
>
> During the discussion the students discover what things they still do not know or fully understand and will therefore require further self-study. This preliminary discussion also leads to the formulation of the learning objectives that will likewise require further study. This is then followed by the self-study phase, in which the students effectively research and investigate the learning objectives, using all available sources. After this self-study, which usually lasts for about two days, the students come together again to re-discuss the same problem or learning task. They report what they have discovered about the learning objectives and discuss any elements of the subject that are still unclear, before attempting to apply what they have learnt to the problem or learning task. During this second discussion the teacher plays a facilitating role, by occasionally asking questions that will require the students to think more deeply, and encourage them to put into practice and evaluate what they have learned.

In other words, in problem–based learning, the solving of a problem by the learners themselves is central, with the teacher or a coach acting in a supporting role.

The use of problem solving as an instructional method, however, completely ignores human working memory limitations, as Kirschner, Sweller, and Clark and Sweller explained. Working memory is very limited in duration and capacity. Baddeley described how information stored in working memory and not rehearsed is lost within 30 seconds, and the capacity of working memory is limited to only a small number of seven plus or minus two elements (according to Miller) or even four plus or minus one element (according to Cowan). When actively processing rather than merely storing information, the number of items that can be processed may only be two or three, depending on the nature of the processing required (Sweller, van Merriënboer, & Paas).

The interactions between working memory and long-term memory are even more important than the direct processing limitations. The limitations of working memory only apply to new, yet to be learned information that has not been stored in long-term memory. When dealing with previously learned information stored in long-term memory, the limitations disappear because an experienced problem solver has constructed cognitive schemas in long-term memory that can be used to solve new problems. These schemas are handled as one element in working memory. But in the absence of cognitive schemas, as is the case for novice learners in school, problem solving is only possible thanks to weak methods such as means—ends analysis, which requires the student to consider differences between the goal state and the given state of the problem, and to search blindly for solution steps to reduce those differences. Problem solving through means—ends analysis or other weak methods is the only way of attaining a problem goal in the absence of useful cognitive schemas. This process is exceptionally expensive in terms of working memory capacity, because the problem solver must continually hold and process in working memory the current problem state, the goal state, the relations between goal state and problem state, the solution steps that could reduce the differences between the two states, and any subgoals along the way. More importantly, it bears no relation whatsoever to schema construction processes concerned with learning to recognize problem states and their associated solution steps; that is, with learning to solve problems. Learning to solve problems and problem solving are thus two very different and incompatible processes!

Several alternatives to conventional problem solving have been devised to teach problem solving in more efficient ways, including the use of goal-free problems, worked-out examples and completion problems (see Sweller et al., for an overview). Goal-free problems do not permit problem solvers to extract differences between a current problem state and a goal state because no goal is specified. To solve goal-free problems, a learner considers the problem state encountered and finds a solution step that can be applied, yielding a new problem state for which the learner can find another solution step, and so on. With regard to working memory, a goal-free strategy requires nothing more than each problem state and any solution step that can be applied to that state, which drastically reduces working memory load. It is precisely this combination that is required for the construction of cognitive schemas. Studying worked-out examples also eliminates means—ends search and cognitive load. In contrast to conventional problems, worked-out examples focus students' attention on relevant problem states and associated solution steps, enabling them to construct useful cognitive schemas. An alternative to worked-out examples is provided by completion problems, because they overcome the disadvantage of worked-out examples, that they do not force learners to carefully study them. Completion problems are problems for which a given state, a goal state and a partial solution are provided to learners, who must complete the partial solution. Like worked-out examples, completion problems decrease cognitive load, but unlike worked-out examples, they force learners to study them because they otherwise will not be able to complete the solution correctly.

There is overwhelming evidence[2] that goal-free problems, worked-out examples and completion problems are much more effective than conventional problem solving to teach problem-solving skills and reach transfer of learning; that is, the ability to solve new problems in a domain. Problem solving as an instructional method only becomes effective when learners have already developed useful cognitive schemas in a domain. Fading guidance strategies, as Renkl and Atkinson explain, are critical to support the development process of novice problem solvers into more experienced problem solvers. An effective fading-guidance strategy is, for example, the "completion strategy", which uses completion problems as a bridge between worked-out examples (i.e., completion problems with a full given solution) and conventional problems (i.e., completion problems without a given solution). In a completion strategy, learners start with the study of worked-out examples, then complete increasingly larger parts of given partial solutions, and only independently solve conventional problems after lengthy and substantial practice.

And why does problem-based education seem to score so poorly in the professional literature? Research shows that in practice it is not really suitable for acquiring new knowledge. Some studies have even recorded negative effects in terms of knowledge acquisition, which means that students can sometimes even learn the wrong things. If, however, you use problem-based learning to apply previously acquired knowledge to a new

---

[2] Available from the authors.

problem, then it has a significantly positive effect. In other words, problem-based learning is very suitable for applying and honing existing skills and for making connections between different concepts. But it is far less appropriate for acquiring new knowledge or insights. This leads to the conclusion that it is very important for the teacher to play an active role in thinking about the different solution strategies and in providing new insights.

:-| The use of problem-based learning to learn new content does not have a positive learning effect. But there is a positive learning effect if you use problem-based learning to further explore and remember something that the learner already knows.

REFERENCES

Baddeley, A. (1992). Working memory. *Science, 255*, 556–559.

Baddeley, A. (2000). The episodic buffer: A new component of working memory? *Trends in Cognitive Sciences, 4*, 417–422.

Cowan, N. (2001). The magical number 4 in short-term memory: A reconsideration of mental storage capacity. *Behavioral and Brain Sciences, 24*, 87–114.

Dochy, F., Segers, M., Van den Bossche, P., & Gijbels, D. (2003). Effects of problem-based learning: A meta-analysis. *Learning and Instruction, 13*, 533–568.

Dolmans, D. D. (2010, 27 June). *Innoveren om beter te leren* (Inaugurele rede, Maastricht University) [Innovating to learn better (Inaugural address, Maastricht University)]. Maastricht: Maastricht University. Retrieved July 8, 2012, from <http://www.maastricht-university.nl/web/file?uuid=b63e23d7-e5a2-4056-8a94-9efe1df320f7&owner=0d667d 2d-a0b0-439a-9adc-2b4dca0a88cc>.

Gijbels, D., Dochy, F., Van den Bossche, P., & Segers, M. (2005). Effects of problem-based learning: A meta-analysis from the angle of assessment. *Review of Educational Research, 75*, 27–61.

Kirschner, P., Sweller, J., & Clark, R. (2006). Why minimal guidance during instruction does not work: An analysis of the failure of constructivist, discovery, problem-based, experiential, and inquiry-based teaching. *Educational Psychologist, 41*(2), 75–86.

Miller, G. A. (1956). The magical number seven, plus or minus two: Some limits on our capacity for processing information. *Psychological Review, 63*, 81–97.

Newman, M. (2004). *Problem based learning: An exploration of the method and evaluation of its effectiveness in a continuing nursing education programme.* London: Middlesex University.

Popper, K. (1999). *All life is problem solving.* London: Routledge.

Renkl, A., & Atkinson, R. K. (2003). Structuring the transition from example study to problem solving in cognitive skill acquisition: A cognitive load perspective. *Educational Psychologist, 38*(1), 15–22.

Sweller, J. (1999). *Instructional design in technical areas.* Camberwell, Australia: ACER Press.

Sweller, J., van Merriënboer, J. J. G., & Paas, F. (1998). Cognitive architecture and instructional design. *Educational Psychology Review, 10*, 251–296.

van Merriënboer, J. J. G. (1997). *Training complex cognitive skills.* Englewood Cliffs, NJ: Educational Technology Publications.

van Merriënboer, J. J. G., & Kirschner, P. A. (2007). *Ten steps to complex learning* (2nd ed.). Hillsdale, NJ: Erlbaum/Taylor and Francis.

MYTH 8

Boys Are Naturally Better at Mathematics than Girls

Are there really biological or genetic reasons that would cause or allow one gender to perform better than the other, for example that boys are better at mathematics than girls? This is an idea that is widely believed, and not just among teachers: boys and girls are different. Girls are better linguistically and boys are better at mathematics. In the past there were several studies that seemed to confirm this, such as the Programme for International Student Assessment (PISA) findings of 2003 and 2009. Even so, the idea is now coming under increasing pressure. For example, in the Trends in International Mathematics and Science Study (TIMSS) the results per country sometimes show that girls score as well as and sometimes better than boys at mathematics. Moreover, a metastudy by Stoet and Geary concluded that the past research on which the "difference" idea is based was not always scientifically reliable. They criticized the past reports that claimed to verify these differences. Although they found that differences did often exist, usually in favor of the boys but sometimes in favor of the girls, in general these differences were relatively small.

A study by Kane and Mertz based on international data from 86 countries has provided evidence to suggest that some of the typical ideas about gender and mathematical ability are open to reasonable doubt. In particular, it questions the widely held assumption that girls are worse at mathematics because boys and girls are biologically different.

Jonathan Kane and Janet Mertz, both professors at the University of Wisconsin (Kane, a professor of mathematical and computer sciences; Mertz, the senior author of the study and a professor of oncology), extensively tested the different biological, social/cultural and economic factors that may explain the discrepancy in mathematical performance between boys and girls, and concluded that not one of these hypotheses could be proven scientifically by the data. In fact, the results of their analyses showed that, in general, girls outperformed boys in mathematics by about five points in the 2003 and 2007 TIMSS.

The researchers linked the difference in performance to social and cultural factors, rather than biological ones. They arrived at this insight by comparing the data from the different countries. They established that in some countries there is no difference at all between the mathematics results of boys and girls. More specifically, it was clear that it was primarily in Western countries that boys systematically do better than girls. As stated in the article, "it is much more reasonable to attribute differences in math performance primarily to country-specific social factors" than to gender issues (Kane & Mertz).

As far as boys and girls in the same class are concerned, the researchers concluded that having separate classes for girls does not seem to benefit them. This was evident from the experience of separate classes that exist in Muslim countries, previously investigated by Steven Levitt of *Freakonomics* fame. One author of the Wisconsin study, Janet Mertz, comments: "The girls living in some Middle Eastern countries, such as Bahrain and Oman, had, in fact, not scored very well, but their boys had scored even worse, a result found to be unrelated to either Muslim culture or schooling in single-gender classrooms". She continues: "Bahraini boys may have a low average math score because some attend religious schools, whose curricula include little mathematics. Also, some low-performing girls drop out of school early, so that the tested sample is not representative for the whole population. For this reason, we believe it is much more reasonable to attribute differences in math performance to country-specific social factors" (Fryer & Levitt).

A 2014 meta-analysis of gender differences in scholastic achievement, by Daniel and Susan D. Voyer, shows something completely different. Their analysis of research spanned the period between 1914 and 2011 in more than 30 countries, based on 502 effect sizes drawn from 369 samples reflecting the grades of 538,710 boys and 595,332 girls. They found a small but significant female advantage for the overall sample of effect sizes. Noteworthy was that the largest female advantage was for language courses and the smallest for mathematics courses. In other words, girls had higher achievement across the board, even for mathematics!

It is of interest here that the authors studied school achievement as opposed to scores on standardized achievement tests. Their reason was that "[S]chool marks reflect learning in the larger social context of the classroom and require effort and persistence over long periods of time, whereas standardized tests assess basic or specialized academic abilities and aptitudes at one point in time without social influences" (Voyer & Voyer).

The conclusion was that despite the commonly held idea (actually the stereotype) that boys do better in mathematics and science than girls, girls have achieved higher grades than boys throughout their school years for nearly a century. They state, "Although gender differences follow essentially stereotypical patterns on achievement tests in which boys typically score higher on math and science, females have the advantage on school grades regardless of the material" (Voyer & Voyer).

Why is this the case? The authors posit that a combination of cultural and social factors might explain the results obtained; and by this we mean why the difference between girls and boys — with girls performing better — in mathematics is so small. They state, "the fact that parents tend to attribute math performance to abilities for males and to efforts for females might also lead males and females to approach school work differently. Specifically, the differential attributions made by parents might lead them to encourage more effort in females than in males, at least in math courses. This differential amount of encouragement could account in part for the slight female advantage in math" (Voyer & Voyer). In other words, if parents (and possibly teachers) did not accept this stereotype and act accordingly, the difference between girls and boys would be even larger! Finally, they note with respect to using achievement instead of standardized scores, that "research has shown girls tend to study in order to understand the materials [school achievement], whereas boys emphasize performance [on standardized tests], which indicates a focus on the final grades ... Mastery of the subject matter generally produces better marks than performance emphasis, so this could account in part for males' lower marks than females".

Crisis? What Crisis?

The above-mentioned study (Voyer & Voyer) shows that panic-driven claims that there is a gender crisis — or actually a boy crisis (including its related crisis of the feminization of education and the recurring call for single-sex classrooms, which we will discuss further in this book) — where the cry is that education needs to be drastically revamped because boys are now lagging behind girls in school achievement, are based on quicksand because girls' grades have been consistently higher than boys' grades across almost a century, with no significant changes in recent years. The authors of the study state, "The fact that females generally perform better than their male counterparts throughout what is essentially mandatory schooling in most countries seems to be a well-kept secret, considering how little attention it has received as a global phenomenon".

This has been backed up by a piece of Norwegian research which shows that it is primarily a willingness to practice that determines whether someone is good at mathematics, and that even if someone is good at one specific type of mathematics, innate abilities are not enough to skip practice to be good in other areas of mathematics (Sigmundsson, Polman, & Lorås).

In summary, we can conclude that in many studies boys do indeed achieve better scores for mathematics than girls, but in other studies girls sometimes score better than boys. However, the overall differences are so small that it should not be a matter for concern. The gender of the pupil is not a good predictor of mathematical performance.

But there is more. Imagine a world in which there are no words for numbers. Would you still be able to make calculations? The answer is probably "no". This became apparent from a study of the Pirahã tribe, who live in the Amazon rainforest (Everett & Madora). They have just three words to describe quantity: *hòi* means "small number or quantity"; *hoì* means "slightly bigger number or quantity" and *baàgiso* means "reason to meet" or "the largest number of quantity". The tribal community is one of the few communities in the world that is completely anumerical. And what transpires? Its members do indeed have difficulty with mathematical calculations.

How is this relevant to the general belief that boys are better at mathematics and girls are better at languages? It is relevant because it shows that this premise is simply not true. Statistics show that girls who are verbally stronger are often also stronger in mathematics; because to be good at mathematics — as the Pirahã prove in a reverse sense — you need to have good language skills.

In short, the entire boy—girl difference idea is a classic example of what thinking in boxes and self-fulfilling prophecies can lead to. The difference does not exist: so don't believe it.

:-\ Girls are not inherently less good at mathematics than boys; it's as simple as that.

REFERENCES

Everett, C., & Madora, K. (2011). Quantity recognition among speakers of an anumeric language. *Cognitive Science*, *36*(1), 130—141.

Fryer, R. G., Jr., & Levitt, S. D. (2009). *An empirical analysis of the gender gap in mathematics.* National Bureau of Economic Research (No. w15430).

Kane, J. M., & Mertz, J. E. (2012). Debunking myths about gender and mathematics performance. *Notices of the American Mathematical Society, 59,* 10–21.

Sigmundsson, R., Polman, R. C. J., & Lorås, H. (2013). Exploring individual differences in children's mathematical skills: A correlational and dimensional approach. *Psychological Reports, 113*(1), 23–30.

Stoet, G., & Geary, D. C. (2012). Can stereotype threat explain the gender gap in mathematics performance and achievement? *Review of General Psychology, 16*(1), 93–102.

Voyer, D., & Voyer, S. D. (2014). Gender differences in scholastic achievement: A meta-analysis. *Psychological Bulletin, 140,* 1174–1204.

Wei, W., Lu, H., Zhao, H., Chen, C., Dong, Q., & Zhou, X. (2012). Gender differences in children's arithmetic performance are accounted for by gender differences in language abilities. *Psychological Science, 23,* 320–330.

MYTH 9

In Education, You Need to Take Account of Different Types of Intelligence

In recent years, the educational world has been in thrall to Howard Gardner's theory of multiple intelligences, first launched by this American psychologist in 1983. According to Gardner, an intelligence is "a biopsychological potential to process information that can be activated in a cultural setting to solve problems or create products that are of value in a culture". It is — if we look at it in a clinical way — not an ability to learn, but an ability to process information through different intelligences, with these different intelligences being represented in different parts of the brain.

Why is this idea so attractive to so many people? In part, because it means that someone who fails to score well in a classic general intelligence quotient (IQ) test may turn out to be intelligent in some other, more specific way. It transforms the idea that all children should have equal chances to achieve all that they can achieve into an idea that all children are both equal with respect to some form of intelligence while unique in that their intelligences differ. It fits very well in the social-democratic philosophies that have flourished since the middle of the last half of the previous century, namely the essential equality of all people. One can see — in this age of anti-intellectual, anti-elitist populism — the attractiveness of this idea that there is not one "unfair" concept of universal intelligence "g", but rather that we are all Einsteins but in our own right.

Gardner identified the following intelligences:
- verbal/linguistic intelligence (word smart)
- mathematical/logical intelligence (maths smart)
- visual/spatial intelligence (picture smart)
- musical/rhythmical intelligence (music smart)
- bodily—kinesthetic intelligence (movement smart)
- interpersonal intelligence (people smart)
- intrapersonal intelligence (self smart)
- naturalist intelligence (nature smart).

One important thing to be aware of is the fact that the things included in this list are, according to Gardner, not fixed or permanent. Over time, new intelligences may be added and redundant ones may disappear. The most recent addition is existential intelligence (philosophically smart), meaning a well-developed understanding of religion, philosophy and the meaning of life.

Teachers who follow this theory have done much valuable work, because they recognize the differences in people. We would not dream of criticizing the value of this work, but the foundations on which it is based do seem to be rather shaky. In particular, there is one person who believes that this theory has often been incorrectly interpreted in the educational world, and that person is Howard Gardner himself!

A myth that irritates me is that people place my intelligences on the same foot-ing as learning styles. Learning styles say something about how people approach everything they do. If you are good at planning, people expect you to have a plan for everything you do. My own research and observations lead me to suspect that this is a wrong assumption.

If we are talking about multiple intelligences, we mean that we react indi-vidually in different ways to different types of content, such as language, music or other people. This is something completely different from a learning style.

You may think that a child is a visual learner, but you cannot say that with my theory of multiple intelligences. I would say that you have a child who is spatially aware, who has the ability to visualize things easily in space, and that we can build on this strength if we want to teach the child something new.

But this is not all. In the same interview Gardner complains about other aspects of the way his theory is translated into educational practice.

Another myth that is widely believed is that, because we have seven or eight intelligences, we need to develop the same number of different tests, so that each child's performance for each individual intelligence can be measured. This is a perversion of the theory. It is falling into the same error as the classic IQ test and then multiplying that error several times over. Personally, I am against the measuring of intelligences, except when this is used for a specific learning objective. For example, if we want a better understanding of the past history of the child, or we want to help it with its maths or we want to map out what might be a good starting-point for helping that specific child.

This interview dates from 1997, but in a 2013 opinion piece, Gardner repeated the same refutation of learning-styles thinking using his multiple intelligences theory (Strauss).

We now know that intelligences are not the same as learning styles (just as well, because we know what that might mean!), but are they really intelligences in the sense that Gardner claims?

In preparation for this section, we read dozens of articles about multi-ple intelligences. The best summary of the arguments was provided by

Daniel Willingham, a cognitive psychologist at the University of Virginia. He thinks that what Gardner called "intelligences" are actually "talents".

> Why are we referring to musical, athletic, and interpersonal skills as intelligences? Gardner was certainly not the first psychologist to point out that humans have these abilities. Great intelligence researchers — Cyril Burt, Raymond Cattell, Louis Thurstone — discussed many human abilities, including aesthetic, athletic, musical, and so on. The difference was that they called them talents or abilities, whereas Gardner has renamed them intelligences. (Willingham, 2004)

Willingham believes — and even Gardner himself has suggested something similar — that the theory would never have received so much attention if the name "intelligences" had not been used. Willingham argues that this terminology is not correct. According to him, the term "intelligence" has always referred to the kind of thinking skills that make a child successful in school. After all, the first intelligence test was devised precisely to predict the likelihood of this success; if it was important in school, it was included in the intelligence test.

There are a number of problems with the theory of multiple intelligences. First, according to Lynn Waterhouse in her 2006 article in *Educational Psychologist*, at that point in time there were no published studies that offered evidence of the validity of multiple intelligences. While proponents of the theory, for example Chen, argue that "a theory is not necessarily valuable because it is supported by the results of empirical tests" (p. 22) and that "intelligence is not a tangible object that can be measured" (p. 22), these arguments do not exempt the theory from the need for validating empirical data. She continues that Gardner himself makes it next to impossible to validate the "intangible theorized constructs" since measurement requires clearly defined components for the intelligences, but that Gardner himself stated that he will not define such components! This is like justifying that paranormal experiences did not happen in a controlled setting by saying that they did not occur because the "vibes" in the test situation were not right. Even if all people in a soccer stadium give "vibes" that gravity does not exist, the beer that I am holding will still fall to the ground if I let it slip out of my hand.

Another problem posed by Waterhouse is that research has shown that many of the categories of intelligence that Gardner differentiates correlate very highly with each another and thus cannot really be considered to be separate intelligences. Cognitive performance on skills related to verbal—linguistic, logical—mathematical and visual—spatial tasks, as well as many memory tasks, have been shown be highly related. In other words, general intelligence. She concluded:

> Enthusiasm for the use of the theory in classroom practice should be tempered by the awareness that the lack of sound empirical support makes it likely that its application will have little real power to enhance pupil learning beyond that stimulated by the initial excitement of something new. (Waterhouse, 2006)

John White, Emeritus Professor of Philosophy of Education at the Institute of Education University of London, in discussing his problems with Gardner's theory of multiple intelligences, presents a number of problems in relation to the theory. First, it is a theory of development. The theory assumes that what occurs or unfolds in the biological realm is also found in the mental realm. White posits two problems with this developmentalism, namely:

- In the biological realm it is so that in the seed/initial state, "biological seeds, plant or animal, have within them the power to unfold into more complex stages, given appropriate environmental conditions". While a newborn human also has certain inborn capacities such as the power to see and hear things, to desire for food and so forth, these capacities do not have "within them the power to unfold into more complex forms". They may change and become more sophisticated (whatever that may mean to different people) but they do not unfold into these. The changes are cultural products into which people are socialized. They are what makes one person crave a hamburgers and fries while another craves oysters and foie gras, what makes one person go to a wrestling match and another to an opera. One is not better than the other, but the original desires and powers to eat and see have become sophisticated in different, sociocultural ways.
- The mature state (Gardner's end-state) is clear in physical contexts. A fully grown human, worm or plant is one that can grow no further. While all biological entities continue to change, the changes that occur are either changes that maintain a steady state or changes towards the entity's inevitable deterioration; they are not towards further growth as is the case with respect to learning. If we were to apply Gardner's ideas to the mind, what we are actually saying is that we all have mental ceilings in each of Gardner's intelligences that we can either maintain (i.e., we will never know any more and we can only maintain what we have learnt until our point of biological maturity) or lose (i.e., as our brains inevitably deteriorate).

But his major concern "is not with MI [multiple intelligences] theory for its own sake but with its present influence in the educational world. If I am right, the eight or nine intelligences have not been shown to exist. If so, what are the implications for the school reforms based on the theory? As things are now, children are being encouraged to see themselves . . . as having innately given strengths in certain areas. This is part of their self-understanding. But if the theory is wrong, they may be getting a false picture of themselves".

In other words, multiple intelligences is more a booster of self-esteem than a prescription for teaching and learning (Gardner himself warned that he has proposed a scientific theory that should not be mistaken for a prescription for schooling). White continues that, in his opinion, there are better ways of improving self-esteem, "ones based on fact rather than illusion" and that see-ing one's intelligence in all of those pigeonholes [our words] "can be just as limiting to children's self-perception as IQ theory used to be. In some ways it is only a pluralistic version of this older determinism".

The educational supporters of Gardner's theories assumed that his new intelligences had roughly the same meaning and so drew the conclusion that if people have a particular type of intelligence, then the schools should teach it. This could lead to an interesting discussion about the proper function of schools, but the truth of the matter is that the theory actually reverses the original meaning of intelligences. This does not exempt you from your obligation as a teacher to find out as much as you can about the different talents of your pupils, so that you can then make best positive use of these talents. Just remember that they are probably not intelligences in the sense that Gardner meant.

A Well-Researched Alternative? Guilford's Structure of Intellect Model

In 1955, J. P. Guilford — an early proponent of the idea that intelligence is not a unitary concept — first presented his *structure of intellect model* (Figure 9), which he continued to revise through the years based on empirical psychometric research. In that model, a person's intelligence can be categorized by 180 different components in three different inde-pendent dimensions or categories:

- six *operations*: cognition, memory recording, memory retention, diver-gent production, convergent production, evaluation
- six *products*: units, classes, relations, systems, transformations, implications
- five *contents*: visual, auditory, symbolic, semantic, behavioral.

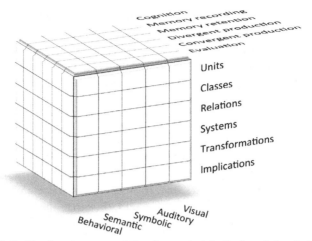

Figure 9 Guilford's structure of intellect model. *Designed by Pedro De Bruyckere, based on Guilford, J. P. (1988). Some changes in the structure of intellect model.* Educational and Psychological Measurement, 48, 1—4.

Since the dimensions are independent, there are theoretically 150 different components of intelligence ($6 \times 6 \times 5 = 180$).

Sources

Guilford, J. P. (1967). *The nature of human intelligence.* New York: McGraw-Hill.

Guilford, J. P. (1988). Some changes in the structure of intellect model. *Educational and Psychological Measurement, 48,* 1—4.

Guilford, J. P., & Hoepfner, R. (1971). *The analysis of intelligence.* New York: McGraw-Hill.

:-| We are more inclined to regard multiple intelligences as a kind of philosophy rather than a proven theory. We refrain from calling it a myth, but it is a theory that has the potential to become a myth, if taken too seriously.

REFERENCES

Adey, P. (2012). From fixed IQ to multiple intelligences. In P. Adey, & J. Dillon (Eds.), *Bad education* (pp. 199—214). Maidenhead: Open University Press.

Checkley, K. (1997). The first seven . . . and the eighth intelligence: A conversation with Howard Gardner. *Educational Leadership, 55*(1), 8—13.

Gardner, H. (1983). *Frames of mind: The theory of multiple intelligences.* New York: Basic Books.

Geake, J. (2008). Neuromythologies in education. *Educational Research*, *50*, 123−133.

Strauss, V. (2013, October 16). Howard Gardner: "Multiple intelligences" are not "learning styles". Retrieved March 31, 2014, from <http://www.washingtonpost.com/blogs/answer-sheet/wp/2013/10/16/howard-gardner-multiple-intelligences-are-not-learning-styles/>.

Waterhouse, L. (2006). Multiple intelligences, the Mozart effect, and emotional intelligence: A critical review. *Educational Psychologist*, *41*(4), 207−225.

White, J. (2005). *Howard Gardner: The myth of multiple intelligences* London: Institute of Education Viewpoint No. 16.

Willingham, D. T. (2004, Summer). Reframing the mind. *Education Next*. Retrieved May 30, 2012, from <http://educationnext.org/reframing-the-mind/>.

MYTH 10

Our Memory Records Exactly What We Experience

As a separate issue from learning, remembering what you have learned is an important part of daily life and therefore an important part of education as well. Some people have holes in their memory; others are capable of remembering a great deal. But there is bad news: nobody's memory is perfect. In fact, everything that we remember, everything that is recorded in our long-term memory, is the result of incoming information that we have processed (consciously or unconsciously) in the past. Imagine that you are walking along a corridor at school. While you are walking from one classroom to another, you are being constantly bombarded by sensory stimuli, but you will only remember the things that make an impact on your attention, the things on which you then focus. You will recall the delicious smell of the spaghetti sauce wafting up from the school canteen (it is nearly lunchtime and you are starving) but you might not notice the poster for the next school party (you are not really a party animal).

You sometimes hear people claim that they have a photographic memory. In 1970, a Harvard scientist called Charles Stromeyer III published an article in *Nature* in which he described the remarkable case of Elizabeth, who really did seem to have the perfect memory: she could memorize everything she saw. It is worth pointing out how unique she is: no one had ever done it before her and no one has ever done it since. In more recent times, she has refused to retake the same test, following her marriage to . . . Charles Stromeyer III.

The first question we need to ask is: What exactly is memory? This, however, is not an easy question to answer.

First, in psychology, memory is the process in which information is encoded, stored and retrieved. Via encoding, information from the world reaches our senses. Via storage, we maintain some of that information over longer or shorter periods of time. And via retrieval we locate and return that stored information.

Second, theories of cognition and cognitive architecture such as in the multistore model of memory proposed by Atkinson and Shiffrin (1968) discern at least three types of memory, namely sensory memory, working memory (also called short-term memory) and long-term memory (Figure 10).

Sensory memory is where it all begins. Information — actually stimuli from the world — reaches one or more of our five senses. In typical educational and learning situations this is via the ears or eyes, though in some types of learning the other three senses can also play a role, such as taste if one is learning to cook, smell if one is learning about aromatics in chemistry or flowers in botany, and touch if one is learning a sport or a medical student is learning to palpate a patient. Via the five senses, information enters sensory memory, where relevant information will be selected to be sent to working memory. In this respect sensory memory acts as a kind of buffer for stimuli received through the five senses, which are retained accurately, but very briefly. Important here is selection, since our senses are constantly "receiving" information from the environment (think of all the sounds in the room in which you are now sitting) but you only "register" what you attend to. It is even the case that you sometimes choose to deliberately ignore some incoming sensory stimuli.

Short-term or *working memory* is what you are using at this very moment to process this text (stimuli that have entered your sensory register through attention and recognition). It acts as a kind of "scratchpad" for temporary recall of the information that is being processed at any point in time. To understand this sentence, for example, you need to hold the beginning of the sentence in mind while the rest is read. This is a task carried out by the short-term or working memory. You use it for all of your conscious activities and it is the only memory that you can monitor. Everything else — content and function — is concealed until brought into working memory. This memory, as Miller and Baddeley describe, is

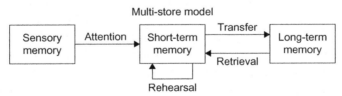

Figure 10 Atkinson and Shiffrin's multistore model of memory. *Reprinted from Atkinson, R. C., & Shiffrin, R. M. (1968). Human memory: A proposed system and its control processes. In K. W. Spence & J. T. Spence (Eds.),* The psychology of learning and motivation *(Vol. 2) (pp. 89–195). New York: Academic Press. Reprinted within the STM Permissions Guidelines (see http://www.stm-assoc.org/permissions-guidelines/ and http:// www.stm-assoc.org/2015_01_29_STM_Permissions_Guidelines_2014.pdf).*

very limited in that it can only hold about seven items or elements of information at any one time, which are lost if you do not do anything with them within a few seconds. You, as a reader, probably experience this limit when you are asked to read a very long and complicated sentence with many clauses and subclauses. At the end of the sentence, you no longer know what you have read and then have to read it again. Furthermore, because short-term/working memory is also used to organize, contrast, compare or work on that information, you probably can only process two or three items of information simultaneously as opposed to merely holding that information. Finally, short-term/working memory is seen not as one monolithic structure, but rather a system embodying at least two mode-specific components: a visuospatial sketchpad (e.g., for written words and pictures) and a phonological loop (e.g., for sounds) coordinated by a central executive which "calls up" information from elsewhere in the brain.

Long-term memory is, in contrast, what you use to make sense of and give meaning to what you are doing now. It is the repository for more permanent knowledge and skills and includes all things in memory that are not currently being used but which are needed to enable understanding. Short-term memories can become long-term memory via *consolidation*, in which we rehearse what we have placed in that memory and make meaningful associations between that information and information already stored — in schemas — in our long-term memory. Most cognitive scientists believe that the storage capacity of long-term memory is unlimited and is a permanent record of everything that a person has learned. You are not directly conscious of long-term memory. Awareness of its contents and functioning is filtered through working (conscious) memory.

Finally, there are other types of memory, which deal less with where and how something is sensed, processed and stored, but rather with the type of information. For example:

- *Declarative memory* deals with conscious and explicit recall and consists of information that we have explicitly stored and explicitly try to retrieve. This declarative memory can be further subdivided into *semantic memory*, which concerns facts, meanings, concepts and knowledge about the external world taken independent of context; and *episodic memory*, which concerns — usually — serial events and experiences specific to a particular context, such as a time and place in our lives. A subset of episodic memory is autobiographical memory, which deals with particular events within one's own life.

- In contrast to declarative memory, *procedural memory* is based not on conscious recall, but rather on implicit learning. This type of memory is primarily found, for example, in learning motor skills, and involves repetition and practice. A characteristic of procedural memory is that the things that are remembered are automatically translated into actions, and thus are sometimes very difficult to describe. In German this is known as *Fingerspitzengefühl* (literally: fingertips feeling) and in English we often call it tacit knowledge.

- *Topographic memory* is the ability to orient oneself in space, to recognize and follow an itinerary, or to recognize familiar places.

- *Flashbulb memories* are clear episodic memories of unique and highly emotional events. People remembering where they were or what they were doing when they first heard the news of President Kennedy's assassination or of 9/11 are examples of flashbulb memories.

There are a small number of people who have an eidetic memory, which is more common among the relatively young and the relatively old (Searleman). This resembles a photographic memory, which allows them to recall images that they have seen. But the recalled image is never an exact copy of the original. With this type of memory, what you see is colored by what you know or by what you expect to see, and therefore cannot be regarded as perfectly photographic.

As a general rule, we remember very little detail. Our brain stores only the most necessary elements and simply fills in the fine detail when we need to remember something. In this way, it may seem as though we remember something fully, but much of this hasty "filling in" is often not correct. This is because:

- Memory is general and even blurred, in that the images that we consider to be stored in our memory (that is, in our mind's eye) are less clear and information rich than the actual perception itself.

- Memory often stores (i.e., encodes) perceptual information automatically and unconsciously in a general verbal form and not as an image. For example, with respect to a room, we store the information that a room was big, small, noisy, calm, bright, dimly lit, etc. One of the authors recently went back to his old high school gym, which he remembered as being really big, only to be shocked by how small it was.

- Memory fills in gaps via a process of reconstruction that makes use of pieces of information from other sources such as pre-existing schemas and other memories. We interpret what we see so that it fits our schemas (Piaget called this *assimilation*) and mix them with other memories, either personal or vicarious (e.g., through reading something in a book, hearing something on the radio, or seeing something in a film or on television).
- Memory systematically distorts perception in systematic ways according to systematic biases. What we know determines what we see and how we experience it, and not the other way around.
- Memory is personal as we all interpret events in terms of our own world view. This is the basis of all constructivist learning principles. Different people seeing the same event or reading the same text will interpret and remember it differently.
- Memory changes over time (the original trace deteriorates) and with retelling (the trace is continually updated with new information). As we recall an event over and over, we drop details from earlier versions and add new details to later versions. All things being equal, accuracy declines with each new version.

Research conducted by Mark Snyder and Seymour Uranowitz indicates, for example, that stereotypes can often play a role in the recall process. They gave their test subjects a detailed text to read, outlining the life story of a woman, Betty K. One half of the test group was told that Betty was heterosexual; the other half that she was a lesbian. Both groups were then given a memory test about what they had read. Snyder and Uranowitz were able to conclude that people "adjusted" their recollections to coincide with their image of Betty (heterosexual or lesbian); for example, their memories about her relationship with her father and how she spent her free time.

The manner in which questions are asked also has an influence on what we remember. In 1974, Elisabeth Loftus and John Palmer conducted a now legendary experiment to prove this point. They showed their test subjects a slide depicting a car accident. The test subjects were then asked questions about the content of the slide. But some of the questions were deliberately suggestive. For example, on the slide a "stop" sign was clearly visible, but one of the questions suggested that it was actually a "give way" sign. People who were asked the suggestive question more frequently reported seeing a "give way" sign than the people who were asked the same question in a non-suggestive way. This all goes to prove that your memory is not always as reliable as you might think.

But I Saw It with My Own Eyes!

The following is attributed to Alan Baddeley in his book *Your memory: A user's guide*:

Australian eyewitness expert Donald Thomson appeared on a live TV discussion about the unreliability of eyewitness memory. He was later arrested, placed in a lineup and identified by a victim as the man who had raped her. The police charged Thomson although the rape had occurred at the time he was on TV. They dismissed his alibi that he was in plain view of a TV audience and in the company of the other discussants, including an assistant commissioner of police. The policeman taking his statement sneered, "Yes, I suppose you've got Jesus Christ, and the Queen of England, too". Eventually, the investigators discovered that the rapist had attacked the woman as she was watching TV — the very program on which Thomson had appeared. Authorities eventually cleared Thomson. The woman had confused the rapist's face with the face that she had seen on TV.

Source

Baddeley, A. D. (2004). *Your memory: A user's guide*. Richmond Hill, Canada: Firefly Books.

:-\ Don't trust your memories; they are never 100% correct. There is always a certain degree of selection and distortion. As a teacher, it is important for you to understand this.

REFERENCES

Atkinson, R. C., & Shiffrin, R. M. (1968). Human memory: A proposed system and its control processes. In K. W. Spence, & J. T. Spence (Eds.), *The psychology of learning and motivation* (Vol. 2, pp. 89—195). New York: Academic Press.

Baddeley, A. D. (1992). Working memory. *Science*, *255*, 556—559.

Bower, G. H. (1975). Cognitive psychology: An introduction. In W. K. Estes (Ed.), *Handbook of learning and cognitive processes: Volume 1: Introduction to concepts and issues* (pp. 25—80). Hillsdale, NJ: Erlbaum.

Gilbert, D. T. (2006). *Stumbling on happiness*. New York: A. A. Knopf.

Kapur, N. (2011). *The paradoxical brain*. Cambridge, MA: Cambridge University Press.

Lilienfeld, S. O. (2010). *50 great myths of popular psychology: Shattering widespread misconceptions about human behavior* Chichester, UK: Wiley-Blackwell.

Loftus, E., & Palmer, J. (1974). Reconstruction of automobile destruction: An example of the interaction between language and memory. *Journal of Verbal Learning and Verbal Behavior, 13*, 585–589.

Miller, G. A. (1956). The magical number seven, plus or minus two: Some limits on our capacity for processing information. *Psychological Review, 63*, 81–97.

Searleman, A. (2007, March). Is there such a thing as a photographic memory? And if so, can it be learned? *Scientific American*. Retrieved July 9, 2012, from <http://www.scientificamerican.com/article/is-there-such-a-thing-as/>.

Snyder, M., & Uranowitz, S. W. (1978). Reconstructing the past: Some cognitive consequences of person perception. *Journal of Personality and Social Psychology, 36*, 941–950.

Willingham, D. T. (2009). *Why don't students like school? A cognitive scientist answers questions about how the mind works and what it means for the classroom*. San Francisco, CA: Jossey-Bass.

MYTH 11

School Kills Creativity

One of the most viewed online videos on education is the RSA Animate video of *Changing education paradigms* by Sir Ken Robinson, famous for his three — not dissimilar — TED talks. We could discuss a lot of aspects of this video, but one main idea has struck many chords with people: school kills creativity.

In the video, Robinson describes the "alternative uses task" or "alternative uses test", originally developed by Guilford in 1967. In this test examinees are asked to list as many possible uses for a common household item (such as a brick, a paperclip or a newspaper).

Robinson explains that a genius is someone who can find over 200 uses for a paperclip, and that the majority of children who are under six are in fact geniuses before we start to school them to become "normal", with an average of 10—15 possible uses. Robinson does not quote research here, but a 1993 book by Land and Jarman called *Breakpoint and beyond: Mastering the future — today*, in which they discussed their 1968 study where 1600 three- to five-year-olds were given a similar creativity test to Guilford's, used by NASA to measure divergent thinking in engineers and scientists. They then retested the same children at 10 years of age and again at 15 years of age.

So, school kills creativity because children become less divergent thinkers. Still, there are some issues with this claim.

First of all, Robinson makes creativity and genius synonyms, but are they? Actually, it was Guilford (see myth 9 on multiple intelligences) who was one of the researchers in the 1950s and 1960s who started the debate over whether intelligence (as measured by IQ) and creativity are part of the same process (which is called the conjoint hypothesis) or represent distinct mental processes (the disjoint hypothesis). However, the correlations between IQ and creativity are low (Batey & Furnham).

Another possible explanation of the relationship between IQ and creativity is "the threshold hypothesis", as proposed by Ellis Paul Torrance, who developed a test based on Guilford's original task. This threshold hypothesis argues that you need a high degree of intelligence but that this is not enough to be creative. Kim's 2005 meta-analysis, examining whether this hypothesis was correct, found only small correlations between IQ and creativity tests and did not support the threshold theory.

But Robinson does not see genius as something you have or you don't have, and the same seems to go for creativity. He uses this one piece of research to show that everybody is born creative and genius and school does a really bad job.

Sawyer notes in his first chapter in his great review on the science of creativity that there are indeed many different views on the concept and that these views have changed over time. The idea of the child as born creative and society gradually corrupting them as they grow up originates "from the 19th-century Romantic era-belief that children are more pure, closer to nature ..." (p. 25). This is closely related to the view made popular by Rousseau in his book *Emile*.

But is it true? If we look at the changes during childhood, the view of people such as Piaget or Vygotsky is that when children are learning something new, they basically are constructing or *creating* new knowledge. Play is also an important element for creativity and, for instance, Sawyer describes how five-year-olds engage much more in improvisational play than three-year-olds. So, a child is not necessary born creative, but by learning becomes more creative ... but maybe not by learning after the age of six, when formal school really begins?

Well, first of all, there is an intriguing relationship between the amount and quality of pretend play and a child's measured creativity years later (correlation, not proven causation).

But as we learn more ... most research indicates with becoming older we become more creative. Some research (e.g., Torrance) mentions a *fourth-grade slump*, but other more recent research did not find this slump. And if there is one it's probably not because of school. Runco concluded "... that the fourth-grade slump, if it occurs isn't due to the highly structured school system, as Torrance thought; rather, if it occurs, it results from normal maturational processes, as children enter a 'literal' or 'conventional' stage in thinking and moral reasoning more generally, as part of a necessary developmental path towards the adult's 'postconventional' stage" (in Sawyer, p. 74). Sawyer concludes that it is misleading to refer to developmental changes as "slumps".

What can we tell about the role of schools in killing creativity? There is a very relevant chapter on education and creativity in the book by Sawyer, with one important paragraph that we need to share:

I believe that schools are essential to creativity. We've learned that creativity requires a high degree of domain knowledge ... Formal schooling is quite good at delivering this domain knowledge to students. Creativity research certainly doesn't suggest that everyone would be more creative if only we got rid of all of the schools! However, schools could better foster creativity if they were transformed to better align with creativity research. (p. 390)

Brainstorming Is Probably One of the Least Effective Methods for Arriving at Original and Creative Solutions

Brainstorming is well known not only in education, but also in the world of work. However, an article in the *New Yorker* magazine set us thinking about the real value of this widely used technique. The article explained how the basic idea of brainstorming was first formulated in 1948 by an advertising executive called Alex Osborn. His book *Your creative power* was a huge bestseller, but people were particularly fascinated by chapter 33 — the chapter on brainstorming.

But what exactly is brainstorming? It is a creativity technique whose purpose is to generate lots of new ideas about a particular subject in a very short time. The crucial element is that the participants are only allowed to evaluate the ideas afterwards, not during the brainstorming itself.

You have probably taken part in a brainstorming session yourself. But here comes the bad news: it is one of the least successful methods for developing good and creative solutions. Keith Sawyer, a psychologist at the University of Washington, summarizes what science knows about brainstorming as follows:

Decades of research have consistently shown that brainstorming in a group produces fewer ideas than if the same number of people had thought up their own ideas individually, before sharing them collectively.

It might not be so bad if the quality of the ideas resulting from brainstorming was better than the ideas generated by other methods, but even this is not the case. What is true is that people are working more and more collaboratively. Collaboration is positive, but not in the classic form of the brainstorming session. There are several methods that do work, but they differ from what we traditionally understand as brainstorming.

In 2003, Charlan Nemeth, a psychology professor at the University of California in Berkeley, divided 265 female students into groups of five.

She gave each group the same problem to solve: "How can we limit the impact of the traffic problem in the San Francisco Bay Area?" She also dictated the working method that the groups needed to follow. The first group was required to work in accordance with the classic brainstorming methodology, not giving any criticism of the suggested ideas until later. The second group was instructed to use what Nemeth called the "debate approach". They were informed that most research had shown that the best method to arrive at a good solution is that you must "spit out" as many ideas as possible — freewheeling — but that research had also shown that the solutions needed to be criticized and discussed for maximum effect. The third group was given no instructions — they could tackle the problem as they saw fit (Nemeth et al.).

The results were clearcut. The brainstorming teams did slightly better than the teams that were left to their own devices, but the "debate" teams were by far the most creative. There was a further knock-on effect as well: when the teams were broken up and the individual participants were asked to think further about the same problem, the members of the brainstorming and free teams came up with an average of only three additional ideas, whereas the members of the debate teams came up with an average of seven extra ideas.

It also is now widely accepted that knowledge workers should work in close proximity to each other: not so close that it is uncomfortable, but close enough for there to be plenty of opportunities for chance encounters. It seems that this is particularly important for researchers. The best research is carried out if people work within 10 meters of each other. Isaac Kohane of the Harvard Medical School summarizes this as follows:

> If you want people to work effectively together, it is important that you create a space where they can bump into each other spontaneously, almost by accident. Even in the internet era, these chance meetings are important for results.

Sources

Feinberg, M., & Nemeth, C. (2008). *The "rules" of brainstorming: An impediment to creativity?* Berkeley, CA: University of California (Institute for Research on Labor and Employment Working Paper Series, Working Paper No. Irwps-167-08).

Lee, K., Brownstein, J., Mills, R., & Kohane, I. (2010). Does collocation inform the impact of collaboration? *Plos ONE*, 5(12), e14279 Available at <http://www.plosone.org/article/info%3Adoi%2F10.1371%2Fjournal.pone.0014279>.

Nemeth, C. J., Personnaz, M., Personnaz, B., & Goncalo, J. A. (2003). *The liberating role of conflict in group creativity. A cross cultural study.* Institute for Research on Labor and Employment.

Osborn, A. F. (1957). *Applied imagination* (1st ed.). New York: Scribner.

Sawyer, R. K. (2012). *Explaining creativity: The science of human innovation.* Oxford: Oxford University Press.

:-\ Maybe schools are not fostering and nurturing creativity enough, but they definitely do not kill it!

REFERENCES

Batey, M., & Furnham, A. (2006). Creativity, intelligence, and personality: A critical review of the scattered literature. *Genetic, Social, and General Psychology Monographs, 132,* 355–429.

Guilford, J. P. (1967). *The nature of human intelligence.* New York: McGraw-Hill.

Kim, K. H. (2005). Can only intelligent people be creative? A meta-analysis. *Prufrock Journal, 16*(2–3), 57–66.

Land, G., & Jarman, B. (1993). *Breakpoint and beyond: Mastering the future — today.* New York: HarperCollins.

Robinson, K. (2010, October 14). RSA Animate — Changing education paradigms. Retrieved May 31, 2014, from <https://www.youtube.com/watch?v = zDZFcD GpL4U&feature = kp>.

Runco, M. A. (2003). *Critical creative processes.* Cresskill, NJ: Hampton Press.

Torrance, E. P. (1968). A longitudinal examination of the fourth grade slump in creativity. *Gifted Child Quarterly, 12*(4), 195–199.

Torrance, E. P. (1981). Predicting the creativity of elementary school children (1958–80) — and the teacher who "made a difference". *Gifted Child Quarterly, 25*(2), 55–62.

MYTH 12

Ninety-Three Percent of Our Communication Is Non-Verbal

This myth is sometimes known as the Mehrabian myth, after Albert Mehrabian (1939–), emeritus professor of psychology at the University of California, Los Angeles. He carried out research into the ways in which verbal and non-verbal communication relate to each other in pro- portional terms. This research resulted in what is often known as the 7–38–55 rule. This rule expresses the ratios between the three different elements we use to communicate and give meaning:

- The words you use account for 7% of meaning.
- The intonation of your voice counts for 38% of meaning.
- Your body language counts for 55% of meaning.

As with the theory of multiple intelligences, the inventor of the theory was none too happy with the way his ideas were subsequently interpreted and used. First, Mehrabian himself cautioned: "Please note that this and other equations regarding relative importance of verbal and nonverbal messages were derived from experiments dealing with communications of feelings and attitudes (i.e., like–dislike). Unless a communicator is talking about their feelings or attitudes, these equations are not applicable".

In an interview with the BBC, Mehrabian was asked point- blank whether 93% of our communication is non-verbal, to which he answered: "Of course not. And every time I hear my results being incor- rectly quoted in this way, I cringe inside. It must be obvious to anyone with a little bit of common sense that this cannot be right".

In an e-mail to Max Atkinson, reproduced in his book *Lend me your ears*, Mehrabian wrote: "I am obviously uncomfortable about misquotes of my work. From the very beginning I have tried to give people the cor- rect limitations of my findings. Unfortunately the field of self-styled 'cor- porate image consultants' or 'leadership consultants' has numerous practitioners with very little psychological expertise".

Talk about the durability of a myth. Even the original researcher is not able to expunge this monster that has gone on to live a life of its own.

Cries and Whispers

One of the authors, an American by birth, went to see a movie shortly after first arriving in The Netherlands. Having been in the country for two whole weeks and having no functional knowledge of the Dutch language he chose a film that sounded as if it was in English — *Cries and whispers*, directed by Ingmar Bergman — only to sit down and experience a very visual film in Swedish (the original title is *Viskningar och rop*) with Dutch subtitles. Do you really think that Paul — or do you think that you — could possibly grasp 93% of the communication in that film without the words, even though the actors were very expressive?

By the way, according to IMDB, this was the plot (which none of us ever got): When a woman dying of cancer in early twentieth century Sweden is visited by her two sisters, long-repressed feelings between the siblings rise to the surface.

Let's look at this rationally. You are reading these words without hearing us or seeing us, and yet you no doubt clearly understand the point we are trying to make. And there are plenty of other examples: a telephone conversation; talking to your partner while she is in the bathroom and you are in the kitchen. Of course, things can always go wrong with verbal communication and the non-verbal does also play an important role, but please remember that Mehrabian's original research investigated the way people communicate their emotions. He never intended that his findings should be applied to all forms of communication between people.

In addition to the author's comments and common sense, there is a third reason to find the myth unusable. The experiments were not what one would call ecologically valid and usable in real-world communication. For example, in one of Mehrabian's experiments the participants had to determine the positive ("dear", "thanks" and "honey"), negative ("brute", "don't" and "terrible") or neutral ("oh", "maybe" and "really") content of these nine words. Each was then read in a positive, neutral or negative tone of voice. In another, these vocalizations of the words were combined with photographs of people looking positive, negative or neutral. The participants were asked to judge whether the words were positive, negative or neutral based on the combined word/tone or word/picture combinations. This is where the statistics came from. Mehrabian claimed that in these experiments — a completely artificial, non-naturalistic design — the face conveyed 55% of the information, the voice 38% and the words just 7%. He showed in these specific experiments how tone of voice or facial expression can often override a word's meaning in conveying a positive or negative feeling.

Unfortunately, and this is as bad as if not worse than the learning pyramid myth, Mehrabian's limited experimental findings have been taken out of context, repeated, misunderstood, reworded, and so forth until "93% of communication is non-verbal" has become accepted as reality.

What does this myth show? Well, it shows that people recognize that non-verbal communication is important. And it is. But why do they need to exaggerate its importance to such a ludicrous extent? That is an entirely different question!

:-\ Even the inventor of this myth is irritated by the way his percentages are (mis)used. They are only accurate (possibly) if someone is talking about his or her feelings, but not in any other case!

If You Don't Learn a Language When You Are Young, You Lose the Chance to Learn That Language

There are lots of myths about learning languages. One of them is that it is best to learn a language when you are young, because it will cost you much more time and effort to learn it in later life. This myth has its origins in the theory of critical periods formulated by Eric Lenneberg in 1967 and the experiments of Konrad Lorenz in the 1970s. It is also a typical feature of the development theories of Piaget and others. One of the conclusions offered by Lenneberg was that the first language must be learnt during puberty: this would not be possible at a later age because of changes in the brain.

This theory has been broadened to include a second or foreign language. However, many modern-day researchers now regard the theory of critical periods as a myth. They argue that there is no such thing as critical periods for human learning. There may well be sensitive periods, periods during our lives when we find it easier to learn. But this does not mean that we become "incapable" of learning as we get older. When they are born, children have the ability to distinguish between different vocal sounds, but as they get older this ability deteriorates. For example, Japanese people find it increasingly difficult to tell the difference between the "l" and the "r" sound. This is a process that begins between the sixth and twelfth months of life.

For many things, the idea of "the earlier, the better" is indeed true, but the concomitant idea that after a certain period it is "too late" to learn certain skills is far too pessimistic. Much has been written on the plasticity of the human brain. And while we must not exaggerate this plasticity (if there was more, there would be far fewer serious consequences resulting from brain trauma), there is certainly enough to help us with learning in later life.

Research carried out in 2003 by Pallier et al. showed that it is even possible to forget your original mother tongue (something the American-born author of this book, to a certain degree, experiences every day as his English slowly transforms into Dunglish, making him often ask his colleagues "How do you say XXX in English?"). Their study showed that Korean children who had been adopted up to the age of eight years by people living in rural France had completely forgotten their original mother tongue in adulthood. They were effectively given a "new" mother tongue. It must be noted, however, that in all these cases there was no further contact with the Korean language as they were growing up.

:-\ Are there critical periods for learning a (second) language? It becomes more difficult after a sensitive period, but it is certainly not impossible.

Sources

Bruer, J. T. (1999). *The myth of the first three years: A new understanding of early brain development and lifelong learning*. New York: Free Press.

Byrnes, J. P. (2001). *Minds, brains, and learning: Understanding the psychological and educational relevance of neuroscientific research*. New York: Guilford Press.

Goswami, U. (2006). Neuroscience and education: From research to practice? *Nature Reviews Neuroscience*, 7(5), 406–413.

Lenneberg, E. H. (1967). *Biological foundations of language*. New York: Wiley.

Pallier, C., Dehaene, S., Poline, J. B., LeBihan, D., Argenti, A. M., Dupoux, E., et al. (2003). Brain imaging of language plasticity in adopted adults: Can a second language replace the first? *Cerebral Cortex*, *13*, 155–161.

REFERENCES

Atkinson, M. (2004). *Lend me your ears*. New York: Oxford University Press.

Mehrabian, A. (1972). *Nonverbal communication*. Chicago, IL: Aldine-Atherton.

Mehrabian, A. (1981). *Silent messages: Implicit communication of emotions and attitudes*. Belmont, CA: Wadsworth.

Mehrabian, A. (2011). "Silent messages": A wealth of information about nonverbal communication. Retrieved September 2, 2012, from <http://www.kaaj.com/psych/smorder.html>.

Mehrabian, A., & Ferris, S. R. (1967). Inference of attitudes from nonverbal communication in two channels. *Journal of Consulting Psychology*, *31*, 248–452.

So, What Exactly Do We Know about Learning?

If our summary so far has dampened your spirits (because you now know that some methods that you are using are not as effective as you thought), take heart! Here is a summary of the methods for which scientific evidence of their effectiveness does exist.

FEEDBACK

Feedback can be one of the most important influences on our ability to learn — if it is done properly. If not done properly, its effects can be negative rather than positive. In their 2007 summary article, Hattie and Timperley distinguished four levels at which you can give feedback:

- *Task-oriented* feedback: "You began your lesson with a concrete example; as a result, your lesson was much clearer".
- *Process-oriented* feedback: "You are not well enough prepared to deal with the material to be learned".
- *Self-regulatory* feedback; in other words, feedback about how to direct attention, feelings and behavior: "Even if you are no longer confident about it, it is still better to try and complete this exercise first.
- *Person-oriented* feedback: "You're really good at this!"

Guasch, Espasa, Alvareza, and Kirschner, in studying teacher feedback and peer feedback in collaborative writing, give this a tweak, speaking of corrective, suggestive and epistemic feedback. They describe the different types as:

- *Corrective* feedback: this refers to comments about the assignment requirements and the adequacy of the content (e.g., This is not what is requested; This concept is not correct).
- *Suggestive* feedback: this includes advice on how to proceed or progress and invites exploration, expansion or improvement of an idea (e.g., Giving an example at the end of this argument or paragraph would make your point much clearer).
- *Epistemic* feedback: this refers to requests for explanations and/or clarifications in a critical way (e.g., Do you think that this idea reflects what the author highlights in his/her study?).

These different types and levels are often intermixed; for example, the task-oriented and the person-oriented levels: "Well done, you're really clever!" However, it seems that the most effective type of feedback is to move though the different levels in stages, from task-oriented to process-oriented and then on to self-regulation. This also true for the types spoken of by Guasch et al., for example the combination of epistemic feedback and suggestive feedback (e.g., Do you think that this sentence is convincing enough? We recommend you reread the article referenced and identify the similarities and differences between the theories presented. It can help you to carry out the task in a more adequate way).

It is also important that you do not give too much feedback at the same level. For example, if you give too much feedback about what to do and not enough about how to do it, it is possible that your pupils (or employees) will focus too heavily on just the task. Feedback at the self-regulatory level is only effective if the learner is convinced that greater effort and attention will lead to the desired result.

It also seems that written comments have a much greater impact than just a vague figure such as 5/10. If you give both a figure and a comment, research shows that the pupils focus almost exclusively on the figure and hardly read the comment.

THE BASIS OF REMEMBERING: PROCESSING AND EMOTION

Although it is certainly possible to drill some kinds of lesson content into pupils, if you really want them to remember things you need to work in one of two ways: you need to make them think about the things you want them to remember or you need to link those things to emotions. In our ninth myth about remembering, we gave an example of someone walking along a school corridor, who only remembers the things that particular sensations force him or her to focus on. This is why curiosity also helps you to remember things. As a teacher, it is a good idea to identify the key information that you want your public to remember at the end of the lesson, lecture or meeting. Once you have done this, try and formulate a suitable (and preferably surprising) question or problem-solver that will lead your public in the direction you want them to go. It is crucial that the question is experienced by the learner as being a problem, something that needs to be thought about carefully.

As an alternative, emotions are also a good way to stimulate the memory. Certain smells and sounds, perhaps even a song, are easy to remember if they are associated with a particular emotion. Surely you are not one of those people who has forgotten the song played for his opening wedding dance?

LEARNING THROUGH CONCRETE EXAMPLES

People are not made to think too abstractly. Make sure that you translate your ideas in a down-to-earth manner, so that the learner can link these ideas to things in his or her own life. You can often do this with sensory references: how does something smell, taste or feel?

A specific form of concrete learning relates to the importance of storytelling. Stories help us to remember things more easily. Cognitive research has shown that our brain reacts differently to stories than to other forms of information. It is almost as if stories are "psychologically privileged". We understand stories better, remember them more accurately and prefer listening to them. If you are preparing your lesson, think carefully about how you can work the essence of your learning content into a good story. And don't forget: good stories usually contain strong characters, a conflict and complications leading to the resolution of that conflict (Schank & Abelson).

GIVE YOUR LEARNERS VARIETY AND SURPRISE

People quickly get used to the status quo. But if something in our environment changes, we immediately give it more attention. This means that a good starting point is to do something new in your lesson every 15 minutes or so. For example, tell a joke or a story, or show a visual image, or look at the lesson's learning content from a different point of view.

MAKE SURE YOU HAVE ENOUGH BREAKS

Different research studies have shown the importance of occasionally stopping with the learning process, so that the learners can actually practice what needs to be learned. You will learn nothing if you don't rest and sleep at the end of a long day's training. And overtraining can also have a limiting effect on learning, if you don't allow enough time for information processing. An experiment conducted by cognitive neurologist Joel Pearson demonstrated that a group of computer trainees who worked for two hours non-stop learned less than a second group who also worked for two hours, but with an hour's break in between (Ashley & Pearson).

BARAK ROSENSHINE'S 10 PRINCIPLES OF GOOD INSTRUCTION

Barak Rosenshine summed up 10 principles of good instruction based on years of research (1) in cognitive science, (2) on the classroom practices of master teachers, and (3) on cognitive supports to help students to learn complex tasks. Although labeled by many as "instructivist" (a politically correct term for those horrible people who would have us teach children instead of letting them discover everything for themselves), Rosenshine suggests that teachers use the 10 principles to help their students to engage with the materials, learn actively, and thus ensure both mastery of the material and enduring understanding of it. These principles are:

1. Review some previous learning every day: Daily review can strengthen previous learning and can lead to fluent recall. (Suggested reading: Miller, 1956; LaBerge & Samuels, 1974.)
2. Present new material in small steps: Only present small amounts of new material at any time, and then assist students as they practice this material. (Suggested reading: Evertson, Anderson, Anderson, & Brophy, 1980; Brophy & Good, 1990.)
2. Ask questions: Questions help students to practice new information and connect new material to their prior learning. (Suggested reading: Good & Grouws, 1979; King, 1994.)
4. Provide models: Providing students with models and worked examples can help students to learn to solve problems more quickly. (Suggested reading: Sweller, 1994; Rosenshine, Chapman & Meister, 1996; Schoenfeld, 1985.)
5. Guide student practice: Successful teachers spend more time guiding the students' practice of new material. (Suggested reading: Evertson et al., 1980; Kirschner, Sweller & Clark, 2006.)
6. Check for student understanding: Checking for student understanding at each point can help students to learn the material with fewer errors. (Suggested reading: Fisher & Frey, 2007; Dunkin, 1978.)
7. Obtain a high success rate: It is important for students to achieve a high success rate during classroom instruction. (Suggested reading: Anderson & Burns, 1987; Frederiksen, 1984.)
8. Provide scaffolds for difficult tasks: The teacher provides students with temporary supports and scaffolds to assist them when they learn

difficult tasks. (Suggested reading: Pressley, & Woloshyn, 1995; Rosenshine & Meister, 1992.)

9. Require and monitor independent practice: Students need extensive, successful independent practice in order for skills and knowledge to become automatic. (Suggested reading: Rosenshine, 2009; Slavin, 1996.)

10. Engage students in weekly and monthly review: Students need to be involved in extensive practice in order to develop well-connected and automatic knowledge. (Suggested reading: Good & Grouws, 1979; Kulik & Kulik, 1979.)

REFERENCES

Anderson, L. W., & Burns, R. B. (1987). Values, evidence, and mastery learning. *Review of Educational Research, 57,* 215–224.

Anderson, R. C. (1977). The notion of schemata and the educational enterprise: General discussion of the conference. In R. C. Anderson, R. J. Spiro, & W. E. Montague (Eds.), *Schooling and the acquisition of knowledge* (pp. 415–431). Hillsdale, NJ: Erlbaum.

Ashley, S., & Pearson, J. (2012). When more equals less: Overtraining inhibits perceptual learning owing to lack of wakeful consolidation. *Proceedings of the Royal Society Biological Sciences, 279*(1745), 4143–4147.

Berkowitz, S. J. (1986). Effects of instruction in text organization on sixth grade students' memory for expository reading. *Reading Research Quarterly, 21*(2), 161–178.

Brophy, J. E., & Good, T. L. (1986). Teacher behavior and student achievement. In M. C. Wittrock (Ed.), *Handbook of research on teaching* (3rd ed., pp. 328–375). New York: Macmillan.

Brophy, J., & Good, T. (1990). *Educational psychology: A realistic approach.* New York: Longman.

Brown, J., Collins, A., & Duguid, P. (1989). Situated cognition and the culture of learning. *Educational Researcher, 18,* 32–42.

Collins, A. (1988). *Cognitive apprenticeship and instructional technology.* Cambridge, MA: BBN Labs (Technical Report No. 6899).

Dunkin, M. J. (1978). Student characteristics, classroom processes, and student achievement. *Journal of Educational Psychology, 70,* 998–1009.

Evertson, C. M., Anderson, C. W., Anderson, L. M., & Brophy, J. E. (1980). Relationships between classroom behaviors and student outcomes in junior high mathematics and English classes. *American Educational Research Journal, 17,* 43–60.

Fisher, D., & Frey, A. (2007). *Checking for understanding: Formative assessment techniques for your classroom.* Arlington, VA: Association for Supervision and Curriculum Development.

Frederiksen, N. (1984). Implications of cognitive theory for instruction in problem-solving. *Review of Educational Research, 54,* 363–407.

Gage, N. L. (1978). *The scientific basis of the art of teaching.* New York, NY: Teachers College Press.

Good, T. L., & Grouws, D. A. (1977). Teaching effects: A process–product study in fourth grade mathematics classrooms. *Journal of Teacher Education, 28,* 40–54.

Good, T. L., & Grouws, D. A. (1979). The Missouri mathematics effectiveness project. *Journal of Educational Psychology, 71,* 143–155.

Guasch, T., Esposa, A., Alvareza, I. M., & Kirschner, P. A. (2013). Effects of feedback on collaborative writing in an online learning environment: Type of feedback and the feedback-giver. *Distance Education, 34*, 324–338.

Hattie, J. (2009). *Visible learning: A synthesis of over 800 meta-analyses relating to achievement.* London: Routledge.

Hattie, J., & Timperley, H. (2007). The power of feedback. *Review of Educational Research, 77*(1), 81–112.

King, A. (1994). Guiding knowledge construction in the classroom: Effects of teaching children how to question and how to explain. *American Educational Research Journal, 30*, 338–368.

Kirschner, P. A., Sweller, J., & Clark, R. E. (2006). Why minimal guidance during instruction does not work: An analysis of the failure of constructivist, discovery, problem-based, experiential, and inquiry based teaching. *Educational Psychologist, 41*, 75–86.

Kulik, J. A., & Kulik, C. C. (1979). College teaching. In P. L. Peterson, & W. J. Walberg (Eds.), *Research on teaching: Concepts, findings, and implications* (pp. 70–93). Berkeley, CA: McCutchan.

Laberge, D., & Samuels, S. J. (1974). Toward a theory of automatic information in reading. *Cognitive Psychology, 6*, 293–323.

Miller, G. A. (1956). The magical number seven, plus or minus two: Some limits on our capacity for processing information. *Psychological Review, 63*, 81–97.

Paul, A. M. (2012, July 25). How to get — and keep — someone's attention. Retrieved July 25, 2012, from <http://ideas.time.com/2012/07/25/how-to-get-and-keep-someones-attention/?iid = op-main-lede>.

Pressley, M., & Woloshyn, V. (1995). *Cognitive strategy instruction that really improves children's academic performance* (2nd ed.). Cambridge, MA: Brookline Books.

Rosenshine, B. (2009). The empirical support for direct instruction. In S. Tobias, & T. M. Duffy (Eds.), *Constructivist instruction: Success or failure?* (pp. 201–220). New York: Routledge.

Rosenshine, B. (2010). *Principles of instruction (Band 21 "Educational Practices Series").* Brussels: International Academy of Education and Geneva: International Bureau of Education [Online Document] Retrieved from <http://www.ibe.unesco.org/fileadmin/user_upload/Publications/Educational_Practices/EdPractices_21pdf>.

Rosenshine, B. (2012). Principles of instruction: Research-based strategies that all teachers should know. *American Educator, 36*(1), 12–19, 39. Retrieved May 23, 2014, from <https://www.aft.org/pdfs/americaneducator/spring2012/Rosenshine.pdf> .

Rosenshine, B., Chapman, S., & Meister, C. (1996). Teaching students to generate questions: A review of the intervention studies. *Review of Educational Research, 66*, 181–221.

Rosenshine, B., & Meister, C. (1992). The use of scaffolds for teaching higher level cognitive strategies. *Educational Leadership*, April, 26–33.

Rosenshine, B., & Stevens, R. (1986). Teaching functions. In M. C. Witrock (Ed.), *Handbook of research on teaching* (3rd ed., pp. 376–391). New York: Macmillan.

Rumelhart, D. E., & Norman, D. A. (1978). Accretion, tuning, and restructuring: Three models of learning. In J. W. Cotton, & R. Klatzky (Eds.), *Semantic factors in cognition* (pp. 37–53). Hillsdale, NJ: Erlbaum.

Schank, R. C., & Abelson, R. P. (1995). Knowledge and memory: The real story. In R. S. Wyer, Jr. (ed.), *Knowledge and memory* (pp. 1–85). Hillsdale, NJ: Lawrence Earlbaum Associates.

Schoenfeld, A. H. (1985). *Mathematical problem solving.* New York: Academic Press.

Slavin, R. E. (1996). *Education for all.* Exton, PA: Swets & Zeitlinger.

Spiro, R., Coulson, R., Feltovich, P., & Anderson, D. (1988). *Cognitive flexibility theory: Advanced knowledge acquisition in ill-structured domains.* Champaign, IL: University of Illinois, Center for the Study of Reading (Technical Report No. 441).

Stallings, J. A., & Kaskowitz, D. (1974). *Follow through classroom observations.* Menlo Park, CA: SRI International.

Sweller, J. (1994). Cognitive load theory, learning difficulty and instructional design. *Learning and Instruction, 4,* 295–312.

Willingham, D. T. (2004, Summer). The privileged status of story. AFT. Retrieved November 2, 2012, from <http://www.aft.org/periodical/american-educator/summer-2004/ask-cognitive-scientist>.

Willingham, D. T. (2009). *Why don't students like school? A cognitive scientist answers questions about how the mind works and what it means for the classroom.* San Francisco, CA: Jossey-Bass.

CHAPTER 3

Neuromyths

Contents

Teachers who are more interested in neuroscience in the classroom are more inclined to believe neuromyths.

(Dekker, Lee, Howard-Jones, & Jolles, 2012).

Introduction

In 2007, Susan Pickering and Paul Howard-Jones investigated teachers' views on the role of neuroscience in education. Their findings showed that almost 90% of teaching staff think that neurological insights are important for education, and that teachers are enthusiastic about the idea of incorporating insights from neuroscience in their daily practice. At the same

Urban Myths about Learning and Education
DOI: http://dx.doi.org/10.1016/B978-0-12-801537-7.00004-4

© 2015 Elsevier Inc.
All rights reserved.

time, most scientific publications also warn that neuroscience is a relatively new discipline and that there is a huge gap between what neurologists investigate and what educationalists do with the results of those investigations. Pickering and Howard-Jones' study also revealed that teachers' concept of neuroscience varied widely.

However, this does not prevent countless people in the education profession from telling you everything they know about the relation between the brain and education, which often leads to inconsistencies and inaccuracies. This, of course, is how myths are born. In practice, at the moment it is only the insights of cognitive psychology that can be effectively used in education, but even here care needs to be taken.

Neurology has the potential to add value to education, but in general there are only two real conclusions we can make at present:

- For the time being, we do not really understand all that much about the brain.
- More importantly, it is difficult to generalize what we do know into a set of concrete precepts of behavior, never mind devise methods for influencing that behavior.

One problem is that once we see the word "brain", we immediately become more inclined to believe what is said. In an interesting experiment by David McCabe and Alan Castel, a number of explanations for psychological phenomena were given to two groups of test subjects. One group consisted of neurological experts; the other group consisted of non-specialists. There were four possible answers for each phenomenon:

- a correct explanation
- an incorrect explanation
- a correct explanation supplemented with neurological details that had nothing to do with the phenomenon in question
- an incorrect explanation supplemented with neurological details that had nothing to do with the phenomenon in question.

In both groups, thankfully, the test subjects were usually in agreement with the correct explanation. More remarkable, however, was the fact that among the group of non-specialists the minority who chose the wrong explanation consistently preferred the wrong answer with the unnecessary neurological details to the wrong answer without any details whatsoever.

And this effect increases if you add an image of a brain scan into the equation.

So, what about teachers? Do they believe in neurological myths or not? Research undertaken by Sanne Dekker and colleagues and published in the online journal *Frontiers in Psychology* focused specifically on educators who had indicated an interest in the relationship between neuroscience and education. You would expect this group to be well informed about the difference between "reliable" scientific findings and pseudoscientific "opinions". The survey put forward a list of 32 propositions to 242 people working in the education profession (137 English, 105 Dutch). Fifteen of the 32 propositions, spread randomly throughout the list, were incorrect; in other words, they were neuromyths. Some of these myths will be explored in the pages ahead, such as the contention that "we only use 10% of our brain". The correct statements were things like "boys have bigger brains than girls" and "the left and right halves of the brain always work together". How many of the neuromyths were incorrectly identified as being true? An amazing 49%, half of them. Even more remarkably, the teachers who had a better knowledge of the working of the brain believed more of the myths! In a review article, Howard-Jones compared three additional regions to this data and the prevalence of neuromyths was also high in Turkey, Greece, and China.

These conclusions are disturbing. The teachers who are most interested in applying neuroscience in the classroom are also those who are most inclined to believe in neurological myths. For this reason, we will now look at some of the most stubborn of these myths.

REFERENCES

Bennett, T. (2013). Separating neuromyths from science in education. *New Scientist*, 2932. Retrieved May 15, 2014, from <http://www.newscientist.com/article/mg21929320.200-separating-neuromyths-from-science-in-education.html>.

Bressler, S. L., & Menon, V. (2010). Large-scale brain networks in cognition: Emerging methods and principles. *Trends in Cognitive Sciences, 14*, 277−290.

Dekker, S., Lee, N. C., Howard-Jones, P. A., & Jolles, J. (2012). Neuromyths in education: Prevalence and predictors of misconceptions among teachers. *Frontiers of Psychology, 3*, 429.

Howard-Jones, P. A. (2014). Neuroscience and education: Myths and messages. *Nature Reviews Neuroscience*.

McCabe, D. P., & Castel, A. D. (2007). Seeing is believing: The effect of brain images on judgments of scientific reasoning. *Cognition, 107*, 343−352.

Pantazatos, S. P. (2014). Prediction of individual season of birth using MRI. *NeuroImage, 88*, 61−68.

Pickering, S. J., & Howard-Jones, P. A. (2007). Educators' views of the role of neuroscience in education: A study of UK and international perspectives. *Mind, Brain and Education, 1*(3), 109−113.

MYTH 1

We Are Good Multitaskers

Teachers often ask themselves whether or not pupils who try do every-thing all at the same time are actually able to devote the required degree of attention to each element. Many publications and media sources claim that young people nowadays not only are able to multitask, but also are experts at multitasking. By multitasking, we mean the ability to carry out two or more things that require thinking (i.e., processing of information) simultaneously.

We are tempted to believe that we can multitask because at some level, intuitively, it seems to make sense: it looks as if we are indeed able to per-form multiple actions at the same time. For example, driving a car involves performing a number of actions simultaneously: shifting gears, turning the steering wheel, looking into the mirrors, and so on. Experienced drivers appear to be able to perform all these actions while maintaining a conversa-tion with friends in the car. Or can they? As it turns out, the ability to mul-titask is far more complex than it appears on the surface. An important question is whether humans actually do perform actions simultaneously, or if they really switch between tasks by diverting their attention from one task to another; that is, task-switching.

It turns out that only under special circumstances, where people have so much experience in performing a task that it has become fully automated, can we carry out multiple processes. However, since these processes have become automated, they don't require thought or information processing. Walking and talking at the same time is something most people are able to do, but even then accidents are possible, especially when the conversation is engrossing. When this is the case — especially if the environment is a novel one — we may not register what is in our environment (i.e., we see it but don't process it) and thus trip over a curb, walk into a lamppost, miss the corner where we should have turned off, and so forth. What is clear is that people are not capable of thinking two different thoughts at the same time. In that case, they task-switch, which means that they divide their attention and switch their attention to different cognitive tasks. Because of the often short switches it may appear simultaneous, but it is not. The fact that the brain has strict constraints about the number of cognitive processes it can process is known as the "cognitive bottleneck". A team of researchers led by Michael Tombu has shown the existence of the cognitive bottleneck at the neural-cluster level. These findings imply that executing different cognitive tasks at the same time is much more difficult than we might expect.

For example, have you ever tried to type an e-mail while you are talking to someone on the telephone? It's not easy, is it? Actually, this is a very difficult task. It seems as if each of the tasks that we try to perform distracts us from the other task that we try to do at the same time, even though neither is "rocket science". The result is poor performance on both tasks. While typing, you miss what the other person has said since you were thinking about what you were writing. You heard the person say something but did not process it. It turns out that almost nobody can multitask successfully, whether they are female, generation Y, Z or whatever, or both!

One of the authors of this book has argued in the past that research has proven time and again that the simultaneous execution of tasks inevitably leads to a loss of concentration, the need for longer periods of study and poorer performance. For mastering the content of short texts, "multitaskers" (learners who read and texted "at the same time") needed almost twice as much time and made almost twice as many mistakes as "serial taskers". With reference to learning, we can point specifically to studies carried out at the University of California, Los Angeles, where it was shown that even if you do learn something during multitasking, it is more difficult for you to use what you have learnt later on, because it is much more difficult for your memory to recall. A study by Sanbonmatsu, Strayer, Medeiros-Ward, and Watson at the University of Utah corroborates these claims. Sanbonmatsu and his colleagues looked at the difference between the multitasking activity that people reported about themselves and their actual ability to multitask. The results were very interesting: the self-reported multitasking behavior was negatively correlated with multitasking ability. People who perceive themselves as multitaskers engage more than others in multitasking behavior, but their performance is much worse than they seem to expect.

What the study by Sanbonmatsu and colleagues strongly suggests is that most multitasking may not really be multitasking after all. In reality, multitasking implies continually changing between different tasks. Our brain is well able to do so, but the rapid switching between tasks costs (mental) energy. The end result is that you actually work less efficiently. The so-called "myth of multitasking", as Rosen calls it, is popular because performing more than one task at the same time *appears* to give people emotional gratification. We feel that we accomplish more, which gives a positive feeling. Thus, multitasking is self-reinforcing, as Wang and Tchernev describe it. The pleasure of multitasking overcomes negative cognitive effects in the minds of the "multitaskers".

Still, all this may be a problem of the past, right? It might be that new media teach children how to become better at multitasking. Sadly, the answer to this seems to be negative. This can be illustrated by research that was performed by a team from the Visual Cognition Laboratory at Duke University. Donohue's team investigated whether someone who regularly plays computer games is better at focusing on different tasks at the same time. It turns out that they are not. The test group of gamers was no better at driving and phoning than the control group of non-gamers. Sixty students were asked to play a racing game, while answering questions at the same time (to simulate a telephone conversation). The gamers were much better at the game — as you would expect — but their scores fell significantly once they were required to answer the questions. A large analysis by Wasylyshyn and Verhaeghen of the relation between people's age and their ability to switch between different tasks showed a similar result. When general cognitive decline was taken into account, older people did not perform worse than younger people when being asked to regularly switch between two different tasks.

So, Is Nobody Really Capable of Multitasking?

In all truth, there does seem to be evidence for the existence of a group of people who have the ability to multitask effectively. A research study carried out by Jason Watson and David Strayer in 2010 concluded that their survey population of 200 test subjects contained five "supertaskers", people who were able to do different things at the same time without any noticeable loss of quality. However, it is suspected that these people — as has been already mentioned — are able to switch from one task to another very quickly, rather than actually doing both tasks at the same time. So if you are one of the 2.5% of people who can e-mail and telephone simultaneously, congratulations! You now know that you belong to a very small and privileged minority.

Source
Watson, J. M., & Strayer, D. L. (2010). Supertaskers: Profiles in extraordinary multitasking ability. *Psychonomic Bulletin & Review, 17*, 479–485.

:-\ We often do different things at the same time, but is that really positive? The simultaneous execution of tasks leads to a loss of concentration, the need for longer study periods and poorer performance. Very few people can multitask effectively.

REFERENCES

Donohue, B. J., Eslick, A. N., & Mitroff, S. R. (2012). Cognitive pitfall! Video game players are not immune from dual-task costs. *Attention, Perception & Psychophysics, 74* (5), 1161—1167.

Kirschner, P. A., & van Merriënboer, J. J. G. (2013). Do learners really know best? Urban legends in education. *Educational Psychologist, 48*(3), 169—183.

Rosen, C. (2008). The myth of multitasking. *The New Atlantis, 20*(Spring), 105—110.

Sanbonmatsu, D. M., Strayer, D. L., Medeiros-Ward, N., & Watson, J. M. (2013). Who multitasks and why? Multitasking ability, perceived multitasking ability, impulsivity, and sensation seeking. *PloS ONE, 8*(1), 1—8.

Tombu, M. N., Asplund, C. L., Dux, P. E., Godwin, D., Martin, J. W., & Marois, R. (2011). A unified attentional bottleneck in the human brain. *Proceedings of the National Academy of Sciences of the United States of America, 108*(33), 13426—13431.

Wang, Z., & Tchernev, J. M. (2012). The "myth" of media multitasking: Reciprocal dynamic of multimedia multitasking, personal needs, and gratifications. *Journal of Communication, 62*, 493—513.

Wasylyshyn, C., Verhaeghen, P., & Sliwinski, M. J. (2011). Aging and task switching: A meta-analysis. *Psychology and Aging, 26*(1), 15—20.

MYTH 2

We Only Use 10% of Our Brains

When looking at the end-of-term results of their class, some teachers may take comfort from the thought that their pupils are using only 10% of their brains. If only this were true! For one thing, it would mean that we could engage in much more dangerous action, because the chance of resulting brain damage would be much less. On the other hand, it would be a disaster if brain damage occurred in precisely the "10% region". But these ideas are absurd, as we will show.

In *Scientific American*, Robynne Boyd has argued that this myth dates back to the American psychologist and philosopher William James, who, in his book *The energies of men*, suggested that human beings make use of only a limited part of their physical and mental potential. This "unexploited potential" idea developed into the familiar 10% myth. Others have linked this assertion with Albert Einstein, who is supposed to have used it to indicate his own level of intelligence. This is incorrect, in that no reliable source for this quotation seems to exist (still, neuroscientist John Geake argues that Einstein did mention the 10% statement in a 1920s radio show). The myth seems to have become a part of Western culture. Even Hollywood likes to use it as a plot vehicle, for example in the movie *Limitless*, which revolves around a so-called "smart pill" that allows users to access 100% of their brain abilities. The 2014 movie *Lucy* exploits a similar concept.

Why do we call this claim a myth? Neuroscientist Barry Beyerstein has put forward five arguments to refute it, based on the concepts of brain damage, evolution, brain scans, functional areas and degeneration.

*   *Brain damage.* As already mentioned, the effect of damage to the brain would be much less dramatic if we were using only 10% of its full capacity. Unfortunately, the opposite is true: there is almost no part of the brain that can suffer damage without at least some loss of function. In fact, relatively small amounts of damage to relatively small areas of the brain can have devastating consequences. With the right therapy, the victims of brain damage can sometimes compensate for loss of function through the plasticity of the brain, but that is the exception rather than the rule. Also, the notion that parts of the brain do not serve any particular purpose can have devastating consequences, as

shown by the popularity of frontal lobotomy, a surgical procedure in which most of a person's frontal cortex is removed. Although this does successfully reduce pathological behavior, it has major behavioral side-effects; and to think that António Egas Moniz won the Nobel Prize for Medicine in 1949 for inventing this procedure!

- *Evolution.* Our brains use a lot of energy, in terms of both nutrition and oxygen. Even though the brain makes up only about 2% of our body weight, its energy consumption is about 20% of all available oxygen in the blood. Imagine that the "we only use 10% of our brains" idea is true. This would mean that creatures with a small brain would have an evolutionary advantage. In these circumstances, it is open to question whether we would ever have survived so long with such a large brain. In fact, evolution would probably have ensured that our brain was never allowed to get so big. As Beyerstein concludes: "In the millions of studies of the brain, no one has ever found an unused portion [of the brain]".

- *Brain scans.* New technologies such as positron emission tomography (PET) and functional magnetic resonance imaging (fMRI) allow us to see the activity of the brain in detail. These scans make it clear that there is neural activity throughout the whole brain, even when we are sleeping. Conversely, in cases of serious brain damage there are large areas in the brain where there is no longer any activity at all. This is why we often use the term "brain dead", not to be confused with vegetative state. Brain dead refers to the worst degree of functional brain damage that that is compatible with physical survival following coma.

- *Functional areas.* The human body contains quite a few "leftovers": body parts that evolved in the past, but that we do not need any more for daily life, for example our wisdom teeth. Our bodies even have a remnant of a tail (the coccyx). The question can be asked whether the brain also contains parts that are evolutionarily "outdated". Many years of research have taught us that this does not seem to be the case. The brain is made up of different areas with different functions, which all work together. There is no known part of the brain that does not have a specific function.

- *Degeneration.* Imagine that our brains contain lots of brain cells that we never use. These would gradually die off, since this is what automatically happens to cells that have no useful function; they degenerate and die. In this case, the largest part of the human brain would already have disappeared before we died. But we know that this is not the case under normal circumstances.

In fact, the brain is very flexible in the way it allows cells to die. This is a process called "synaptic pruning", and it forms the foundation for brain development. Without pruning, our brains would never really develop. Years of research have shown that the brain is constantly has developing and that brain function is much more "plastic" than has been assumed. For example, a study by Scholz, Klein, Behrens, and Johansen-Berg revealed that juggling changes the brain in different ways. Both gray and white matter in the brain appear to grow and shrink under the influence of practice. Another famous study that showed this effect was conducted by Maguire and his colleagues, who studied the brains of London taxi drivers. It turns out that the brain areas responsible for maintaining an accurate representation of the complex street layout of London have grown enormously in experienced taxi drivers. Both pruning and plasticity of the brain indicate that an exact measure such as "10%" is far removed from reality.

In view of all these different arguments, how is it possible that the 10% myth continues to be believed by so many people? A few reasons have been touched upon above. In addition to those, it may be the result of all the images of brain scans that have appeared in the media in recent times. These often show limited areas of bright color to denote peaks of brain activity (actually of blood flow) − but this does not mean that the rest is not working at all! Pictures of brain activity are heavily processed and are subjected to different statistical analyses to make clear in which part of the brain there is more activity than in other parts, at any given time. The result is a distorted representation. In short, it is all a matter of lies, damned lies, and brain statistics.

We began this section by stating that the myth may find its origin in William James's idea that people do not tap their full potential, and that a huge amount of it remains unused. Certainly, this is not an unattractive idea. It implies that we all still have room for growth in our lives. One way to achieve such growth is through better use of our brain. This idea is particularly appealing in education, where it is important to focus not just on limitations but also on possibilities for improvement. The brain's plasticity is perfectly suited to this approach. But both growth and improvement are still possible even if we use more than the 10% of our brains stated in the myth. And we do use more, much more − 90% more!

:-\ It may seem that some people are using only 10% of their brain, but this is not the case — we use all of it, all of the time.

REFERENCES

Beyerstein, B. L. (1999). Whence cometh the myth that we only use ten percent of our brains? In S. Della Sala (Ed.), *Mind myths: Exploring everyday mysteries of the mind and brain* (pp. 1—24). Chichester, UK: John Wiley and Sons.

Boyd, R. (2008). Do people only use 10 percent of their brains? *Scientific American*, Retrieved June 13, 2014, from <http://www.scientificamerican.com/article/do-people-only-use-10-percent-of-their-brains/>.

Geake, J. (2008). Neuromythologies in education. *Educational Research, 50*(2), 123—133.

Maguire, E. A., Gadian, D. G., Johnsrude, I. S., Good, C. D., Ashburner, J., Frackowiak, R. S., et al. (2000). Navigation-related structural changes in the hippocampi of taxi drivers. *Proceedings of the National Academy of Sciences of the United States of America, 97* (8), 4398—4403.

Radford, B. (1999). The ten-percent myth. *The Skeptical Inquirer, 23*(2) Retrieved May 15, 2014, from <http://www.csicop.org/si/show/the_ten-percent_myth/>.

Scholz, J., Klein, M. C., Behrens, T. E. J., & Johansen-Berg, H. (2009). Training induces changes in white-matter architecture. *Nature Neuroscience, 12*, 1370—1371.

MYTH 3

The Left Half of the Brain Is Analytical, the Right Half Is Creative

To succeed in life, it is important to be creative. Creativity refers not to some specific ability, but to a more generic aptitude for intelligent problem solving and a knack for looking at problems from a new, fresh perspective. Of course, the brain is heavily involved in creativity, and it can be argued that one important aspect of creativity is the interaction between the brain's two hemispheres. The hemispheres are connected by a large bundle of neural fibers, the corpus callosum. The fact that the two halves of the brain are heavily connected to each other and are in constant communication has not stopped marketing and education gurus from encouraging us to use the right half of our brains more, since this is our innovative, creative, holistic, feminine, Eastern, "yang" side. These same gurus also tell us that we live in a world dominated by the rational, systematic, masculine, Western, "yin" left half of the brain. As Michael Corballis has noted, this asymmetry between the two halves of the brain is considered by many to be unique to humans, although this is not the case. Perhaps you have done a test on the Internet, which showed a turning dancer. The direction in which you see the dancer turn is commonly interpreted as revealing which half of your brain is more dominant. The real explanation for the direction you perceive (and the way it usually changes after staring at the picture for a while) has absolutely nothing to do with the left and right hemispheres and some sort of "dominance". The dancer is an example of a so-called bistable perception or an ambiguous figure: it can be perceived in two ways, with no way being dominant over the other. As Parker and Krug explain, the brain simply picks one perception, and will after a while switch to the other perception.

Lisa Collier Cool described how the concept of different and independent halves of the brain originated during the nineteenth century. Doctors discovered that if one side of the brain was damaged, certain functions would disappear. Modern brain scans have now revealed that the two sides are more closely connected than originally thought, but the basic idea developed in the nineteenth century — that the left side of the brain directs the right side of the body and vice versa (something that was hypothesized by Hippocrates) — is broadly true.

The idea that the left side of the brain is "rational" and the right side "creative" is more recent. It first appeared in a number of popular books in the second half of the twentieth century. From there, it slowly gained a hold in education. Professor Usha Goswami refers to the idea as one of the most troubling of the different neuromyths, because it results in a complete misunderstanding among the public about the relation between neuroscience and education.

What is the current thinking on this matter? As we said, if someone needs to approach a problem creatively, they use their whole brain. It is true that the two halves are different, and that the majority of people do use the left half for most aspects of language, while using the right side for more specialized spatial skills. But still, even for specialized functions such as language, it is clear that the opposite half still plays an important contributory role. The consensus in the neuroscience community seems to be that the study of connectivity in the brain is more interesting than localization of specific functions. Major steps still need to be made in this direction. Steven Bressler and Vinod Menon showed how it is possible to describe brain functioning on a large scale. Central to their notion is dynamic interaction between different areas in the brain. A large study by a group of researchers led by Jared Nielsen also found that although there are localized areas in the brain, it makes no sense to talk about a "left-brained" or "right-brained" network when the whole brain is taken into account. Interestingly, Nielsen and his colleagues also found no difference in brain lateralization between men and women. The analyses that we describe here are forays in an unknown direction, but the future looks promising. Eventually, new discoveries about integrated brain functioning may lead to a rethinking of the way in which cognitive processes occur in the brain.

There is also evidence from research that shows how both halves of the brain are involved in creative processing. In 2004, an experiment by Singh and O'Boyle tested the claim that the two halves of the brain in creative people are used unequally. In their experiment they projected letters at high speed on to the retinas of a group of young people. If participants in the experiment saw the same letter twice, they had to quickly press a button. We already know that through brain lateralization the letters projected on to the left eye end up as images in the right half of the brain and vice versa. This is what makes it a difficult test, involving the coordinated use of both halves of the brain. What transpired? The young people who pressed the button quickest often turned out to be the most creative as well, thereby showing that the combined working of both halves of the brain can be linked to creativity.

What are the biggest dangers associated with this myth? Some have used the idea as a metaphor to indict a world that has become dominated by reason, and reason alone. But this is the same kind of thinking that pigeonholes people in just one of two boxes: rational or emotional. And we have already seen earlier in the book that this kind of restrictive thinking can be a bad idea. Also, the left-brain and right-brain distinction is another example of so-called "neuromarketing", the business involved in highly lucrative selling and endorsing of products that the makers say or claim are specifically geared to the "whole brain" or the "creative brain". An experiment by Annukka Lindell and Evan Kidd revealed the effectiveness of neuromarketing: consumers preferred a training program that was called "Right Brain" over a training that was simply called "Right Start". Again, the use of the word "brain" gives people a feeling of a strong scientific basis. If it's in the brain, it must be true!

For this reason and for the reasons above, we would not recommend the training packages that are now available to specifically develop the right side of your brain.

:-\ Although thinking and creativity require a good connection between both halves of your brain, there is no reason to assume a "left-brained" and "right-brained" style of thinking.

REFERENCES

Bressler, S. L., & Menon, V. (2010). Large-scale brain networks in cognition: Emerging methods and principles. *Trends in Cognitive Sciences, 14*, 277–290.

Cool, L. C. (2011). 5 Brain myths, busted. Retrieved June 18, 2014, from <http://www.q8medix.com/news-2822/5-Brain-MythsBusted>.

Corballis, M. (2014). Left brain, right brain: Facts and fantasies. *PloS Biology, 12*(1), e1001767.

Geake, J. (2008). Neuromythologies in education. *Educational Research, 50*(2), 123–133.

Goswami, U. (2004). Neuroscience and education. *British Journal of Educational Psychology, 74*, 1–14.

Lindell, A. K., & Kidd, E. (2013). Consumers favor "right brain" training: The dangerous lure of neuromarketing. *Mind, Brain, and Education, 7*(1), 35–49.

Nielsen, J. A., Zielinski, B. A., Ferguson, M. A., Lainhart, J. E., & Anderson, J. S. (2013). An evaluation of the left-brain vs. right-brain hypothesis with resting state functional connectivity magnetic resonance imaging. *PloS ONE, 8*(8), 1–11.

Parker, A. J., & Krug, K. (2003). Neuronal mechanisms for the perception of ambiguous stimuli. *Current Opinion in Neurobiology, 13*, 433–439.

Parker-Pope, T. (2008). The truth about the spinning dancer. *New York Times,* Retrieved June 18, 2014, from <http://well.blogs.nytimes.com/2008/04/28/the-truth-about-the-spinning-dancer/index.html>.

Singh, H., & O'Boyle, M. W. (2004). Differences in interhemispheric interaction during global/local processing in mathematically gifted adolescents, average ability youth and college students. *Neuropsychology, 18,* 371–377.

MYTH 4

You Can Train Your Brain with Brain Gym and Brain Games

Brain training is hot. Training your brain, which means training your problem-solving skills, your hand—eye coordination, your memory or any other combination of cognitive abilities seems to have replaced dieting as a "must-do" fad. All kinds of wonderful new tools have been developed for this purpose in recent years, such as Brain Gym® or Brain Games, with Nintendo's Brain Age™ perhaps being the best known of all. The reason is simple: brain training has grown into a major business. Worldwide revenues in 2012 exceeded more than $1 billion, and they may well surpass $6 billion by 2020. The popularity of training programs for the brain raises questions about their effectiveness. Does regular practice with brain games improve cognitive functioning, and can these changes have a permanent effect? A number of scientific studies have tried to find out, but the results have been unequivocally disappointing.

For example, in 2010 the British television program *Bang goes the theory* tested brain games that claimed to improve the memory and reasoning skills of its users. In total, 11,430 people participated in this experiment. The trial involved 8692 participants aged between 18 and 60 years who were asked to play one of the games three times a week for six weeks, with a minimum game time of 10 minutes a day. In addition, there was a control group of a further 2738 people. These people were asked not to play a game but instead to surf the Internet for the same amount of time, to try and find the answers to a number of general questions. At the end of the trial period, the same IQ test was administered to all participants. The results of this test were clear: there was no difference between the performance of the game group and that of the Internet group. In fact, the Internet surfing group scored higher than the game group on some elements of the test. Although the experiment was conducted for television (and was criticized for this reason), it had a sound scientific base. Adrian Owen of the Cognition and Brain Sciences Unit at Cambridge University and his colleagues published their findings in the respected journal *Nature*. Their report concludes with a crystal-clear verdict: "We believe that these results confirm that six weeks of regular brain training confers no greater benefit than simply answering general knowledge questions using the Internet".

So far, so bad, but how about the popular Nintendo games? Stuart Ritchie from the University of Edinburgh and his colleagues conducted research on Brain Gym, and also reviewed the evidence relating to brain training on Nintendo consoles. Their conclusion is that this training is not effective. The same lack of effect was found with respect to Brain Gym, a series of physical movement exercises designed to improve your brain. Ritchie found that other, more traditional brain enhancers — such as drinking lots of water (which prevents the brain from drying out) or using cod-liver oil (rich in omega-3) — could also be dismissed. Apparently, it's not easy to affect the brain through simple means.

A report commissioned by the UK government and carried out by the Education Endowment Foundation reviewed educational interventions informed by neuroscience (Howard-Jones, 2014). The report points out that there is some evidence for the effectiveness of a few specific interventions, but that any differences that are found in research usually disappear as soon as more rigorous analytical methods are applied to the data. This is the case, for example, with Cogmed Working Memory Training (© CWMT; www.cogmed.com). Cogmed was developed with the goal of being able to improve working memory in children with attention-deficit/hyperactivity disorder (ADHD). A working memory deficit has been found to be one of the main characteristics of ADHD. In a thorough study, Anil Chacko from the City University of New York and colleagues administered either a CWMT active or a CWMT passive (control) treatment to 85 children with ADHD. They found only limited results: working memory did improve a little for children in the CWMT active condition, but this improvement could only be found when specific memory tests were administered. No discernible improvement in normal functioning could be found. Chacko concludes that Cogmed should not be considered effective for treating children with ADHD.

What Cogmed does show is that there are methods that can improve the working of our memory, but they are often devised for the learning of very specific types of content. For example, you can try mnemonic tricks, repetitive sequences of the same stimulus or making mind maps, which are designed to give a particular meaning to the things you want to remember. A mind map, as the name suggests, requires you to mentally map out a concept clearly and concisely, but without the need to think in too much detail about a specific formulation. You do this by using a graphic schedule (often known as an information tree), starting from a central subject that you can then link to related concepts and other subsidiary matters.

Still, it is important to note that training effects have been shown to be limited. In a 2013 study by Tyler Harrison and colleagues, participants followed a specific training regime to improve the size of their working memory. The study showed how people's working memory capacity did improve: they were able to use their memory more effectively on tasks that were similar to the training tasks. However, the ability to better use your memory does not seem to spread to more general cognitive improvements. Harrison et al. looked at fluid intelligence, which involves problem solving and logical thinking. Improving working memory capacity did not have any effect on the fluid intelligence scores of the people who participated in the training.

All the research seems to point in one direction: training can help people in learning to apply strategies that improve working memory capacity. The word "brain" is misleading since any training necessarily involves the brain. There is as yet no evidence at all that brain training that is aimed at improving general cognitive abilities such as fluid intelligence will in any way be effective: just don't expect to become smarter from playing video games.

In October 2014, 73 psychologists, cognitive scientists and neuroscientists from around the world signed an open letter stating that companies marketing "brain games" that are meant to slow or reverse age-related memory decline and enhance other cognitive functions are exploiting customers by making "exaggerated and misleading claims" that are not based on sound scientific evidence.

To end this section on a positive note, there are some things that are known to be healthy for your brain. These are: using it regularly, taking exercise and eating a balanced diet. Did you expect anything else?

Or You Could Start Chewing . . .

Curiously enough, it appears that bubblegum also has a positive (very) short-term effect on the brain. Craig Johnston of the Baylor College of Medicine found that chewing gum helps to reduce stress and improve concentration, and thus helps academic performance. Opinion on this matter is still divided, though, not least because Johnston's research was sponsored by chewing gum business William Wrigley Jr. Even if it is true, it is not clear whether its beneficial effect is caused by the chewing motion or by an injection of sugar into the system.

As a result, we wouldn't yet recommend you to tell your pupils to chew their way through their exams!

Source

Johnston, C. A., Tyler, C., Stansberry, S. A., Moreno, J. P., & Foreyt, J. P. (2012). Brief report: Gum chewing affects standardized math scoring in adolescents. *Journal of Adolescence*, *35*, 455–459.

Train Your Working Memory Against Depression

While there is hardly any evidence to support the brain improvement claims of the various computer-based commercial packages, Swedish researchers are developing programs that can help to optimize working memory in children with ADHD. Similarly, in The Netherlands, Elke Geraerts and her colleagues at the University of Rotterdam have been working on a series of computer exercises to improve the working memory, specifically as an aid to combat depression.

Sources

Geraerts, E., Hauer, B. J. A., & Wessel, I. (2010). Effects of suppressing negative memories on intrusions and autobiographical memory specificity. *Applied Cognitive Psychology*, *24*(3), 387–398.
Klingberg, T., Fernell, E., Olesen, P. J., Johnson, M., Gustafsson, P., Dahlström, K., et al. (2005). Computerized training of working memory in children with ADHD – a randomized, controlled trial. *Journal of the American Academy of Child & Adolescent Psychiatry*, *44*(2), 177–186.

:-\ Buy a game console for your pleasure – because that is all it is good for. For the time being, there is no evidence that this and other brain gym methods do anything to improve the performance of your brain.

REFERENCES

A Consensus on the Brain Training Industry from the Scientific Community (2015). Retrieved from <http://longevity3.stanford.edu/blog/2014/10/15/the-consensus-on-the-brain-training-industry-from-the-scientific-community>.
Berkman, E. T., Kahn, L. E., & Merchant, J. S. (2014). Training-induced changes in inhibitory control network activity. *Journal of Neuroscience*, *34*(1), 149–157.
Buch, P. (2014). Neuromyths and why they persist in the classroom. Retrieved May 15, 2014, from <http://www.senseaboutscience.org/blog.php/77/neuromyths-and-why-they-persist-in-the-classroom>.
Chacko, A., Bedard, A. C., Marks, D. J., Feirsen, N., Uderman, J. Z., Chimiklis, A., et al. (2014). A randomized clinical trial of Cogmed Working Memory Training in school age children with ADHD: A replication in a diverse sample using a control condition. *Journal of Child Psychology and Psychiatry*, *55*, 247–255.

Harrison, T. L., Shipstead, Z., Hicks, K. L., Hambrick, D. Z., Redick, T. S., & Engle, R. W. (2013). Working memory training may increase working memory capacity but not fluid intelligence. *Psychological Science, 24*, 2409–2419.

Howard-Jones, P. (2014). *Neuroscience and education: A review of educational interventions and approaches informed by neuroscience.* Education Endowment Foundation. Retrieved May 15, 2014, from <http://educationendowmentfoundation.org.uk/uploads/pdf/NSED_LitReview_Final.pdf>.

Owen, A. M., Hampshire, A., Grahn, J. A., Stenton, R., Dajani, S., Burns, A. S., et al. (2010). Putting brain training to the test. *Nature, 465*(7299), 775–778.

Ritchie, S. J., Chudler, E. H., & Della Sala, S. (2012). Don't try this at school: The attraction of "alternative" educational techniques. In S. Della Sala & M. Anderson (Eds.), *Neuroscience in education* (pp. 222–229). Oxford: Oxford University Press.

Smith, B. (2014). Do brain training programs really make you smarter? Retrieved May 15, 2014, from <http://www.redorbit.com/news/science/1113038003/do-brain-training-programs-work-010214/>.

MYTH 5
Men Have a Different Kind of Brain than Women

Obviously, men are different from women; at least, physical differences are observable. People also have all sorts of ideas about gender differences in thinking. Some of these ideas are clearly stereotypes, but for others things are less clear. The question boils down to this: Is there such a thing as the male brain and the female brain? And if there is, should we take account of differences between male and female brains in the classroom?

We know that male and female brains do differ from each other in terms of form and function. On average, the male brain is larger than the female brain. This fact led the famous neurologist Pierre-Paul Broca to assume that men must be more intelligent than women (a claim that was socially acceptable during Broca's days in the nineteenth century). Also, the language area in the female brain is, in general, more active than the same area in the male brain. Still, it is far from clear what these observable differences actually mean in practice. We have already seen that boys and girls perform differently in different subjects (even to the point that girls were shown to be better in all subjects in a metastudy of school results over the past 100 years), such as mathematics, but we concluded that this was more the result of cultural factors than biological ones. In other words, the observed differences between performance between boys and girls seem to be unrelated to brain differences.

To date, no empirical proof has been offered to show that boys and girls learn in a different way from each other. Nor has it been scientifically proven that women are better at multitasking or that their brains are designed to behave more empathically. It is certainly true that women score better than men in empathy tests ... except in the tests where the men are told that they usually do better than women! A study by researchers from Cambridge University looked at many aspects of the brains of men and women with the aim of improving neuropsychiatric diagnosis and eventual treatment. This large meta-analysis compared data reported in 167 articles (selected from an initial giant stack of 5600 relevant articles). Apart from the obvious differences, such as brain size, differences were found in the amygdala (a brain area involved in memory and emotion) and the hippocampus (an area involved in processing memories). The researchers note that they cannot predict how differences in brain structures influence actual behavior. Even though differences in brain physiology provide a welcome source for ideas about behavioral gender differences, these are not substantiated by facts.

This brings us back to the danger of thinking in terms of boxes. The British psychologist Cordelia Fine warns us to be on our guard against "neurosexism". By placing too much emphasis on possible but unsubstantiated differences between the brains of men and women, there is a risk that we will create new and prejudicial sexual stereotypes. Although the concept of neurosexism and the book by Fine were heavily criticized by some neuroscientists, there is certainly a growing consensus that there exists a tendency to overstress gender-based differences. We tend to look for and focus on small differences between two groups, whereas we underestimate or even ignore the much larger differences within groups. If we look at the things our brains are most actively engaged in, we find no relevant differences between the way men and women observe the world, the way they learn new things, the way they store memories or how they communicate with each other.

A study by Janet Hyde has shed new light on this last aspect, although her conclusions may so some extent by colored by her basic premises. This is a general issue in research on gender differences; it is often very difficult to distinguish between opinions and facts. In her research Hyde did not search for differences, but instead for similarities between men and women. Of course, she was able to observe many similarities. Consequently, she was able to dispel a few classic ideas about men and women, by establishing that:

- Women do not really talk more than men.
- Women only reveal marginally more personal details about themselves than men.
- Men and women are equally capable of interrupting; this is largely a question of social status — if the woman has the lead, she will be more inclined to butt in.

As we have already stated, in practice there are more differences within the sexes than between the sexes. But this fact implies that the claim that single-sex education will be more effective than mixed education is wrong. We will look at this subject again later in the book.

:-\ Yes, the brains of boys and girls are in some ways different, but there are more similarities than differences. You should not use these differences as an argument.

REFERENCES

Fine, C. (2010). *Delusions of gender: How our minds, society, and neurosexism create difference.* New York: W.W. Norton.

Hyde, J. S. (2005). The gender similarities hypothesis. *American Psychologist, 60,* 581–592.

Ruigrok, A. N. V., Gholamreza, S.-K., Meng-Chuan, L., Baron-Cohen, S., Lombardo, M. V., Tait, R. J., et al. (2014). A meta-analysis of sex differences in human brain structure. *Neuroscience & Biobehavioral Reviews, 39,* 34–50.

Voyer, D., & Voyer, S. D. (2014). Gender differences in scholastic achievement: A meta-analysis. *Psychological Bulletin, 140,* 1174–1204.

MYTH 6

We Can Learn While We Are Asleep

It may be every student's dream: to be able to learn while you're asleep! The idea that it could be possible to learn new information during sleep (also known as hypnopedia) is not new. Sleep-learning has always been a popular topic in fiction. Also, there is a business element involved: in the past cassette tapes were sold with the intention that they would be put on "repeat" while sleeping, while nowadays digital files are sold through the Internet with the same intention. Experiments to see whether sleep-learning is really possible were already being carried out during the Second World War. It was hoped that secret agents would be able to more quickly learn the dialects of the regions into which they were to be parachuted if they continued learning foreign languages while they were sleeping.

Russian research has suggested that the idea is a valid one, but their scientific methods were not wholly reliable. In particular, it was not clear why it seemed to work with one person, but not with another. Moreover, the Russians failed to check to what extent the test subjects did or did not sleep throughout the night. This may help to explain why scientists in the West have never been able to come up with comparable results.

Research has established that after an operation, people were able to remember things that were said during their operation, while they were anaesthetized. But this is not the same as learning in your sleep, because the state of being under anesthesia is not comparable with the sleep state. It lacks the depth of sleep and second, it is more like a chemically induced and reversible coma, in which relatively little brain activity is registered.

So, unless you recorded yourself speaking the text or you never actually sleep, we are afraid that the recording you play on your smartphone throughout the night won't help you much when exam time comes around.

Yet, perhaps there is a little bit of hope. A study by researchers from the Weizmann Institute of Science in Israel has shown that there is a way in which you *can* learn during your sleep. It is similar to the way the Russian neurologist Ivan Pavlov conditioned his dogs to salivate. In other words, we are not talking about learning content, but more a kind of classical conditioning. The dogs learned to associate receiving food with the sound of a bell. Over time, they began to salivate in anticipation every time they heard the bell. It now appears that this same mechanism can be applied to people, not with sound — which would probably wake the person up — but with smell. While asleep, test subjects heard a tone, following which an aroma was released. A pleasant aroma followed one tone and a less than pleasant aroma followed a different tone. What happened? The following day — while awake — test subjects reacted to both tones as though the "learnt" aroma was about to be released. This means that while they were sleeping, their brain did learn to associate a tone with a smell.

Of course, this is not really learning but rather, at most, very low-order learning at the same level as simple operant conditioning. Further research is needed to explore whether it is possible to extend this to real learning. In the meantime, we recommend not letting those recordings disturb your beauty sleep just yet.

Sleep and School: Why not Begin at 11 o'Clock?

Research by Russell Foster, a professor of neuroscience at Oxford University, has suggested that the students' memories function better during tests conducted at 2 pm than at the "ungodly" hour of 9 am. For this reason, he argues in favor of starting school at the more reasonable hour of 11 o'clock.

The most important reason for this, according to Foster, is that young people sleep too little. Why do they sleep so little? Because teenage life is overfull (e.g., homework, friends, Internet, television, parents, parties, sports) and they drink too many caffeine-rich drinks. Moreover, during this period of their lives their sleeping rhythms change. The research was formally conducted in an English school, but the results only made the British media, and to date have not been published in any scientific journal.

Source
Rosen, D. (2009). Sleeping angels. Should high school start at 11am? *Psychology Today*, Retrieved June 14, 2014, from <http://www.psychologytoday.com/blog/sleeping-angels/200903/should-high-school-start-11-am>.

:-\ People can be conditioned in their sleep; for example, to associate particular smells with particular tones. But can we actually learn content in our sleep? Dream on!

REFERENCES

Arzi, A., Shedlesky, L., Ben-Shaul, M., Oksenberg, A., Hairston, I. S., & Sobel, N. (2012). Humans can learn new information during sleep. *Nature Neuroscience, 15,* 1460—1465.

Schwartz, R. S., Brown, E. N., Lydic, R., & Schiff, N. D. (2010). General anesthesia, sleep, and coma. *New England Journal of Medicine, 363*(27), 2638—2650.

MYTH 7

Babies Become Cleverer if They Listen to Classical Music

In 1993, an influential article was published in the scientific journal *Nature*. The researchers, from the University of California, claimed that after listening for just 10 minutes to a Mozart piano sonata (K448), a group of university students were able to perform a series of spatial reasoning tests — as part of the standard Stanford–Binet Intelligence Scale — noticeably better than a control group which was played a tape of "ordinary" relaxing music, whatever that is. The improved spatial reasoning was sometimes interpreted as a claim that listening to Mozart could temporarily raise your general IQ by 8 or 9 points! This finding has gained wide popularity and has become known as the "Mozart effect". The inevitable Mozart CDs for babies soon followed. Even now, there are multiple web stores selling MP3 recordings geared at "stimulating your baby's brain". In 1998, the governor of Georgia even set aside $105,000 of the state budget to provide every child born in the state of Georgia (approximately 100,000 per year) with a tape or CD of classical music. The governor was quoted in *The New York Times* as stating: "No one questions that listening to music at a very early age affects the spatial, temporal reasoning that underlies math and engineering and even chess".

It is clear that this research had a high score for reliability on the checklist at the back of this book, but (once again) the conclusions reported in the media went far beyond what the researchers had actually said. For one thing, the improvement in reasoning in the group that listened to Mozart was only noted immediately after the playing of the Mozart sonata. Also, the effect seemed to last only for a very brief time. It was never claimed to be a lasting effect.

The Mozart effect has been a welcome research topic, and multiple studies have tried to replicate the effect, sometimes with (limited) success. Versna Ivanov and John Geake (Geake is mentioned elsewhere in this book as a "myth buster") found some evidence for the Mozart effect, although listening to music by Johann Sebastian Bach proved to be just as effective. One obvious question is whether it is necessary to play music by Mozart to improve one's cognitive skills. Maybe music that we personally enjoy can be just as, or even more effective than Mozart. In that case, classical music should not have any specific advantage over other types of music: it's just a matter of personal preference. Studies like the one by Ivanov and Geake provide evidence that backs up this claim. Donna Lerch and Thomas Anderson analyzed and compared many of the Mozart effect studies. They came to the following general conclusion:

The music of Wolfgang Amadeus Mozart is both physically and aesthetically accessible to the general public. A number of studies have indicated that listening to Mozart's work may temporarily increase cognitive skills. Other studies have found no statistically significant "Mozart effect". It is unfortunate that the media and commercial ventures have taken the initial modest, unverified study and conjured up a pseudo-science which gave rise to, and which continues to promote, a full-blown industry.

One of the companies that discovered to their own cost and shame that they should never have become involved with such products is Disney. The "Baby Einstein (TM)" CDs were a profitable and successful business venture for Disney. In 2007, however, a study by Zimmerman, Christakis, and Meltzoff caused a large stir among the public when they reported that their research showed that the products in the Baby Einstein series could actually lead in some cases to a worsening rather than an improvement of language ability. This study was hotly contested and a number of matters still remain unclear. A reanalysis of the data from Zimmerman et al.'s 2007 experiment by Ferguson and Donnellan led them to conclude that it is not possible to make strong inferences from the data from the 2007 experiment, but Zimmerman strongly disagrees. The matter remains contested; even so, after many complaints, in 2009 Disney organized repayment for disgruntled parents, admitting that its products had been incorrectly marketed as "educational".

So, does a bit of music have no positive effect on the brain at all? Actually, there may be one long-lasting effect that is of interest. However, it does not involve merely listening to music, but practicing and playing a musical instrument yourself. Research has shown that older adults benefit from music training early in life. Even when people have not played a musical instrument for decades, their neural processing of sounds is improved over people who had no music practice early in life. These "trained" older people experience fewer difficulties understanding speech, even in crowded environments. This leads us to conclude that smart parents do not force their children to listen to Mozart, but encourage them to create their own music instead.

:-\ Classical music will not make your children any smarter.

REFERENCES

Dana Foundation (2009). *Neuroeducation: Learning, arts, and the brain.* New York: Dana Press.

Ferguson, C. J., & Donnellan, M. B. (2014). Is the association between children's baby video viewing and poor language development robust? A reanalysis of Zimmerman, Christakis, and Meltzoff (2007). *Developmental Psychology, 50*(1), 129–137.

Ivanov, V. K., & Geake, J. G. (2003). The Mozart effect and primary school children. *Psychology of Music, 31*(4), 405–413.

Lerch, D., & Anderson, T. (2000). The Mozart effect: A closer look. Retrieved June 14, 2014, from <http://lrs.ed.uiuc.edu/students/lerch1/edpsy/mozart_effect.html>.

Lilienfeld, S. O. (2010). *50 great myths of popular psychology: Shattering widespread misconceptions about human behavior.* Chichester, UK: Wiley-Blackwell.

Mehr, S. A., Schachner, A., Katz, R. C., & Spelke, E. S. (2013). Two randomized trials provide no consistent evidence for nonmusical cognitive benefits of brief preschool music enrichment. *PloS ONE, 8*(12), e82007.

Rauscher, F. H., Shaw, G. L., & Ky, K. N. (1993). Music and spatial task performance. *Nature, 365*, 6447.

Sack, K. (1998). Georgia's governor seeks musical start for babies. Retrieved from <http://www.nytimes.com/1998/01/15/us/georgia-s-governor-seeks-musical-start-for-babies.html>.

White-Schwoch, T., Woodruff Carr, K., Anderson, S., Strait, D. L., & Kraus, N. (2013). Older adults benefit from music training early in life: Biological evidence for long-term training-driven plasticity. *Journal of Neuroscience, 33*(45), 17667–17674.

Zimmerman, F. J., Christakis, D. A., & Meltzoff, A. N. (2007). Associations between media viewing and language development in children under age 2 years. *Journal of Pediatrics, 151*(4), 364–368.

MYTH 8

We Think Most Clearly When We Are Under Pressure

It has become a staple of many popular action movies. About two-thirds into the movie, the hero gets into serious trouble. All hope seems lost. It is right at that moment of maximum pressure that the hero has his or her finest hour, and saves the day. This idea is also part of our culture: when we are forced to think under pressure, we come up with better solutions more quickly. It has become a cliché — but is it actually true?

At first hearing, it doesn't sound illogical. As soon as our adrenaline begins to flow, we are capable of much more than in a normal situation (you've heard of the woman who lifted up the car that her child was under). What happens in stress situations is that our bodies show a physiological fight-or-flight response. As part of this, our brains become supercharged with powerful hormones. The fight-or-flight response facilitates a quick reaction to emergency situations. Also, a bit of pressure makes us more alert and helps us to create new memories. Still, everything in moderation. If stressful situations happen too often, they can have a negative effect on the brain. Some researchers argue that too much stress can even cause permanent brain damage. For example, researchers from the Yale University School of Medicine have shown that learned helplessness in rats, which is a typical stressful condition, leads to damage in the hippocampus, the area in the brain that controls memory formation. The same seems to be true for humans. In particular, our memory can suffer if it is subjected to too much stress, so that we have more trouble remembering and recalling things. A large review study at the Center for Studies on Human Stress at McGill University showed that the relation between the level of stress and cognitive performance as measured, for example, in hippocampal volume follows an inverted-U shape. That is, there is an optimum level of performance that depends on the amount of stress: both too little and too much stress degrades performance.

Other studies have shown that the related emotion of fear can also have a negative effect on how children perform at school and can actually limit their ability to learn. For example, considerable research has been carried out into so-called "maths anxiety". An analysis of the Programme for International Student Assessment (PISA) results for 2003 showed that the countries with above-average performance in mathematics were also the countries with the lowest incidence of maths anxiety. The question is: Which causes which? Is it the case that if you're good at math this leads to less anxiety? Or is it that if you have less anxiety, you perform better? Or is there possibly a third factor that influences both?

Mullainathan and Shafir describe how we seem to have a limited amount of what they call mental "bandwidth" and that we use a bit of that bandwidth each time we address a problem (e.g., fear or stress because of poverty or time restraints). This used bandwidth then cannot be used for learning.

:-\ You do not think "better" under pressure and you learn less well if you are frightened.

REFERENCES

Franklin Institute. (2004). The human brain — Stress. Retrieved June 18, 2014, from <http://learn.fi.edu/learn/brain/stress.html>.

Hajszan, T., Dow, A., Warner-Schmidt, J. L., Szigeti-Buck, K., Sallam, N. L., Parducz, A., et al. (2009). Remodeling of hippocampal spine synapses in the rat learned helplessness model of depression. *Biological Psychiatry, 65*(5), 392—400.

Hattie, J. (2009). *Visible learning: A synthesis of over 800 meta-analyses relating to achievement.* London: Routledge.

Lee, J. (2009). Universals and specifics of math self-concept, math self-efficacy, and math anxiety across 41 PISA 2003 participating countries. *Learning and Individual Differences, 19*(3), 355—365.

Lupien, S., Maheu, F., Tu, M., Fiocco, A., & Schramek, T. (2007). The effects of stress and stress hormones on human cognition: Implications for the field of brain and cognition. *Brain and Cognition, 65*(3), 209—237.

Mullainathan, S., & Shafir, E. (2013). *Scarcity: Why having too little means so much.* New York: Macmillan.

Does It Help to Have a Correct Knowledge of How the Brain Works?

Right, so what have we learned so far? Most of us cannot multitask, we use all of our brain (both the left and the right halves), we prefer to have our sleep undisturbed and babies prefer this too (no Mozart, thank you), and we do not necessarily perform better under pressure. The fact that many people, including many teachers, still believe in some or all of these myths is a cause for real concern. We have shown that knowledge about the brain is taken seriously (and usually rightfully so), and will in all probability have a direct impact on teaching practice. So if this knowledge is faulty, the impact on educational practice cannot be anything else than negative. We therefore need to ensure the use of correct knowledge so that it can have a positive — rather than a negative — effect.

It is likely that part of the potential of every pupil in class is unused at the moment. This is a matter of concern, and appropriate action may be taken, as long as it is clear that it has nothing to do with the pupil's brain.

Over the years, numerous studies in the field of educational psychology have shown that learning requires active effort on the part of the learner in order to be effective. It is better to be honest with your pupils — and their parents — on this score, rather than offer false hopes that learning will happen by itself, almost like magic. Learning is hard, and it can be argued that it is important for learning to be hard to be more effective. As Lev Vygotsky stated at the beginning of the twentieth century, real learning takes place in a learner's zone of proximal development: that narrow region where learning is challenging but not *too* hard. However, putting pupils under pressure — as is sometimes the case with speed tests — can also have a clear negative effect, particularly for pupils who are more sensitive to being placed in a stressful situation.

Teachers who treat boys and girls differently are in danger of creating a self-fulfilling prophesy: they may encourage pupils to behave in accordance with the stereotypes that have been set for them; a process sometimes referred to as the "stereotype threat", an effect that has been researched with sometimes positive and sometimes negative results.

The idea that there is some kind of general training method that can help us to improve the working of our brain and the way we think is an old one. We have shown that these general methods are mostly ineffective. The implication for education is that we should not become fixated on disciplines that we believe can help our pupils to think better. In the past, these were thought to be classical languages such as Latin and Greek; nowadays you see many schools devoting extra attention to chess. Even computer programming has been touted as a method to improve logical problem solving. Both are certainly useful and entertaining pastimes, just as Latin and Greek are fascinating subjects, but the idea that they will somehow hone your "analytical skills" should be taken with a very large pinch of salt.

REFERENCES

Cimpian, A., Mu, Y., & Erickson, L. C. (2012). Who is good at this game? Linking an activity to a social category undermines children's achievement. *Psychological Science*, *23*(5), 533–541.

Ganley, C. M., Mingle, L. A., Ryan, A. M., Ryan, K., Vasilyeva, M., & Perry, M. (2013). An examination of stereotype threat effects on girls' mathematics performance. *Developmental Psychology*, *49*(10), 1886–1897.

Howard-Jones, P. (2014). *Neuroscience and education: A review of educational interventions and approaches informed by neuroscience*. Education Endowment Foundation. Retrieved May 15, 2014, from <http://educationendowmentfoundation.org.uk/uploads/pdf/NSED_LitReview_Final.pdf>.

Lupien, S., Maheu, F., Tu, M., Fiocco, A., & Schramek, T. (2007). The effects of stress and stress hormones on human cognition: Implications for the field of brain and cognition. *Brain and Cognition*, *65*(3), 209–237.

Willingham, D. T. (2009). *Why don't students like school? A cognitive scientist answers questions about how the mind works and what it means for the classroom*. San Francisco, CA: Jossey-Bass.

CHAPTER 4

Myths about Technology in Education

Contents

It is not the medium that decides how effectively learners learn.

One of the most frequently cited reasons for justifying the need for change in education, or at least for labeling it as old fashioned, is the enormous technological (r)evolution our world has undergone in recent years. It is now almost impossible to imagine, but 25 years ago only a very small number of people had access to the Internet; access to the World Wide Web started to become popular in 1993 when the first widely used graphical web browser, Mosaic, was released. Nowadays, we have the Internet in our pocket, in the form of a smartphone, which has exponentially more computing power than the Apollo Guidance

Urban Myths about Learning and Education
DOI: http://dx.doi.org/10.1016/B978-0-12-801537-7.00005-6
© 2015 Elsevier Inc.
All rights reserved.

Computer that put the first men on the moon! Schools with desks, black-boards or whiteboards and — perish the thought — books seem like some kind of archaic institution; an institution which, even if it does use a digi-board or a learning platform, does so in a manner that still bears a suspi-ciously strong resemblance to the way things were done in the past.

We could talk for hours — or in our case write for pages — about whether society's fixation on technological change is a classic example of chronocentrism: the tendency to regard the period in which you live as being special or even unique. It is difficult to assess whether or not we are currently living through a period of great change, precisely for that rea-son: because we are living through it. We are too close to make the judg-ment. Is our chronocentrism another myth perhaps? Who can say? It certainly makes for a fascinating discussion.

In this section we will be looking at miracle tools and talking about digital natives, but also about the fear that technology is making us more stupid. And there is one more thing we are curious about: are you read-ing these words on paper or from a screen?

MYTH 1

New Technology Is Causing a Revolution in Education

School television, computers, digital boards, iPads. It was thought that all these new tools would — or will — change education beyond recognition. But if you look at the research of someone like Larry Cuban, it seems that classroom practice has remained pretty stable during recent years. Even Microsoft cofounder Bill Gates — who you would hardly suspect of being against technology in education — summarized his view on the matter as follows: "Just giving people devices has a really horrible track record".

The correct use of tools and resources nevertheless does have the potential to change education. Very often these change phenomena are general rather than specific. For example, the influence of the printed word is gigantic, but this influence — like so many other tools and resources — is anchored in society as a whole. You need to come down to the level of something like the blackboard if you want to consider a resource that has specifically changed education.

In 1983, Richard Clark published a definitive study on how it was pedagogy and not the medium that made a difference in learning, stating that instructional media are "mere vehicles that deliver instruction but do not influence student achievement any more than the truck that delivers our groceries causes changes in our nutrition". It is not that he thought that media selection was irrelevant. In his words, good instruction should "package essential instructional methods based on available resources and the cost-effectiveness qualities of media attributes for specific learners and learning goals" (p. 23). In 1994 he went as far as to make a daring prediction; namely, that media would never influence education. He based this position on his opinion that, at that time, there was no proof to show that a medium was capable of ensuring that pupils and students could learn more effectively. He saw the medium as a means, a vehicle for instruction, but the essence of learning remained in the hands of the teacher.

We are now 20 years further down the line and the question needs to be asked: Does Clark's belief still hold true? During those 20 years we have seen the explosion of almost unimaginable technological possibilities. Even so, Clark and Mayer continue to assert that nothing has fundamentally changed. They argue that 60 years of comparative studies about teaching methods and teaching resources all confirm that it is not the medium that decides how effectively the learners learn. Clark and Feldon confirm that the effectiveness of learning is determined primarily by the way the medium is used and by the quality of the instruction accompanying that use. When media (or multimedia) are used for instruction, the choice of medium does not influence learning. Hattie described, for example, how instructional methods such as learner control and explanative feedback that are more effective within conventional environments are also more effective within computer-based environments.

This can be called the *method-not-media* hypothesis, as tested in a study by Sung and Mayer. In their research, students received an online multimedia lesson on how a solar cell works that consisted of 11 narrated slides with a script of 800 words. Focusing on the instructional media being used, students received the lesson on a desktop computer (i.e., an iMac) in a lab or on a mobile device (i.e., an iPad) in a courtyard. But they also used different instructional methods. Students received a continuous lesson with no headings (standard method) or a segmented lesson in which the learner clicked on a button to go to the next slide, with each slide having a heading corresponding to the key idea in the script for the slide (enhanced method). By combining changes in both medium and method, we can see what matters most. Across both media, the enhanced group outperformed the standard group on a transfer test, yielding a method effect on learning outcomes for both desktop and mobile media. Across both methods, looking at the medium, the mobile group produced stronger ratings than the desktop group on self-reported willingness to continue learning, yielding a media effect on motivational ratings for both standard and enhanced methods. Effective instructional methods can improve learning outcomes across different media, whereas using handheld instructional media may increase students' willingness to continue to engage in learning. We will return to the motivational aspects when discussing the next myth.

A Hype Cycle Instead of a Hype?

Gartner Inc., an information technology (IT) research and advisory firm, has been producing hype cycles since 1995 to describe the evolutions in technology in many different areas of industry and services, including education (Figure 11).

A hype cycle, in Gartner's interpretation, comprises five phases:

1. *Technology trigger*: The first phase of a hype cycle is the "technology trigger" or breakthrough, product launch or other event that generates significant press and interest. This could be the release of a tablet computer such as the iPad; in earlier days it could be the breakthrough of television. Both technologies delivered such claims.

2. *Peak of inflated expectations*: In the next phase, a frenzy of publicity typically generates overenthusiasm and unrealistic expectations. This is the moment when you get claims that the iPad or television will change education forever. Maybe this new technology will even make traditional schools obsolete. At the time of writing this piece, massive online open courses (MOOCs) seem to be in this situation, but there is a big chance that when you read this, these will be in the next phase of the hype cycle.

3. *Trough of disillusionment*: Technologies enter the trough of disillusionment because they fail to meet those unrealistic expectations and quickly become unfashionable. This is the moment when one colleague (you know who) will say that he was right in not adopting the new technology for his class.

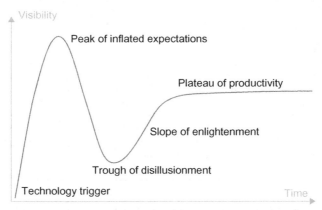

Figure 11 Gartner hype cycle. *Designed by Jeremy Kemp, based on Gartner Inc. (2013, July 3). Hype cycle research methodology. Retrieved from <http://www.gartner.com/technology/research/methodologies/hype-cycle.jsp>, released under the GNU Free Documentation License, downloaded from <http://en.wikipedia.org/wiki/Hype_cycle#mediaviewer/File:Gartner_Hype_Cycle.svggr1>.*

4. *Slope of enlightenment*: Although the hype may be over and the press and their representatives may have stopped saying both good and bad things about the technology, some teachers continue through the slope of enlightenment, and experiment to understand the benefits and practical application of the technology.

Nowadays, for example, we use a lot of video in class. It may not be like traditional "school television", with TV taking over the role of the teacher, but rather short fragments incorporated into the lesson. This brings (educational) video into the last phase of the hype cycle:

5. *Plateau of productivity*: A technology reaches the plateau of productivity as its benefits have become widely demonstrated and accepted.

This model of the hype cycle originates from a for-profit organization, and although it is often used this does not mean that it is a proven model. Richard Veryard notes some important issues concerning this cycle. First, all technologies appear to have the same eventual outcome, which is strange. Second, and even more strange, is that all the points are perfectly on the line. Veryard concludes, "To a scientific mind, this is a strong clue that the coordinates are not based on any real objective measurement, and that the curve itself is not subject to scientific investigation or calibration. The curve itself is based on a standard engineering pattern". Third, Veryard thinks it is strange that the shape of the line has not altered (or accelerated) in 10 years, while all the evidence points to a shifting (shrinking) curve.

Still, bearing this in mind, it can be a handy tool to look at technology in and outside education.

Sources

Jarvenpaa, H., & Makinen, S. J. (2008). Empirically detecting the hype cycle with the life cycle indicators: An exploratory analysis of three technologies. In *IEEE International conference on industrial engineering and engineering management, 2008 (IEEM 2008), Singapore* (pp. 12–16). Piscataway, NJ: IEEE.

Linden, A., & Fenn, J. (2003). *Understanding Gartner's hyper cycles*. Stamford, CT: Gartner Strategic Analysis Report No. R-20-1971.

Veryard, R. (September 16, 2005). Technology hype curve. Retrieved April 14, 2014, from <http://demandingchange.blogspot.be/2005/09/technology-hype-curve.html>.

If we look at the influence of technology on the effectiveness of instruction, the picture is not fully clear. This can partly be explained by the fact that relatively little research has been carried out that involves the comparison of two similar groups, one group learning with and the other group learning without the benefits of a new technology. The different metastudies on this subject, analyzed by John Hattie, reveal a considerable variation in results. A review by Hew and Cheung on the implementation of technology, more specifically Web 2.0 tools such as wikis, blogs and virtual worlds, in K-12 and higher education, suggests that actual evidence regarding the impact of those technologies on student learning is as yet fairly weak. There are still a number of studies that point to a positive gain in learning terms (e.g., the review by Rüther describes positive effects on mathematics and sciences), but the majority equate the positive learning effect resulting from the good use of technology with good teaching. The crucial factor for learning improvement is to make sure that you do not replace the teacher as the instrument of instruction, allowing computers to do what teachers would normally do, but instead use computers to supplement and amplify what the teacher does.

A 2009 metastudy about e-learning did, however, tentatively conclude that the use of both e-learning and contact education — which is known as blended learning — produces better results than lessons given without technology. This is also the case when you use computer-game based learning; the role of instruction still needs to have a real significant learning effect, as Wouters and Van Oostendorp conclude in their meta-analysis. Such instructional support may appear in several forms, such as providing feedback, scaffolding and giving advice.

Still, there remain some questionable claims that technology can change, by itself, the present system of education. Clark and Feldon summarize:

- Multimedia instruction accommodates different learning styles and so maximizes learning for more students. As we explained in Myth 1, the idea of learning styles in itself is already an urban myth in education.

- Multimedia instruction facilitates student-managed constructivist and discovery approaches that are beneficial to learning. We also discussed the element of discovery in education in Myth 6. Clark and Feldon conclude on this claim that "Discovery-based multimedia programs seem to benefit experts or students with higher levels of prior knowledge about the topic being learned. Students with novice to intermediate levels of prior knowledge learn best from fully guided instruction". In fact, this is again a similar conclusion to the one we saw earlier on and is an extra example of how the medium does not influence the learning. Prior knowledge is an individual difference that leads to learning benefits from more guidance at low to moderate levels but not at higher levels, regardless of the media used to deliver instruction.

- Multimedia instruction provides students with autonomy and control over the sequencing of instruction. Although technology can deliver this, the more important question is whether this is a good thing or not. Letting students decide the pace of learning, e.g., by pausing or slowing down videos or presentations, is beneficial to learning. But only a small group of students has the benefit of being given the chance to select the order of lessons, learning tasks and learning support. For the majority of students this has a mostly negative influence on learning.

:-\ The medium seldom influences teaching, learning and education, nor is it likely that one single medium will ever be the best one for all situations.

REFERENCES

Clark, R. (1983). Reconsidering research on learning from media. *Review of Educational Research, 53*, 445−449.

Clark, R. E. (1994). Media will never influence learning. *Educational Technology Research and Development, 42*(2), 21−29.

Clark, R. E., & Feldon, D. F. (2014). Ten common but questionable principles of multimedia learning. In R. E. Mayer (Ed.), *The Cambridge handbook of multimedia learning* (2nd ed., pp. 151−173). Cambridge: Cambridge University Press.

Clark, R. C., & Mayer, R. E. (2011). *E-learning and the science of instruction: Proven guidelines for consumers and designers of multimedia learning.* San Francisco, CA: Pfeiffer.

Cuban, L. (2009). *Oversold and underused: Computers in the classroom.* Harvard, MA: Harvard University Press.

Hattie, J. (2009). *Visible learning: A synthesis of over 800 meta-analyses relating to achievement.* London: Routledge.

Hew, K. F., & Cheung, W. S. (2013). Use of Web 2.0 technologies in K-12 and higher education: The search for evidence-based practice. *Educational Research Review, 9*, 47−64.

Means, B., Toyama, Y., Murphy, R., Bakia, M., & Jones, J. (2009). Evaluation of evidence-based practices in online learning: A meta-analysis and review of online learning studies. Technical Report. Washington, DC: Center for Technology in Learning.

Rüther, K. (2012). ICT en leerprestaties − Een systematische review naar de invloed van ICT op leerprestaties in exacte vakken in het voortgezet onderwijs. Thesis, University of Twente.

Sung, E., & Mayer, R. E. (2013). Online multimedia learning with mobile devices and desktop computers: An experimental test of Clark's methods-not-media hypothesis. *Computers in Human Behavior, 29*, 639−647.

Wouters, P., & Van Oostendorp, H. (2013). A meta-analytic review of the role of instructional support in game-based learning. *Computers & Education, 60*, 412−425.

Young, J. R. (2012). A conversation with Bill Gates about the future of higher education. *Chronicle,* Retrieved June 27, 2012, from <http://chronicle.com/article/A-Conversation-With-Bill-Gates/132591/>.

MYTH 2

The Internet Belongs in the Classroom Because It Is Part of the Personal World Experienced by Children

How often have you heard this said? And it sounds so logical, doesn't it? At the same time, many teachers have discovered to their cost that just using information and communications technology (ICT) in their lesson "randomly", in an unstructured way, does not always have lasting success. The problem is that most research studies have been evaluations of relatively short-term projects. The research by Sung and Mayer mentioned in Section 5.1 focuses on the liking of a medium during the actual test, which for a student actually lasted for about 12 minutes. Also note that in this research being motivated because of the medium (with an effect size d of 0.60) did not help the learning as much as the chosen pedagogical approach (with an effect size d of 0.67). But when we discuss implementing technology and the Internet in the classroom, people do not argue for using it once or only for a short period, but for long-term implementation. Therefore, it is the impact over a longer period that really needs to be determined.

A study by the Canadian Higher Education Strategy Associates described how students had a preference for "ordinary, real life" lessons rather than e-learning or the use of some other technology. It was a result that surprised the researchers. "It is not the portrait we expected, whereby students would embrace anything that happens on a more highly technological level. On the contrary – they really seem to like access to human interaction, a smart person at the front of the classroom".

The findings also revealed that the more technology was used to teach a particular course, the lower the number of students who felt they were able to get something out of that course. While the 1380 students from 60 Canadian universities questioned for this survey were generally satisfied with the courses they received, the level of satisfaction fell significantly when more digital forums, online interactions or other technological elements were involved. Yet, at the same time, more than half the respondents said that they would skip a lesson if there was more information or a comparable video lesson online.

Although these results at first glance seem to be fairly negative for e-learning, the responses to some further questions were more positive.

The majority of students (59.6%) said that they would like a larger electronic content in their courses. When asked what they would specifically like to see online, 53.6% answered that they would like more online course notes, with 46.4% advocating more recordings of lessons on the web.

These finding are broadly in keeping with the results of a 2011 literature study by Chris Jones and Binhu Shao, which investigated the expectations of young people with regard to new forms of education and ICT. They reached the following conclusions.

- The gap between the students and their teachers is not great, and certainly not so great that it cannot be bridged. In fact, the relationship is determined by the requirements teachers place on their students to make use of new technologies. There is little evidence that students (in further education) expect the use of these new technologies.
- In all the studies consulted, the students persistently report that they prefer moderate use of ICT in their courses. "Moderate" is, of course, an imprecise term that is difficult to quantify.
- Students do not naturally make extensive use of many of the newest technologies, such as blogs, wikis and virtual worlds. Students who need or are required to use these technologies in their courses are unlikely to object to them, but there is not a natural demand among students for any such use.

Maybe this will change as technology becomes more and more normal. However, a study on students in Glasgow found little change; these students appeared to conform to fairly traditional pedagogies, albeit with minor uses of technology tools that deliver content. Research comparing traditional books with e-readers shows that students prefer paper.

The sad thing is that even if students did prefer to use technology in school, this does not mean that they would learn more. In 2005, Clark and Feldon concluded, "The best conclusion at this point is that overall, multimedia courses may be more attractive to students and so they tend to choose them when offered options [yet] ... student interest does not result in more learning and overall it appears to actually result in significantly less learning than would have occurred in 'instructor led' courses". A decade later, based on 10 years of extra research, Clark and Feldon stand by this conclusion.

In her latest book, danah boyd [she writes her name in lower case letters] describes the main reasons for young people to use technology. These reasons are mainly social, such as sharing information with each other, and meeting each other online and in real life. They do discuss school stuff with each other, but the role of this technology is very different from Facebook or their iPhone or Android phone being a learning machine.

Three Profiles of Students Using Technology in Education: Instrumental Users, Separators and Integrators

The second phase of the Digital Learners in Higher Education project, from which we took the Canadian research mentioned earlier, uncovered some important insights into how learners in higher education think about and using digital technologies for social and academic purposes, and how they separate and integrate their uses. The paper has been submitted for review, but Mark Bullen has already published it online to share their insights (Bullen & Morgan, 2013).

The three profiles of students using technology are:

* *Instrumental users (or tool-limited, tool-specific users)* generally used only one or two technology tools, or only one or two functions of a tool. In other words, instrumental users mediated their activity using limited technology resources (tools), or used a technology for a specific activity or more narrowly defined object (e.g., gaming versus connecting with others).
* *Separators* consciously or unconsciously separated their academic and social practices. In activity theory terms, the social and academic lives remain as separate activity systems, where boundary crossing is avoided. While the same tools may be part of both systems, for the most part the community and rules mediate the activities differently and therefore these shared tools do not function as boundary objects.
* *Integrators* have overlapping social and academic practices in both the types of tools they use and their practices. In other words, there is evidence of boundary objects and boundary crossing, which have been negotiated by the subject.

Source
Bullen, M., & Morgan, T. (2013). Digital learners in higher education: Implications for teaching, learning & technology. Retrieved April 14, 2014, from <https://app.box.com/s/oie8y6mi8062ftq8g05d>.

You are not going to hear us say that the Internet has no place or should play no role in the classroom. On the contrary, it clearly has and does. But it must be used for valid content and didactic reasons. In this context, it is also worth noting that the expression of this current myth is usually related to the following myth.

:-\ It sounds simple, but the most important thing about ICT is that pupils/learners must experience it and its use as added value in terms of learning (i.e., that the learning experience is more efficient, effective and/or enjoyable); otherwise, they will lose interest. As a separate issue, it is important that the world of education should not become isolated from what is happening in the real world.

REFERENCES

boyd, d. (2007). *Why youth (heart) social network sites: The role of networked publics in teenage social life* ((pp. 119–142)). *MacArthur foundation series on digital learning — Youth, identity, and digital media volume.* Cambridge, MA: MIT Press (pp. 119–142).

boyd, d. (2014). *It's complicated: The social lives of networked teens.* New Haven, CT: Yale University Press.

Bullen, M., Morgan, T., & Qayyum, A. (2011). Digital learners in higher education: Looking beyond stereotypes. *Proceedings of the ED MEDIA conference,* Lisbon, July 1, 2011.

Clark, R. E., & Feldon, D. F. (2005). Five common but questionable principles of multimedia learning. In R. Mayer (Ed.), *The Cambridge handbook of multimedia learning* (pp. 97–117). New York: Cambridge University Press.

Clark, R. E., & Feldon, D. F. (2014). Ten common but questionable principles of multimedia learning. In R. E. Mayer (Ed.), *The Cambridge handbook of multimedia learning* (2nd ed., pp. 151–173). Cambridge: Cambridge University Press.

Friedrich, H. F., & Hron, A. (2010). Factors influencing pupils' acceptance of an e-learning system for secondary schools. *Journal of Educational Computing Research, 42* (1), 63–78.

Gros, B., Garcia, I., & Escofet, A. (2012). Beyond the net generation debate: A comparison of digital learners in face-to-face and virtual universities. *International Review of Research in Open and Distance Learning, 13*(4) Retrieved November 22, 2012, from <http://www.irrodl.org/index.php/irrodl/article/view/1305/2311>.

Jones, C., & Shao, B. (2011). *The net generation and digital natives: Implications for higher education.* York: Higher Education Academy.

Kaznowska, E., Rogers, J., & Usher, A. (2011). *The state of e-learning in Canadian universities, 2011: If students are digital natives, why don't they like e-learning?* Toronto: Higher Education Strategy Associates.

Margaryan, A., Littlejohn, A., & Vojt, G. (2011). Are digital natives a myth or reality? University students' use of digital technologies. *Computers & Education, 56*(2), 429–440.

Sung, E., & Mayer, R. E. (2013). Online multimedia learning with mobile devices and desktop computers: An experimental test of Clark's methods-not-media hypothesis. *Computers in Human Behavior, 29*(3), 639–647.

Woody, W. D., Daniel, D. B., & Baker, C. A. (2010). E-books or textbooks: Students prefer textbooks. *Computers & Education, 55*(3), 945–948.

MYTH 3

Today's Digital Natives Are a New Generation Who Want a New Style of Education

Digital natives! Whenever the question of digital innovation in education is discussed, this is a term that immediately comes to the surface. Synonyms include the "net generation" or "Homo zappiens" or the "app generation", as Howard Gardner has called them. But this idea should be avoided. Even the person who coined the term digital natives, Marc Prensky, admitted in his most recent book *Brain gain* that the term is now obsolete. Does this mean that we will not hear this term in the future? No, unfortunately not. When we began to count how often we heard the term used on the radio, we came to an average of twice per week over a fairly lengthy period (during the writing of this book, in fact). This cost us quite a few radios, because we have an inclination to throw something at the radio or throw it somewhere irretrievable whenever we hear those two little words . . . digital natives. Ugh!

Worst of all is the fact that this "concept" is one of the reasons most frequently cited to support the argument for radical change in the education system. So, for the sake of clarity, here — hopefully for the last time — are the very good arguments for consigning this term to the dustbin of educational history.

The concept of digital natives is usually used to describe young people who were born in the digital world and for whom all forms of ICT are natural. The adults who were born earlier are therefore "digital immigrants", who try with difficulty to keep up with the natives. Marc Prensky first coined both terms in 2001. With this concept he referred to a group of young people who have been immersed in technology all their lives, giving them distinct and unique characteristics that set them apart from previous generations, and who have sophisticated technical skills and learning preferences for which traditional education is unprepared. As Kirschner and van Merriënboer note, Prensky's coining of this term — and its counterpart digital immigrants for people who are not digitally native — was not based on research into this generation, but rather created by rationalizing phenomena that he had observed.

As the idea became popular, extra claims were added to the initial concept. Erika Smith, of the University of Alberta, describes eight claims in the different present discourses on digital natives:

1. *They possess new ways of knowing and being.* The main idea behind this claim is that there is an urgent need for both educational institutions (administrators, educators) and parents to recognize and adapt to digital native learners who possess new learning styles and/or different ways of knowing and being. Wim Veen — who coined the name "Homo zappiens" — adds to this claim that for digital natives for "learning is playing" and "school is for meeting friends rather than learning". Therefore, from this viewpoint, education as it is today is in big trouble as it is a part of old ways of schooling (i.e., old ways of being and knowing), often associated with digital immigrants.

2. *They are driving a digital revolution transforming society.* Another dominant claim Smith sees is that there is a pressing need to acknowledge and accept that a digital revolution is transforming society. Many argue that this revolution is especially evident within and important for higher education, but with tablet schools popping up in many countries, this argument can be heard for all ages.

3. *They are innately or inherently tech-savvy.* Within digital native discourse, students are seen as innately or inherently tech-savvy, desiring and using digital technology in all arenas, as opposed to older educators — aka digital immigrants — who lack tech-savviness. Ask many parents and teachers and they will agree, as these kids have helped many of them with technology.

4. *They are multitaskers, team-oriented and collaborative.* Net generation students are often said to be multitaskers, team-oriented and collaborative, something we tackled in the first neuromyth we discussed.

5. *They are native speakers of the language of technologies.* Purported as native speakers of the language of technologies, digital natives are often seen as having unique viewpoints and abilities, especially regarding their unique aptitude for the language of technology.

6. *They embrace gaming, interaction and simulation.* According to this sixth digital native claim, gaming, interaction, and simulation (i.e., multi-linear, visual, virtual environments) are both embraced by and well suited to the net generation.

7. *They demand immediate gratification.* The net generation is often portrayed as demanding immediate gratification, with short attention spans and no tolerance for delays. They may not want it all, but they want it now.

8. *They are reflecting and responding to the knowledge economy.* As a last claim, Smith describes how proponents of digital native notions often present a strong relationship between the needs of the net generation and the knowledge economy (i.e., students as consumers, demanding customer satisfaction), specifically within the context of the information age.

Smith concludes that there is little to no proof for these claims, and she is not alone. A meta-analysis conducted in 2008 by Bennett, Maton, and Kervin had already shown that there was little hard evidence to support the use of this terminology.

A New Form of ADHD

As Kirschner and van Merriënboer see it, children today seem to be suffering from a new form of ADHD (attention deficit hyperlink disorder) where learners at the computer behave like butterflies fluttering across the information on the screen, touching or not touching pieces of information (i.e., hyperlinks), quickly fluttering to the next piece of information, unconscious to its value and with no plan. This *butterfly defect* was first signaled by Salomon and Almog. Kirschner and van Merriënboer conclude that learners are often seduced (Richard Mayer spoke of seductive details in learning materials) into clicking the links, forgetting what they are looking for. This "fluttering" leads, at best, to a very fragile network of knowledge. Many a quest ends in a quagmire of possibly interesting, but irrelevant pieces of information.

This form of "ADHD" can hurt even the brightest students when in class, as research by Ravizza, Hambrick, and Fenn shows, describing how non-academic Internet use during class negatively predicts examination scores.

Sources
Kirschner, P. A., & van Merriënboer, J. J. G. (2013). Do learners really know best? Urban legends in Education. *Educational Psychologist, 48*(3), 1—15.

Mayer, R. E. (2005). *The Cambridge handbook of multimedia learning.* Cambridge: Cambridge University Press.

Ravizza, S. M., Hambrick, D. Z., & Fenn, K. M. (2014). Non-academic Internet use in the classroom is negatively related to classroom learning regardless of intellectual ability. *Computers & Education, 78,* 109—114.

Salomon, G., & Almog, T. (1998). Educational psychology and technology: A matter of reciprocal relations. *Teachers College Record, 100,* 222—241.

But maybe the concept of digital natives was more a kind of prediction, and we just had to wait. Perhaps today's young generation *are* true digital natives. If we look at the research performed in high-tech Hong

Kong by David M. Kennedy and Bob Fox, the answer is more than nuanced. Kennedy and Fox investigated how first year undergraduate students used and understood various digital technologies. They discovered, like danah boyd did with the American teenagers, that the first year undergraduate students at Hong Kong University (HKU) do use a wide range of digital technologies.

The students use a large quantity and variety of technologies for communication, learning, staying connected with their friends and engaging with the world around them. But they are using them primarily for "personal empowerment and entertainment". More importantly, Kennedy and Fox describe that the students are "not always digitally literate in using technology to support their learning. This is particularly evident when it comes to student use of technology as consumers of content rather than creators of content specifically for academic purposes".

Margaryan, Littlejohn, and Vojt reported that university students — that is bona fide card-carrying digital natives — use only a limited range of technologies for learning and socialization; "... the tools these students used were largely established technologies, in particular mobile phones, media player, Google, Wikipedia. The use of handheld computers as well as gaming, social networking sites, blogs and other emergent social technologies was very low". This finding has been supported by a number of other researchers (e.g., Selwyn; Williams & Rowlands) who found the same, namely that university students do not really have a deep knowledge of technology, and what knowledge they do have is often limited to basic office suite skills, e-mailing, text messaging, Facebook and surfing the Internet.

When looking at the same topic in another continent, Europe, the large-scale EU Kids Online report of 2011 placed the term "digital natives" in first place on its list of the 10 biggest myths about young people and technology. Just 36% of Europe's 9—16-year-olds said that they knew more about the Internet than their parents.

Kirschner and van Merriënboer add to this list of studies other research in different countries such as Austria, Australia, Canada, Switzerland and the USA, which all comes to the same conclusion: there is no such thing as a generation of digital natives.

The literature study by Jones and Shao, previously mentioned in Section 5.2 when discussing our second myth about technology in education, reveals that if you want to see a connection between (non-existent) digital natives and education, then the reality of the situation needs to be approached with the necessary degree of nuance. In particular, the following conclusions from their report should be hung above the bed of every educational guru:

- There is no evidence to suggest that there is a single new generation of young students entering higher education. Terms such as the "net generation" and "digital native" do not accurately describe the processes of change that are taking place, which are most probably the result of a more diverse and more complex inflow.
- There is no evidence of a consistent demand from students to change the pedagogic forms of (higher) education (e.g., by allowing more team or group work). But this does not necessarily mean that they would be opposed to such changes (see also when discussing our second myth about technology in education).

The researchers therefore conclude that the existence of a new generation of students, defined as digital natives, cannot be cited as a reason for radical changes to the existing educational structure. The different studies that they compared showed that young students do not form an integrated new generation in the manner that the term "digital natives" implies, and that these students do not have any specific demands in terms of the use of ICT in education.

A further important conclusion from the evaluations made by Jones and Shao is that political choices need to be made explicitly and should not be blurred by arguments about a "change of generation" that simply does not exist. As a result, the myth means that we often overlook the need for the further development of our young people's digital skills within the education system.

> :-\ Digital natives are a myth in their own right. There is no evidence that this current generation needs different education or different work forms within education than the previous generations.

REFERENCES

Bennett, S., Maton, K., & Kervin, L. (2008). The "digital natives" debate: A critical review of the evidence. *British Journal of Educational Technology, 39*(5), 775–786.

Bullen, M., Morgan, T., Belfer, K., & Qayyum, A. (2009). The net generation in higher education: Rhetoric and reality. *International Journal of Excellence in E-Learning, 2*, 1.

Bullen, M., Morgan, T., & Qayyum, A. (2011). Digital learners in higher education: Generation is not the issue. *Canadian Journal of Learning & Technology, 37*, 1.

Gardner, H., & Davis, K. (2013). *The app generation: How today's youth navigate identity, intimacy, and imagination in a digital world.* New Haven, CT: Yale University Press.

Gros, B., Garcia, I., & Escofet, A. (2012). Beyond the net generation debate: A comparison of digital learners in face-to-face and virtual universities. *International Review of Research in Open and Distance Learning, 13*(4) Retrieved November 22, 2012, from <http://www.irrodl.org/index.php/irrodl/article/view/1305/2311>.

Jones, C., & Shao, B. (2011). *The net generation and digital natives: Implications for higher education.* York: Higher Education Academy.

Kennedy, D. M., & Fox, B. (2013). "Digital natives": An Asian perspective for using learning technologies. *International Journal of Education & Development Using Information & Communication Technology, 9,* 1.

Kirschner, P. A., & van Merriënboer, J. J. (2013). Do learners really know best? Urban legends in education. *Educational Psychologist, 48*(3), 169–183.

Livingstone, S., Haddon, L., Görzig, A., & Olafsson, K. (2011, September). *EU kids online – Final report.* Retrieved September 22, 2011, from <http://www2.lse.ac.uk/media@lse/research/EUKidsOnline/EUKidsII%20(2009-11)/EUKidsOnlineIIReports/Final%20report.pdf>.

Margaryan, A., Littlejohn, A., & Vojt, G. (2011). Are digital natives a myth or reality? University students' use of digital technologies. *Computers and Education, 56,* 429–440.

Prensky, M. (2001). Digital natives, digital immigrants. *On the Horizon, 9,* 5.

Prensky, M. (2012). *Brain gain: Technology and the quest for digital wisdom.* New York: Palgrave Macmillan.

Reeves, T.C., & Oh, E.J. (2008). Do generational differences matter in instructional design? Retrieved August 10, 2012, from <http://blogs.ubc.ca/dblinks/files/2011/08/DoGenerationalArticle_ID.pdf>.

Selwyn, N. (2009). The digital native – Myth and reality. *Aslib Proceedings: New Information Perspectives, 61,* 364–379.

Smith, E. E. (2012). The digital native debate in higher education: A comparative analysis of recent literature. *Canadian Journal of Learning & Technology, 38,* 3.

Veen, W. (2006). Homo zappiens. Retrieved March 16, 2011, from <http://www.hansonexperience.com/blog/2006/12/slides_van_de_p.html>.

Veen, W., & Vrakking, B. (2006). *Homo zappiens: Growing up in a digital age.* London: Network Continuum Education.

Williams, P., & Rowlands, I. (2007). *Information behaviour of the researcher of the future: Work package II.* London: University College London.

MYTH 4

The Internet Makes Us Dumber

In recent years a number of authors — often neurologists — such as Susan Greenfield or Manfred Spitzer, in his 2012 book *Digitale Demenz* (Digital dementia), have appeared from a new group of technological critics who seem to agree that we are all becoming more stupid because of the technology we are using. Often referring to the plasticity of the brain, they argue that Internet is rewiring our brains and this is bad. It is certainly true that the Flynn effect has come to a halt in some countries. The Flynn effect is the substantial and long-sustained increase in intelligence test scores measured in many parts of the world from roughly 1930 to the present day.

The reasons for this halt, however, are neither uniform nor clear. James Flynn, who gave the name to this effect in his 2012 book, already has doubts about whether the effect actually measures that we really have become smarter. There are other plausible reasons for the rise in the test scores, such as education more closely mimicking intelligence quotient (IQ) tests. Research by Woodley, Nijenhuis, Must, and Must even suggests that the better scores on IQ tests result from increased guessing on harder test items.

Were the Victorians Cleverer than Us?

In a meta-analysis from 2013, Woodley, te Nijenhuis, and Murphy describe how they found an intriguing reversal of the Flynn effect, stating that the average intelligence of the people in the nineteenth century was higher than the present average. Their logic is that (1) the average reaction time of people as measured in different experiments has gone up since 1889, and (2) reaction time is negatively related to g (general intelligence), so that (3) the average g must have decreased since then. It has to be said, however, that the logic that leads these researchers to this conclusion requires multiple inferences, some of which are of doubtful accuracy. We can conclude that, even if g has decreased over time, this does not seem to reflect a general decline in intelligence.

Source

Woodley, M. A., te Nijenhuis, J., & Murphy, R. (2013). Were the Victorians cleverer than us? The decline in general intelligence estimated from a meta-analysis of the slowing of simple reaction time. *Intelligence, 41*(6), 843–850.

As a result, it is not easy to say whether the Internet might be partly responsible for the halt in the phenomenon, as we do not know for certain what actually caused the Flynn effect. Some authors, such as Steven Johnson, even see the use of (new) media as an important contributory factor in the rise of average IQ that has been evident in recent years.

Nowadays we are relying more and more on technology. As an illustration of this fact, Betsy Sparrow, a professor at Columbia University in New York, has described the "Google effect". Together with her team, she discovered that students remember information more easily if they think that this information is not likely to be available on the Internet. Her study also revealed that students are better able to remember where to find something on the Internet than they are at remembering the information itself. In this respect, the popular "Google" search engine is increasingly acting as a kind of "external memory".

But is this really evidence to show that the Internet is making us dumber? To be honest, we don't know. At the moment there is no conclusive, empirical proof that decides the issue one way or the other. Although Nicolas Carr has provided many indications in his book *The shallows*, his arguments are personal and anecdotal, rather than scientific. Perhaps Steven Pinker is right when he says that we are now making better use of our brains by using Google for "unnecessary information", just as we now use a satnav instead of a map. And in the final analysis, we certainly know more now than we did in the past. So why should we be more stupid?

In an opinion piece from 2010 in reaction to the publication of the book by Nicholas Carr, Christopher Chabris and Daniel Simons, two leading neurologists, want to prove the digital alarmists wrong. They argue that Google is not making us stupid, PowerPoint™ is not destroying literature and the Internet is not really changing our brains:

> The appeals to neural plasticity, backed by studies showing that traumatic injuries can reorganize the brain, are largely irrelevant. The basic plan of the brain's "wiring" is determined by genetic programs and biochemical interactions that do most of their work long before a child discovers Facebook and Twitter. There is simply no experimental evidence to show that living with new technologies fundamentally changes brain organization in a way that affects one's ability to focus. Of course, the brain changes any time we form a memory or learn a new skill, but new skills build on our existing capacities without fundamentally changing them. We will no more lose our ability to pay attention than we will lose our ability to listen, see or speak.

Still, there are reasons to consider being careful with the total amount of screen time that children may have in a normal day. The American Academy of Pediatrics (AAP, 2006) warns that studies have shown that excessive media use can lead to attention problems, school difficulties, sleep and eating disorders, and obesity. This view has been confirmed by a study by researchers from Iowa State University. Therefore, the AAP recommends no more than one to two hours of screentime a day for children two years and older. Hattie also describes a clear negative impact of excessive television consumption on learning. Note that many of these studies examined the influence of television rather than the influence of interactive technology such as smartphones and social media. Also note that most of these studies found a correlation rather than a causal relation; that is, there may be other reasons why children who watch a lot of television may have poorer school results.

Be Aware of Sesame Street?

The idea that the media are shrinking the attention span of children goes back to the late 1960s. As children watched more television, the idea became popular that because of the brevity and fragmentation of commercials, and the relatively short segments of programs such as Sesame Street, the attention span of children and teenagers had reduced (Newman, 2010).

Although the idea has been around for a long time, Schmidt and Anderson conclude that no evidence has been found to support the claim that watching television harms children's ability to pay attention. They do see possible positive and negative effects of television on children, but these have nothing to do with the form of the media, but rather the content. For example, watching a program such as Sesame Street has a proven positive effect on learning for preschoolers, while watching (pure) entertainment programs can have a negative impact on their learning.

Sources

Newman, M. Z. (2010). New media, young audiences and discourses of attention: From Sesame Street to "snack culture". *Media, Culture & Society, 32*(4), 581—596.

Schmidt, M. E., & Anderson, D. R. (2007). The impact of television on cognitive development and educational achievement. In N. Pecora, J. P. Murray, & E. Wartella (Eds.), *Children and television: Fifty years of research* (pp. 65—84). Mahwah, NJ: Lawrence Erlbaum Associates.

:-| The discussion continues to rage. Those in the "Internet makes us stupid" camp have no solid evidence to support their claim. There is more to say for the "Internet makes us smarter" argument.

REFERENCES

American Academy of Pediatrics (2006). Media and children. Retrieved April 10, 2014, from <http://www.aap.org/en-us/advocacy-and-policy/aap-health-initiatives/Pages/Media-and-Children.aspx>.

Carr, N. G. (2010). *The shallows: What the Internet is doing to our brains.* New York: W.W. Norton.

Chabris, S., & Simons, D. (2010). Digital alarmists are wrong. *Los Angeles Times,* Retrieved December 26, 2013, from <http://articles.latimes.com/2010/jul/25/opinion/la-oe-chabris-computers-brain-20100725>.

Flynn, J. R. (2012). *Are we getting smarter?: Rising IQ in the twenty-first century.* Cambridge: Cambridge University Press.

Gentile, D. A., Reimer, R. A., Nathanson, A. I., Walsh, D. A., & Eisenmann, J. C. (2014). Protective effects of parental monitoring of children's media use: A prospective study. *JAMA Pediatrics, 168*(5), 479—484.

Hattie, J. (2009). *Visible learning: A synthesis of over 800 meta-analyses relating to achievement.* London: Routledge.

Johnson, S. (2005). *Everything bad is good for you: How today's popular culture is actually making us smarter.* Grand Rapids, MI: Riverhead Publishing.

Pinker, S. (2010). Mind over mass media. *The New York Times,* Retrieved June 13, 2010, from <http://www.nytimes.com/2010/06/11/opinion/11Pinker.html>.

Smart, P. (2010). Cognition and the web. In 1st ITA Workshop on Network-Enabled Cognition: The contribution of social and technological networks to human cognition, Maryland, USA. Retrieved June 9, 2012, from <http://eprints.soton.ac.uk/271824/1/Cognition_and_the_Webv13.pdf>.

Sparrow, B., Liu, J., & Wegner, D. M. (2011). Google effects on memory: Cognitive consequences of having information at our finger-tips. *Science, 333*(6043), 776—778.

Spitzer, M. (2012). Digitale Demenz *[Digital dementia]* Munich: Droemer Knaur.

Swain, F. (2011). Susan Greenfield: Living online is changing our brains. *New Scientist,* 2823.

Woodley, M. A., te Nijenhuis, J., Must, O., & Must, A. (2014). Controlling for increased guessing enhances the independence of the Flynn effect from *g*: The return of the Brand effect. *Intelligence, 43,* 27—34.

MYTH 5
Young People Don't Read Any More

Of course young people read. They read a lot. As Hall Sorrell and Hopper explain, teenagers constantly read what is available to them through the different forms of technology that continue to evolve. But when people think that young people today read less, it's not about reading websites or text messages, it's about reading books.

In 2010, *Reader's Digest* in the UK conducted a survey into the reading habits of some 2000 adults and 700 children (see *The Telegraph*, 2010). The results revealed that:

- One in five children hardly ever reads a book.
- One in three never reads a book.
- One in 20 children has never read a book.

These figures support a perception that many people seem to have; namely, that young people and children don't read anymore, and certainly not for pleasure. But is a survey in a popular monthly magazine a reliable source for such a sweeping claim?

Perhaps more scientifically gathered data could tell us more. A 2007 report, "To read or not to read", describes a significant decline in reading by youngsters in the USA in the previous 20 years. The study compared data from 1982 and 2002 and found that less than one-third of the 13-year-olds were daily readers. The percentage of 17-year-olds who read nothing at all for pleasure doubled over the same 20-year period. Yet the amount they read for school or homework stayed the same. However, these data are already quite old and stem from the beginnings of the digital area.

The Programme for International Student Assessment (PISA) study carried out by the Organisation for Economic Co-operation and Development looks not only at learning results, but also at the learning behavior of the respondents. These behavioral aspects are then further developed in smaller, theme-based PISA articles. In 2011 one of these reports was devoted to "Young people and reading for pleasure". The most important conclusions of this article are as follows:

- On average, two out of three students read every day for pleasure.
- The percentage of students who reported that they read for enjoyment daily dropped in the majority of OECD countries between

2000 and 2009, but in some countries that proportion increased. In the USA, the average remained the same. Many of the countries that saw a drop were countries that had a very high average in 2000. Some of the countries that saw an increase were countries that had a relatively low average in 2000.

- The extent to which young people read for relaxation corresponds with better overall PISA results, but it should be noted that this is only a correlation, not a causality.
- Boys and girls from families with a higher socioeconomic status read more than young people from families with a lower socioeconomic status; moreover, the gap between the two has increased between 2000 and 2009.

PISA 2012 did not focus on reading, so we do not have any new OECD figures yet. A 2012 report, "Stage of life", polled teenagers about their reading habits and found that 77.7% of them said that they read at least one extra book per month for personal pleasure that is not required for school. Nearly a quarter (24.5%) read five or more books per month outside school. These figures are much higher than the PISA figures, but this probably is due to the way they selected the teenagers. In the USA, the PEW Research Center examined the reading habits of the American audience in 2012, youth included. Book readers under the age of 30 consumed an average of 13 books in the previous 12 months and a median of six books; in other words, half of book readers in that age cohort had read fewer than six and half had read more than six. Still, even in these digital times, libraries remain important to many (American) youngsters. PEW found that in the 12 months before the survey in 2013, 53% of Americans aged 16 and older had visited a library or bookmobile, 25% had visited a library website, and 13% had used a handheld device such as a smartphone or tablet computer to access a library website.

Which Is Best: Print, Screen or Audio?

With more and more possibilities to access information, it is interesting to examine which way is best. When examining the evidence it becomes clear that there is still much research needed on this topic. The research mentioned here needs more replication and further examination. A metareview in 1992 by Dillon suggests that reading electronic textbooks — despite the sometimes different perception — does take more time, but comprehension is not affected. Research since than shows less consistent results: a slight majority has confirmed these earlier conclusions, but almost as many have found few significant differences in reading speed or comprehension between paper and screens. In a 2013 literature review for *Scientific American*, Ferris Jabr concludes that when it comes to intensively reading long pieces of plain text, paper and ink may still have the advantage.

A 2013 study at the University of Waterloo in Ontario, Canada, examined how our minds respond to various forms of reading material. In this study, 235 test participants engaged with three excerpts of *A short history of nearly everything*, a popular science book by Bill Bryson. The participants read one of the excerpts silently from a computer screen, read the second excerpt aloud off the screen, and listened to the third as the screen went blank. During each of the three ways of reading, the participants were tested for three cognitive impacts: mind-wandering, memory and interest. Mind-wandering was measured with a prompt that appeared on the screen from time to time, asking participants whether or not they had been paying attention. Memory was measured with a short true-or-false quiz after the excerpt. Interest was measured by participant rating. The results showed that the option of reading aloud led to the least amount of mind-wandering. Listening to the passage led to the most mind-wandering. The option of listening to the passage was also associated with the poorest memory performance and the least interest in the material.

Sources

Dillon, A. (1992). Reading from paper versus screens: A critical review of the empirical literature. *Ergonomics*, *35*(10), 1297−1326.

Jabr, F. (2013). The reading brain in the digital age: The science of paper versus screens. *Scientific American*, *11*. Available in <http://www.scientificamerican.com/article/reading-paper-screens/>.

Noyes, J. M., & Garland, K. J. (2008). Computer- vs. paper-based tasks: Are they equivalent? *Ergonomics*, *51*(9), 1352−1375.

Sousa, T. L. V., Carriere, J. S., & Smilek, D. (2013). The way we encounter reading material influences how frequently we mind wander. *Frontiers in Psychology*, *4*, 892.

As already stated, young people are still doing a lot of reading, and these statistics make clear that a lot of them are reading for pleasure. However, we need to be careful about making too many sweeping assertions, since the reading figures in many countries are falling. Even so, we know that reading continues to be important: both reading by young people themselves and parents reading to their children.

For many years researchers saw a clear correlation between the educational level of parents and the success of their children at school. However, a 20-year-long study under the leadership of Mariah Evans at the University of Nevada has shown that having lots of books in the house, irrespective of both location (in the USA or China) and the academic achievements of the parents, is probably just as important as an influencing factor.

The study concluded that the difference between being raised in a bookless home compared to being raised in a home with a 500-book library has as great an effect on the level of education a child will attain as having parents who are barely literate (three years of education) compared to having parents who have a university education (15 or 16 years of education). Both factors, having a 500-book library or having university-educated parents, propel a child 3.2 years further in education, on average. Having books in the home is twice as important as the father's educational level, and the effect starts to make itself felt from as few as 20 books.

Does this means that massively increasing the distribution of books will lead to a corresponding rise in average points at school? Probably not, but it does argue in favor of projects such as "Reading at Home".

Are We Still Able to Read Long Texts?

In March 2014 an alarming article in the *Washington Post* did the rounds on how serious reading takes a hit from online scanning and skimming. Although several researchers are mentioned in the article, the fact is that we don't know much about it yet. Willingham answers in a response to the article that anyone who comments on this issue (including him and the authors of this book) is, at this moment in time, still guessing. He argues that our brain is less adaptable than we think (cf. Chabris and Simons in Myth 4) and sees a more plausible explanation. He thinks that we are not less capable of reading complex prose, but maybe less willing to put in the work, as our criterion for concluding "this is boring, this is not paying off" has been lowered because online browsing "makes it so easy to find something else to read, watch, or listen to".

Sources

Mount, B. J. (2014). Serious reading takes a hit from online scanning and skimming, researchers say. *The Washington Post*, Retrieved April 17, 2014, from <http://www.washingtonpost.com/local/serious-reading-takes-a-hit-from-online-scanning-and-skimming-researchers-say/2014/04/06/088028d2-b5d2-11e3-b899-20667de76985_story.html>.

Willingham, D. (2014). Don't blame the Internet: We can still think and read critically, we just don't want to. *Real Clear Education*, Retrieved April 17, 2014, from <http://www.realcleareducation.com/articles/2014/04/16/dont_blame_the_web_we_can_still_think_and_read_critically_we_just_dont_want_to_942.html>.

:-| Reading for pleasure is declining in many countries, the USA included. However, this doesn't mean that reading is dead, as many young people are still reading for pleasure.

REFERENCES

Evans, M. D. R., Kelley, J. S., & Treiman, D. J. (2010). Family scholarly culture and educational success: Evidence from 27 nations. *Research in Social Stratification and Mobility*, *28*, 171–197.

Gioia, D. (Ed.), (2007). *To read or not to read: A question of national consequence*. Washington, DC: National Endowment for the Arts.

Hall Sorrell, A., & Hopper, P. F. (2012). Are they reading or not? *National Forum of Teacher Education Journal*, *22*, 3.

Organisation for Economic Co-operation and Development (2011, September). *PISA in focus: Do students today read for pleasure?* (Report No. 8). Retrieved September 15, 2011, from <http://www.oecd.org/pisa/pisaproducts/pisainfocus/48624701.pdf>.

The Telegraph (2010). Literacy concerns as a fifth of youngsters admit hardly ever reading books. *The Telegraph*, Retrieved November 19, 2010, from <http://www.telegraph. co.uk/culture/books/booknews/8114451/Literacy-concerns-as-a-fifth-of-youngsters-admit-hardly-ever-reading-books.html>.

Zickhur, K., & Rainie, L. (2013). *Younger Americans' library habits and expectations*. PEW Research Center. Retrieved April 16, 2014, from <http://libraries.pewinternet.org/files/2013/06/PIP_Younger_Americans_and_libraries.pdf>.

MYTH 6

You Learn Nothing from Games Other than Violence

The use of games in education: people seem to be either for it or against it. But what does the research say? A summary of the professional literature about the learning effect of games carried out by researchers (and gamers) at the University of Connecticut indicates that there is evidence for a learning effect with regard to languages, history and (providing you have a Wii-style console) movement, but that there is no evidence for a similar effect with mathematics and the sciences. A comparative study of the effect of using either a game or a PowerPoint® explanation for the learning of biology and electromechanics concluded that the games — even though they had been consciously designed for learning — were less effective than the PowerPoint lessons with the same content. The most important conclusion of this review is that much more research still needs to be carried out.

There are other aspects that also need to be considered. The above research attempted to establish a correlation between games and the content/objectives of specific subjects. But is it not possible to learn other things from games? What you cannot learn is multitasking. A study by researchers at Duke University makes clear that this skill is reserved for just a privileged few (Donohue, James, Eslick, & Mitroff). But it is possible that games might be able to improve your perception speed?

This was the subject of an experiment carried out at the University of Rochester. The researchers examined two different groups of young people aged between 18 and 25 years. The test group was asked to play 50 hours of action games, such as *Call of Duty 2* or *Unreal Tournament*. A control group was asked to play 50 hours of more relaxed games, such as *The Sims*. After the 50 hours, both groups were asked to complete a series of tests that required making quick decisions. To make these decisions, they first needed to perceive information on a computer (sometimes just visually, sometimes just auditively). They then had to answer a question about the perceived information in the shortest possible time.

The results were remarkable. The reaction time of the action games group was on average 25% quicker than the control group. Researcher Daphne Bavelier concluded: "The players of the action games make more correct decisions per time unit. If you are a surgeon or are standing on a battlefield, this can make all the difference".

The reason for this enhanced speed of decision-making is known as probabilistic inference. When you review a situation, your brain collects visual and auditive information until it has enough to make a reasonable decision. In gamers, this collection process is speeded up. Bavelier adds:

> Decisions are never black and white. The brain is always computing probabilities. As you drive, for instance, you may see a movement on your right, estimate whether you are on a collision course, and based on that probability make a decision: brake or don't brake.

We often hear what has been called the "displacement hypothesis", which assumes that using or being engaged in digital media and using print media negate each other. In other words, they add up to zero, and if teenage boys played videogames less, they would be reading print text more. Lenhart et al. studied this and found that for many youngsters reading is not replaced by videogames, but is actually an integral part of participating and playing. Lenhart and colleagues found that 36% of gamers regularly read game-related texts (e.g., reviews, strategy websites, fan fiction, forum discussions), and this figure increases to 59% if we look at massively multiplayer online games.

Constance Steinkuhler found in four studies that videogames could actually be viewed as a powerful solution to, rather than a cause of, the problem of adolescent boys and reading. In her words:

> Videogames often support a complex textual ecology while sparking youth interest in navigating it, creating opportunities for boys to participate in expansive reading practices ... Reading is an integral part of the ecology of videogame play; the two are not in competition. It may go against the taste of many educators and researchers to assert that the literary worlds of popular culture such as World of Warcraft might be of inherent intellectual value and a powerful way of reengaging young men in literacy classrooms. Yet, we should beware of mistaking discussions of taste for discussions of merit.

But what about the Violence?

There has been a lot of research into the possible effects of violence in media. It goes back to violence in movies and television programs and has moved on to violence in today's computer games. Peter Nikken tried to summarize all possible research on this topic and states that there are indeed possible effects of violence in media. These effects can appear as children becoming more aggressive themselves, but can also be the opposite, that the children who are confronted with violence become more anti-violence. Much has to do with whether the violence is acted by or against a popular hero. Nikken concludes that ± 5% of violent behavior in children can be related to the media they consume. Some groups of children can be more prone to negative effects, including boys, children who already have a violent nature, children who have a difficult home situation and children who have low empathy.

Longitudinal research by Gentile and colleagues confirms this, but also found that pro-social media — videogames, movies or television shows that portray helpful, caring and cooperative behaviors — positively influence behavior regardless of culture.

Sources

Gentile, D. A., Li, D., Khoo, A., Prot, S., & Anderson, C. A. (2014). Mediators and moderators of long-term effects of violent video games on aggressive behavior: Practice, thinking, and action. *JAMA Pediatrics*, *168*(5), 450–457.

Nikken, P. (2007). Kinderen en mediageweld [*Children and media violence*] Amsterdam: SWP.

:-\ You can learn some things from games. Therefore, to say that games have no place in education is jumping to conclusions. However, the claim that games belong in schools as valid learning tools also lacks any real evidence.

REFERENCES

Adams, D. M., Mayer, R. E., MacNamara, A., Koenig, A., & Wainess, R. (2012). Narrative games for learning: Testing the discovery and narrative hypotheses. *Journal of Educational Psychology*, *104*, 235–249.

Coxworth, B. (2010). Sorry, parents — video games are good for the mind. *Gizmag*, Retrieved July 9, 2012, from <http://www.gizmag.com/video-games-increase-decision-making-abilities/16397/>.

Donohue, S., James, B., Eslick, A., & Mitroff, S. (2012). Cognitive pitfall! Videogame players are not immune to dual-task costs. *Attention, Perception & Psychophysics*, *74*(5), 803–809.

Green, S. C., Pouget, A., & Bavelier, D. (2010). Improved probabilistic inference as a general learning mechanism with action video games. *Current Biology, 20*(17), 1573–1579.

Lenhart, A., Kahne, J., Middaugh, E., Rankin Macgill, A., Evans, C., & Vitak, J. (2008). *Teens, video games, and civics.* Washington, DC: Pew Internet and American Life Project.

Steinkuhler, C. (2011). *The mismeasure of boys: Reading and online videogames.* WCER Working Paper. Retrieved from <http://www.wcer.wisc.edu/publications/working-papers/working_paper_no_2011_03.pdf>.

Young, M. F., Slota, S., Cutter, A. B., Jalette, G., Mullin, G., Lai, B., et al. (2012). Our princess is in another castle: A review of trends in serious gaming for education. *Review of Educational Research, 82*, 61–89.

MYTH 7

You Can Help Poor Children to Learn Just by Giving Them Access to Computers

The TED talk by Sugata Mitra is still being shared online. What he has to say is fascinating; namely, that just by a number of computers being placed in the slums of India, children are able to learn spontaneously. In 2013 he received the TED award of $1,000,000 for creating learning environments where illiterate Indian children had access to computers in actual holes-in-walls on the streets of New Delhi slums. To be clear, we have nothing against the good work that the professor tries to do. Mitra's vision is part of what is now called minimally invasive education: education that offers little or no direction, in which the learner is the starting point for everything (or almost everything).

We wanted to know more about this concept and so we investigated the scientific story behind the project. This gave us a more nuanced picture, which (admittedly) is suggested in part in the video, but it nevertheless appeared to us to be more interventionist than you might initially imagine.

What struck us first was the fact that Mitra's research is so infrequently cited in the scientific literature. The majority of the references to his research from 2001 and later are made by Mitra himself or by people from his entourage, and most of these articles appeared in the same journal. This does not necessarily mean anything untoward, but it is unusual, to say the least. Mark Warschauer and Payal Arora also note the lack of independent research on "Hole in the Wall". Both researchers have visited sites where the project took place. Arora came across two unsuccessful Hole in the Wall experiments in two districts: Almora and Hawalbagh in the central Himalayas. She interviewed the students, teachers and other people involved in the project, and describes how the locals had only vague memories of the computers. What they remembered was a far cry from the celebration of free learning. Arora suggests that many "Hole in the Wall" projects failed because of the lack of community help to run them.

Still, the researchers behind the projects claim success in other regions. If we look at the follow-up research by Mitra and his colleagues, a number of very important nuances come to light.

- The approach disadvantages girls, and even with boys there is a very clear pecking order. In other words, the system promotes inequality. This is less evident in the British example, we suspect, probably because the system there was applied within a classroom environment, where the "fight" to decide who could use the computer was more restricted.
- The emphasis in India was quite heavily on gaming and play.
- The project failed in certain regions, in part through vandalism. When the researchers returned to these regions nine months after the project had started, in some cases they found it hard to locate people who could even remember it. This is not necessarily a negative point. As the researchers point out, this is inherent in the limited nature and impact of the project, in contrast with a coordinated policy approach.
- The computer skills learnt were largely basic skills. Without guidance, only a very few learners were able to progress to more complex matters.
- If there was guidance, however, more complex skills could be learned, equivalent to what might be expected of a pupil in a normal school class.

It is also possible to question the research approach used to measure the learning differences between the children who took part in the project and those who did not. (These are the results that Mitra gives in his talk.) Children in the control group were only given questionnaires at the beginning and end of the project, while those in the experimental group were tested every month. It is therefore hardly surprising that a learning effect was noted in the experimental group, since other research in other contexts has proven conclusively that regular testing generally has a positive learning effect (see, for example, the work of Roediger & Karpicke on the testing effect).

The arguments for collaboration and the shared processing of information are compelling — we would not wish to deny that — but guidance and direction are equally crucial, even if it is only in the shape of someone who can ask a series of questions that the learners need to solve.

The project is not unlike the One Laptop Per Child (OLPC) program. Here, another professor, Nicholas Negroponte, former director of the MIT Media Lab, designed a project to put inexpensive, solar-powered laptops and tablets in the hands of children and young people in the least developed countries in Africa, Asia and South America. Again, we don't have anything against the basic goal of the project. OLPC has been the subject of much research interest, but the first large-scale evaluation of the program's impact using randomized control trials happened only recently in Peru. The results are clear:

- The program dramatically increased access to computers.
- There was no evidence that the program increased learning in mathematics or languages.
- The program had some beneficial effects on cognitive skills.

These findings spurred a big debate, as Michale Trucano notes in a blog post on the World Bank website, and such discussions can quickly become about other things. But if we look at the different studies we've examined, the idea of simply providing access to computers does not have a big impact. As Trucano states, dumping hardware in schools, hoping for magic to happen, is just a bad idea. Other elements such as teacher training, class size and decent class material could also be a part of the equation.

In short, it is not our intention to detract from the initiatives, but we feel that the nuances are necessary and important, particularly when we see that many people are basing their opinion of the project exclusively on Mitra's TED talk of good-news messages from other similar organizations. We do not want to stand by and see the creation of yet another myth.

:-| These are noble initiatives, but the scientific literature provides numerous nuances that should not be ignored.

REFERENCES

Arora, P. (2010). Hope-in-the-wall? A digital promise for free learning. *British Journal of Educational Technology, 41*, 689–702 Retrieved April 11, 2014, from <http://www.payalarora.com/Publications/Arora-HopeintheWall.pdf>.

Cristia, J., Ibarrarán, P., Cueto, S., Santiago, A., & Severín, E. (2012). Technology and child development: Evidence from the One Laptop Per Child program. Retrieved April 13, 2014, from <http://www.econstor.eu/bitstream/10419/89035/1/IDB-WP-304.pdf>.

Fairlie, R.W., & Robinson, J. (2013). *Experimental evidence on the effects of home computers on academic achievement among schoolchildren* (NBER Working Paper No. 19060). Cambridge, MA: National Bureau of Economic Research.

Koseoglu, S. (2011). The hole in the wall experiments: Learning from self-organizing systems. Retrieved April 11, 2014, from <http://umn.academia.edu/SuzanKoseoglu>.

McEwan, P. J. (2013). Improving learning in primary schools of developing countries: A meta-analysis of randomized experiments. Unpublished manuscript, Wellesley College.

Mitra, S. (2007). Kid scan teach themselves. TED-talk. Retrieved December 18, 2012, from <http://www.ted.com/talks/sugata_mitra_shows_how_kids_teach_themselves>.

Mitra, S., & Dangwal, R. (2010). Limits to self-organising systems of learning — The Kalikuppam experiment. *British Journal of Educational Technology, 41*(5), 672—688.

Mitra, S., & Rana, V. (2001). Children and the Internet: Experiments with minimally invasive education in India. *British Journal of Educational Technology, 32*(2), 221—232.

Roediger, H. L., & Karpicke, J. D. (2006). Test-enhanced learning taking memory tests improves long-term retention. *Psychological Science, 17*(3), 249—255.

Trucano, M. (2012). Evaluating One Laptop Per Child (OLPC) in Peru. Retrieved April 11, 2014, from <http://blogs.worldbank.org/edutech/node/654>.

Van Cappelle, F. (2004). Investigating the effects of unsupervised computer use on educationally disadvantaged children's knowledge and understanding of computers. Unpublished master's thesis, University of Amsterdam.

Warschauer, M. (2002). Reconceptualizing the digital divide. *First Monday, 7*(7) Retrieved April 11, 2014, from <http://firstmonday.org/article/view/967/888>.

Warschauer, M. (2003). *Technology and social inclusion: Rethinking the digital divide.* Cambridge: MIT Press.

Warschauer, M. (2006). Literacy and technology: Bridging the divide. In D. Gibbs, & K. -L. Krause (Eds.), *Cyberlines 2: Languages and cultures of the Internet* (pp. 163—174). Albert Park, Australia: James Nicholas.

Learning and Technology: A Few Tips

To say that technology in education is a hot topic is something of an understatement. You can use technology in the classroom in many different ways. These can range from simple PowerPoint slides or showing a video during a lesson, through smart boards and the provision of online support material such as teaching aids, to the spectacular massive online open courses known as MOOCs (and all of their offshoots, such as BOOCs, xMOOCs and cMOOCs) that universities are currently using to allow tens of thousands of students worldwide to follow the same studies through video lessons, self-testing and extended forums. Much research has been carried out (and is still being carried out) to investigate the best way to make use of technology for learning purposes both inside and outside the classroom. The tips that we gave earlier in the book in the section on Myths about Learning remain valid here. What now follows are a number of concrete, scientifically based pieces of advice specifically geared for teaching through technology, which we hope educators at all levels will find immediately useful.

- Graphic images with text work better than text alone.
- We hear a lot about multimedia, but in practice the lesson material that we want to offer through ICT often contains too much text. The users of this lesson material learn more if you can regularly supplement the text with clear images that clarify and enhance the content. But this does not mean that you should trivialize or underemphasize your text.
- Richard Mayer's cognitive theory of multimedia learning (based to a large extent on Alan Paivio's dual-coding theory and John Sweller's cognitive load theory). The use of video in the classroom and, by extension, in education generally is currently a subject of heated discussion, not least because of the activities of the Khan Academy™ of Salman Khan, which has placed huge numbers of lessons on YouTube. In the meantime, considerable research has been carried out to establish what makes videos effective − or not. There seem to be a couple of general rules that need to be followed, or rather avoided. Students perform and learn less well with videos when:
  - in addition to animation and a narrator's voice, there are subtitles or regular text summaries of the content
  - the video shows interesting but essentially irrelevant information.

- A good starting point for video lessons on screen is to scrap everything that is not strictly relevant. Trying to brighten up your video lesson with fun images and amusing text is often counterproductive for learning, unless these images and text are "to the point".
- If you are using images in online lesson material or apps, it is recommended that the accompanying text should be spoken rather than written. This allows the learner to concentrate better on the visual information (i.e., no split-attention effect) contained in the image or graphic, without being distracted by too much written text.
- Work with relatively small amounts of learning material, not large chunks.
- For videos, but also for texts and other material, it is advisable when giving online lessons or using classroom technology to divide the content to be learnt into smaller segments. Four segments of five minutes will work much more effectively than one long video of 20 minutes. This has been proven empirically. Research also indicates that this effect is lost if you give the learners control over the pause button, so that they can decide for themselves when to stop and when to carry on. This is clearly a task for the teacher.
- Allow enough practice moments in your video or technology-based lessons.
- Allow the learner control over stopping, going back and repeating dynamic images (video, animations, etc.).
- Even if you are offering lesson packages online, you need to build in at least the same number of practice moments as in traditional lessons, so that learning content can be alternated with practical application. It is advisable to keep these practice moments as practical as possible. In this way, you can forge a direct link with the situations that will confront the learner in later life; for example, in a particular work context.

REFERENCES

Clark, R. C., & Mayer, R. E. (2011). *E-learning and the science of instruction: Proven guidelines for consumers and designers of multimedia learning.* San Francisco, CA: Pfeiffer.

Craig, S. D., Gholson, B., & Driscoll, D. M. (2002). Animated pedagogical agents in multimedia educational environments: Effects of agent properties, picture features and redundancy. *Journal of Educational Psychology, 94*, 428–434.

Fletcher, J. D., & Tobias, S. (2005). The multimedia principle. In R. E. Maye (Ed.), *The Cambridge handbook of multimedia learning.* Cambridge: Cambridge University Press.

Kalyuga, S., Chandler, P., & Sweller, J. (1999). Managing split-attention and redundancy in multimedia instruction. *Applied Cognitive Psychology, 13*, 351–371.

Mayer, R. E., Heiser, J., & Lonn, S. (2001). Cognitive constraints on multimedia learning: When presenting more material results in less understanding. *Journal of Educational Psychology, 93*, 187–198.

Moreno, R., & Mayer, R. E. (1999). Cognitive principles of multimedia learning: The role of modality and contiguity. *Journal of Educational Psychology, 91*, 358–368.

Paivio, A. (1991). Dual coding theory: Retrospect and current status. *Canadian Journal of Psychology/Revue canadienne de psychologie, 45*(3), 255–287.

Sweller, J. (1988). Cognitive load during problem solving. Effects on learning. *Cognitive Science, 12*, 257–285.

CHAPTER 5

Myths in Educational Policy

Contents

Education is often the subject of intense debate in society. How large should our schools be? What should the maximum class size be? Education usually enjoys a generous budget from the state, but is this money always wisely spent?

Let us be clear: we have great respect for policy-makers at all levels in the education system, from ministers to head teachers, and everyone in between. We know that they all need to take account of many, often conflicting, interests.

The following themes deal with questions that often occupy the minds of the educational policy-makers. But we start with an explanation of something that these policy-makers love to do: compare different countries.

Urban Myths about Learning and Education
DOI: http://dx.doi.org/10.1016/B978-0-12-801537-7.00006-8

© 2015 Elsevier Inc.
All rights reserved.

MYTH 1

You Can Justifiably Compare the School Results of Different Countries

We all like to make comparisons. Parents always ask whether their offspring have done "better than average". Schools are also compared with each other, and at international level regional and national authorities also subject themselves to the comparison process. When educational reform is under discussion, the statistics of the PISA come into their own, and until recently Finland was often seen as a source of inspiration for other countries. Why Finland? Because it has scored consistently well in the PISA evaluations over the years, slightly slipping in the 2012 results. But what exactly is PISA?

PISA is the abbreviation for the Programme for International Student Assessment. It is a large-scale international research project that tests the knowledge and skills of 15-year-olds.

This research was carried out for the first time in 2000 and is repeated every three years. In each cycle the same three cognitive domains are investigated: reading ability, mathematical literacy and science literacy. The emphasis is placed on functional skills and knowledge, which will allow people to function actively within society.

These comparative tests are organized under the auspices of the Organisation for Economic Co-operation and Development (OECD), a collaborative venture between 34 different countries that allows them to study, discuss and coordinate their economic policy. Why is an economic organization so concerned about education? Because it believes that high-performing education can have a positive effect on the economy. Within the field of comparative pedagogic studies there is a strong element of increasing economization. How we think and talk about education is shifting away from the question of pedagogic interaction and towards a more output-based approach. That the educational reality is becoming more constricted as a result seems a logical consequence. The more abstractly we look at countries, the easier it is to compare them and the less we are able to take account of the context. It is interesting to discuss whether we are moving in the direction of a uniform education system for an increasingly globalized world, or whether this is just a utopian ideal. The truth is that we live in a "glocal" world: there are global tendencies, but they are translated locally.

Are We Developing a Global Curriculum?

The author of *Finnish lessons*, Pasi Sahlberg, noted an important possible side-effect of the gaining importance of PISA tests worldwide. On his blog, he noted:

> One may also conclude that these international standardized tests are becoming global curriculum standards. Indeed, OECD has observed that its PISA test is already playing an important role in national policy making and education reforms in many countries. Schools, teachers and students are now prepared in advance to take these tests. Learning materials are adjusted to fit to the style of these assessments. Life in many schools around the world is becoming split into important academic study that these tests measure, and other "not-so-important" study that these measurements don't cover. (Sahlberg, 2012)

Source

Sahlberg, P. (December 14, 2012). PISA + TIMSS + PIRLS = GERM? Retrieved April 20, 2014, from <http://pasisahlberg.com/pisa-timss-pirls-germ/>.

Apart from the frequently cited PISA figures, there is a host of other comparative studies, such as the Trends in International Mathematics and Science Study (TIMSS) and Progress in International Reading Literacy Study (PIRLS). These are studies that have a high level of quality control, but where it is also difficult to take account of context.

On a smaller scale, there are also several comparative studies involving a more limited number of countries or regions, where it is possible to look more closely at the contextual detail. These studies are less well known to the public, but nonetheless valid. In this same comparative spirit, education policy-makers also like to visit other countries in search of inspiration. This is certainly one of the simplest but not necessarily one of the best forms of comparable pedagogics. Why do we go to all this trouble? Why is it so important to compare educational systems with each other? Because we want to do better, of course, and perhaps we can learn from those who seem to be doing better already.

Simply copying the approach of these "top" countries is possibly the most stupid thing a country could do. Drawing inspiration from others is always welcome, but as a good educational scientist it is necessary to pause and reflect on *all* the influencing factors. Amanda Ripley visited the different top-performing countries and noted how they differed from each other.

Roger Standaert referred to this in his standard work on comparative pedagogics. According to the professor, we all too often forget that the context in which education happens can be so totally different in other lands and regions that copying elements from those "foreign" education systems, never mind copying the total approach, is unlikely to be successful. For example, the education results from a country that scores well on the PISA list are often inadequately analyzed in relation to the complex totality of processes that are taking place in that country or region, such as demographic evolutions, traditions and natural resources. For this reason, comparing countries can sometimes be confusing. In the comparative report published by Pearson, Finland and South Korea stand in the first and second spots. Yet it is difficult to find two countries that are more different in their educational approach, as Ripley also describes in her 2013 book.

Finland is more progressive, with little emphasis on (standardized) tests and greater focus on equality, creativity and a healthy way of living, whereas in South Korea the approach is fairly traditional, with value attached to technical skills and concrete results. It is for this reason that Standaert warns us that visitors to a country can sometimes be very enthusiastic about something, whereas the country itself can often have doubts about that very same thing. We need to be careful that examples from other countries are not used to legitimize our own political motives.

So You Want to Compare Educational Systems from Different Countries? Where Can You Start?

Comparing educational systems is quite popular, but it is a difficult task as the contexts can be very different. Tests as PIRLS, TIMSS or PISA do a good job in trying to bypass this problem, but still the impact of the context remains.

There are some good resources for getting to know the different educational systems and countries.

- For European countries a good starting point is Eurypedia (https://webgate.ec.europa.eu/fpfis/mwikis/eurydice), which offers comprehensive descriptions of 38 European education systems, usually at national level, but sometimes also at regional level. All information is available in English, with some national information available in the language of the country or region concerned. Aiming at providing the most accurate picture of education systems and the latest reforms in Europe, Eurypedia is a resource tool that is regularly updated and completed by the Eurydice network and its national units (http://eacea.ec.europa.eu/education/eurydice/contacts_national_units_en.php). Powered by MediaWiki, it involves education experts and national ministries responsible for education from across Europe.

- The OECD adds information to its own tool, Education GPS (http://gpseducation.oecd.org/Home), which is *the* source for internationally comparable data on education policies and practices, opportunities and outcomes. Accessible at any time, in real time, the Education GPS provides the latest information on how countries are working to develop high-quality and equitable education systems.
- Educational Quality (SACMEQ, http://www.iiep.unesco.org/en/our-expertise/sacmeq) is an international non-profit developmental organization of 15 ministries of education in southern and eastern Africa that decided to work together to share experiences and expertise in developing the capacities of education planners to apply scientific methods to monitor and evaluate the conditions of schooling and the quality of education.
- The CONFEMEN Programme for the Analysis of Education Systems (PASEC, http://www.confemen.org/le-pasec/, in French), established in 1991, aims to provide information about the evolution of education systems' performance, to contribute to the development and monitoring of education policies. In two decades, over 20 African and Asian countries have been supported by PASEC in conducting national evaluations. In 2012, PASEC established international comparative evaluations, to better meet countries' needs.

There are many more resources. We found these on the website of the New York University library:

- The United Nations Educational, Scientific and Cultural Organization (UNESCO, http://en.unesco.org/themes/education-21st-century) furnishes a wealth of data and publications on educational programs around the world. See especially their statistical data portal (http://www.uis.unesco.org/Education/Pages/default.aspx).
- OECD (http://www.oecd-ilibrary.org/) is the online library of the Organisation for Economic Co-operation and Development. Education literature is well represented in the OECD member countries' documents.
- The Education Policy and Data Center (EPDC, http://www.epdc.org/) provides free global education data, tools for better data visualization, and policy-oriented analysis aimed at improving schools and learning in developing countries.
- Millennium Indicators (http://mdgs.un.org/unsd/mdg/Default.aspx) presents the official data, definitions, methodologies and sources for more than 60 indicators to measure progress towards the Millennium Development Goals (MDGs). The data and analyses are the product of the work of the Inter-agency and Expert Group (IAEG) on MDG Indicators, coordinated by the United Nations Statistics Division.
- World Bank EdStats (http://datatopics.worldbank.org/education/) collects worldwide data on education from national statistical reports, statistical annexes of new publications and other data sources.

- World Development Indicators (http://databank.worldbank.org/data/home.aspx) statistics show country-level detail in a wide variety of areas.
- International Comparisons in Education (http://nces.ed.gov/surveys/international/) (also known as the International Activities Program) supports a variety of activities to provide statistical data for cross-national comparisons of education. Developing indicators and conducting international assessments and surveys are two main area of activity.
- Open Doors (http://www.iie.org/en/Research-and-Publications/Open-Doors) is a comprehensive information resource on international students and scholars studying or teaching at higher education institutions in the USA, and US students studying abroad for academic credit at their home colleges or universities.

Source
Collard, S.. (2014, June 9). International and comparative education. Retrieved June 22, 2014, from <http://guides.nyu.edu/international_education>.

:-| Comparing countries can certainly be a source of inspiration, but education is a complex matter, so that simply copying someone else's approach is not a guarantee of success.

REFERENCES

De Bruyckere, P., & Smits, B. (2009). *Is het nu generatie X, Y of Einstein? [Is it now generation X, Y or Einstein?]*. Mechelen: Wolters/Plantyn.

Economist Intelligence Unit. (2012, November 28). The learning curve (Report). Retrieved November 28, 2012, from <http://thelearningcurve.pearson.com/the-report>.

Feuer, M. J. (2012). No country left behind: Rhetoric and reality of international large-scale assessment (13th ed., William H. Angoff Memorial Lecture, Rep. No. PIC-ANG13). Retrieved October 2, 2012, from <http://www.ets.org/research/policy_research_reports/pic-ang13>.

Lau, J. (2012). How much homework does it take to educate a nation? *New York Times*.

Ripley, A. (2013). *The smartest kids in the world: And how they got that way*. New York: Simon and Schuster.

Sahlberg, P. (2012, December 14). Exclusive! Pasi Sahlberg on TIMSS and PIRLS. Diane Ravitch's Blog. Retrieved December 14, 2012, from <http://dianeravitch.net/2012/12/14/exclusive-pasi-sahlberg-on-timss-and-pirls/>.

Standaert, R. (2007). *Vergelijken van onderwijssystemen [Comparing educational systems]*. Leuven: Acco.

Stewart, W. (2012). Dissemination or contamination? *Times Educational Supplement*.

Vakgroep Onderwijskunde Ugent (2012, January). PISA in een notendop: PISA Vlaanderen [PISA in a nutshell: PISA in Flanders]. Retrieved July 4, 2012, from <http://www.pisa.ugent.be/nl/over-pisa>.

MYTH 2

Class Size Doesn't Matter

There are many things that teachers are convinced are not true (or at least they hope they are not true), but actually turn out to be more true than they think, albeit with a good deal of nuance. One of these things is the influence of class size on learning ability.

Educational policy-makers and politicians across the board and around the world have been toying with the idea for a number of years of increasing class sizes, be they someone in education policy such as Arne Duncan, in education philanthropy (e.g., Bill Gates) or the media (e.g., Malcolm Gladwell), and it is even a topic in the TED talk by PISA head Andreas Schleicher. They all believe that it has been sufficiently proven that this has no influence on school results. This idea keeps popping up, but it goes against the gut feeling of many teachers.

Although it may sound counterintuitive for many people, the policy-makers point to studies such as PISA or Hattie, who found little evidence of impact in the metastudies he examined. In reality, however, the situation is much more complex.

Research has shown that smaller classes are actually better because the pupils pay more attention. However, this is often linked in the same breath to the quality of the teacher, with most researchers thinking that this is a more important learning factor than overall class size. This leads to the reasoning that it is better to have a class of 28−30 pupils with a good teacher than a class of 22−24 pupils with a mediocre teacher. Concomitant to this argument, there is evidence to suggest that class size only makes a difference when there are 16 or fewer pupils, which obviously has significant cost implications.

This theme was the subject of a 2012 interview in *The New York Times* given by Andreas Schleicher, who as top man at the OECD is closely connected with educational reports such as PISA or Education at a Glance. He confirmed that all the OECD reports point in the same direction: if you are forced to choose between a good teacher and a small class, it is better to opt for a good teacher.

But good teachers do not grow on trees, and this is a related problem with small classes: you need more teachers. This is an important point: the shortage of teachers throughout the world is growing all the time, not only in the West but also in developing countries. If you need more teachers, there is a risk that selection criteria will become less strict, so that the number of good new teachers will decline. And if you employ poorer quality teachers, the standard of learning will also decline, so that the benefit of smaller classes is lost before you even begin.

But you can complicate the situation still further by looking at the other side of the coin. How attractive are big classes? And will it be possible to recruit the teachers we need if classes are too large?

A 2014 report by Northwestern University Associate Professor Diane Whitmore Schanzenbach and published by the National Education Policy Center at the University of Colorado, reviewing the evidence, concludes something completely different on the matter of class size:

- Class size is an important determinant of student outcomes, and one that can be directly determined by policy. All else being equal, increasing class sizes will harm student outcomes.
- The evidence suggests that increasing class size will harm not only children's test scores in the short run, but also their long-run human capital formation. Money saved today by increasing class sizes will result in more substantial social and educational costs in the future.
- The payoff from class-size reduction is greater for low-income and minority children, while any increases in class size are likely to be most harmful to these populations.
- Policy-makers should carefully weigh the efficacy of class-size policy against other potential uses of funds. While lower class size has a demonstrable cost, it may prove the more cost-effective policy overall.

Why are Whitmore Schanzenbach's findings in such sharp contrast with the rest of the studies? A lot has to do with the kind of research that you put an emphasis on. Most studies are correlational, rather than showing a clear causal relation.

Let's take PISA as an example. Although PISA surveys are conducted every three years and are therefore longitudinal by nature, they are only longitudinal if you want to compare the evolution of countries, not of individuals, as PISA always looks at 15-year-olds. They can see whether the average class size has an effect on average learning, but it is much harder to guess what the impact of small class sizes in primary education may be later on. The difficulty is that variation in class size is driven by a host of influences. A simple correlation between class size and outcomes is confounded by other factors (e.g., low-achieving or special needs students often are systematically assigned to smaller classes). If this is the case, then a simple correlation would find decreased class size to be negatively associated with achievement.

In his TED talk, Andreas Schleicher compares Luxemburg with South Korea, explaining that Korea has opted to invest in teacher training and not in reducing class size, while Luxemburg has done the opposite, with South Korea outperforming the small European country. If you read the book by Amanda Ripley, who visited all top-performing PISA countries, you'll discover that the classes in South Korea are pretty traditional and not very good, but that after classes have finished, buses take the students to — often expensive — private tutors. The OECD behind PISA admits that after-school education has been a major factor behind the excellent performance of Korean students in international tests, such as PISA. In 2010, around three-quarters of students participated in such courses.

Schanzenbach uses another kind of longitudinal study where pupils are monitored during a longer school — and even life — career. The gold standard in this kind of research is the Student/Teacher Achievement Ratio (STAR) study, an experiment conducted by the Department of Education in the US state of Tennessee during 1985–1989, in which over 7000 students in grade K-3 were randomly placed in class groupings (Finn & Achilles, 1999). There were three possible grouping options:

* small classes (13–17 students per teacher)
* regular classes (22–25 students per teacher)
* regular classes (22–25 students per teacher) with a full-time aide.

STAR is a very relevant study because of the random placement — thus bypassing the difficulties mentioned earlier — and because the nearly 80 schools had to commit to participate for the four-year time-frame. The project included inner city, suburban and rural schools, in both affluent and poor districts.

Looking at the long-term results of the STAR project, Nye and colleagues concluded:

> *The STAR experiment demonstrated that small classes lead to significantly higher achievement for students in reading and mathematics. Analysis of the data collected by the Lasting Benefits Study demonstrate that the positive effects of small classes in early grades result in mathematics, reading, and science achievement gains that persist at least through the eighth grade. As in the case of the initial effects, these effects were remarkably consistent across schools, so lasting benefits were found for all kinds of students in all kinds of schools. (Nye, Hedges, & Konstantopoulos, 1999)*

There are also more recent results pointing in a similar direction. For example, a report from the Southern Regional Education Board concluded that smaller classes are important during the early school years, but have less effect as secondary education progresses. For this reason, it was argued that there is a need to be flexible and objective-specific when dealing with class size. Large classes will always be necessary at some point, for reasons of cost, and if you need to decide where to have large classes, it is better to opt for the older pupils, allowing for students with extra needs.

Finally, a Swedish study suggests that there is another possible positive effect resulting from smaller classes. This study investigated the impact of small classes over a longer period and noted that pupils from smaller classes consistently scored better in academic tests in later years than comparable pupils who had always been in larger classes. The likelihood that a pupil from smaller classes will move on to higher education also increases by 3%, and in later life he or she is also likely to earn a salary that is 3% higher. This sounds great; however, similar research conducted in Norway and The Netherlands did not find any such influence.

Institutions such as the OECD continue to see little effect from smaller class size on their results. However, this discussion is unlikely to die down in the near future.

:-| Some studies show that smaller classes are not necessarily better, but that is just a part of the story. The quality of the teachers seems to be more important than class size, but other studies do suggest that smaller classes also seem to have performed better.

REFERENCES

Barber, M., & Mourshed, M. (2007). *How the world's best-performing school systems come out on top.* McKinsey & Company.

Blatchford, P. (2012). Class size: Is small better? In P. Adey, & J. Dillon (Eds.), *Bad education* (pp. 57–76). Maidenhead, UK: Open University Press.

Blatchford, P., Bassett, P., Goldstein, H., & Martin, C. (2003). Are class size differences related to pupils' educational progress and classroom processes? Findings from the Institute of Education class size study of children aged 5–7 years. *British Educational Research Journal, 29*(5), 709–730.

Brühwiler, C., & Blatchford, P. (2011). Effects of class size and adaptive teaching competency on classroom processes and academic outcome. *Learning and Instruction, 21*(1), 95–108.

Dobbelsteen, S., Levin, J., & Oosterbeek, H. (2002). The causal effect of class size on scholastic achievement: Distinguishing the pure class size effect from the effect of changes in class composition. *Oxford Bulletin of Economics and Statistics, 64*(1), 17–38.

Finn, J. D., & Achilles, C. M. (1999). Tennessee's class size study: Findings, implications, misconceptions. *Educational Evaluation and Policy Analysis*, *21*(2), 97−109.

Finn, J. D., Pannozzo, G. M., & Achilles, C. M. (2003). The "why's" of class size: Student behavior in small classes. *Review of Educational Research*, *73*, 321−368.

Fredriksson, P., Öckert, B., & Oosterbeek, H. (2013). Long-term effects of class size. *Quarterly Journal of Economics*, *128*(1), 249−285.

Gagne, J. (2012). Smart Class-Size Policies for Lean Times. SREB Policy Brief, Southern Regional Education Board (SREB).

Gates, B. (2011). How teacher development could revolutionize our schools. *Washington Post*.

Gladwell, M. (2013). David en Goliath *[David and Goliath]* Amsterdam: Business Contact.

Guttenplan, D. (2012). Comparing the success of nations in schooling. *The New York Times*, Retrieved from <http://www.nytimes.com/2012/11/12/world/europe/12i-ht-educlede12.html?partner=rss>.

Hattie, J. (2009). *Visible learning: A synthesis of over 800 meta-analyses relating to achievement*. London: Routledge.

Institute for Statistics (2011). *The global demand for primary teachers − 2011 update* (UIS/IS/2011/6). Retrieved June 24, 2012, from <http://www.uis.unesco.org/EDUCATION/Documents/IS6-2011-Teachers-EN5.pdf>.

Jones, R. S., & Urasawa, S. (2012). *Promoting social cohesion in Korea*. Paris: OECD Publishing (No. 963).

Leuven, E., Oosterbeek, H., & Rønning, M. (2008). Quasi-experimental estimates of the effect of class size on achievement in Norway. *Scandinavian Journal of Economics*, *110* (4), 663−693.

Matus, R. (2001). Duncan: Better teachers trump smaller class sizes. *Tampa Bay Times*, Retrieved April 2, 2014, from <http://www.tampabay.com/blogs/gradebook/content/duncan-better-teachers-trump-smaller-class-sizes>.

Nye, B., Hedges, L. V., & Konstantopoulos, S. (1999). The long-term effects of small classes: A five-year follow-up of the Tennessee class size experiment. *Educational Evaluation and Policy Analysis*, *21*(2), 127−142.

Ripley, A. (2013). *The smartest kids in the world: And how they got that way*. New York: Simon and Schuster.

Schanzenbach, D. W. (2014). *Does class size matter?* Boulder, CO: National Education Policy Center.

Schleicher, A. (2012). *Use data to build better schools*. TED talk. Retrieved March, 25, 2013, from <http://www.ted.com/talks/andreas_schleicher_use_data_to_build_better_schools>.

MYTH 3

Larger Schools Are Better than Small Ones

For reasons of cost and efficiency, government authorities are inclined to think in terms of schools that are as large as possible. Support services can then be grouped, so that more resources are available for the core tasks. But we wish to focus on another aspect of this issue, namely the effect of school size on learning. Various studies have shown that such a thing as optimal school size may well exist. But what exactly is it? Unfortunately, a number of metastudies contradict each other on this point, and the subject is indeed not an easy one to research, since various factors are at play. Is a school smaller because it is more exclusive or is it larger because it has a good reputation? Moreover, if you look closely at the different studies you will see that the different authors have different ideas about what constitutes "good" education. Some look at the overall picture, while others confine themselves to mathematics results.

In summary, and taking all of the differing factors and opinions into account as far as possible, it seems reasonable to conclude that for secondary education it is best to aim for a size of 600–900 pupils for each autonomous unit. Primary schools with more than 800 pupils should be avoided if at all possible. In this context, it should be noted that some researchers — Hattie for instance — argue that the effect of school size is more important than class size (see the previous myth discussing class size).

But for us there is something much more important than the precise number of pupils in a school, and that is whether or not the school or autonomous unit is sufficiently large to allow well-functioning departmental working, which has a positive effect on the professionalization of the teaching staff. Yet at the same time it is important that the school should not be too large, so that neither the teachers nor the pupils become lost in anonymity. In large, anonymous schools people lose contact with each other, so that the left hand often doesn't know what the right hand is doing. This reduces willingness to accept responsibility.

It is also the case that, ideally, the more heterogeneous the pupil group and the lower their socioeconomic status, the smaller the school should be. Homogeneous pupil populations are better suited to deal with the problems and pressures of larger schools.

You may have noticed that we have deliberately used the terms "school" and "autonomous unit". It may be that particular courses need to be given within the framework of a larger organization, but it is important that the component units retain sufficient independent autonomy, so that they can avoid the problem of anonymity mentioned above.

> :-| The size of a school does have an effect on children's learning. A school must be large enough to allow professionalization, but small enough to encourage people to take responsibility.

REFERENCES

Cotton, K. (1996). *School size, school climate and student performance.* Portland, OR: North-West Regional Educational Laboratory.

Hattie, J. (2009). *Visible learning: A synthesis of over 800 meta-analyses relating to achievement.* London: Routledge.

Leithwood, K., & Jantzi, D. (2009). A review of empirical evidence about school size effects: A policy perspective. *Review of Educational Research, 79*(1), 464–490.

Slate, J. R., & Jones, C. H. (2005). *Effects of school size: A review of the literature with recommendations.* Essays in Education. Retrieved from <www.usca.edu/essays/vol132005/slate.pdf>.

MYTH 4

Separate Education for Boys and Girls Is More Effective than Mixed Education

Because it is increasingly claimed that boys and girls develop differently in biological terms and because it seems that we are "losing" boys from the education system, the question of whether separate schools may be the best way forward is once against coming into prominence.

Because that is what happens, isn't it? Boys move around more, and their noisy, fidgety behavior prevents the girls from learning properly. But is this true? We have already looked at gender differences in the section on Neuromyths. What effect, if any, do these differences have on learning?

In 2011 eight respected scientists published an article in *Science* on this very subject. Their conclusion was that no single reliable study has provided evidence to show that added value will result from providing separate education for boys and girls. They added that, in their opinion, the use of new neurological findings to argue in favor of single-sex education — something that is becoming a trend — is an example of pseudoscience at its worst. These insights confirm the results of an earlier metastudy by Alan Smithers and Pamela Robinson and are confirmed by a metastudy published by the American Psychological Association stating that single-sex education does not educate girls and boys any better than coeducational schools. This last piece of research analyzed 184 studies of more than 1.6 million students from around the world. A separate analysis of only US schools in this study delivered similar findings. In the same vein, the researchers also looked at studies that examined coeducational schools that offered single-sex instruction in certain subjects, and found no significant benefits for boys or girls in these cases.

Part of the problem is that it is very difficult to investigate whether boys and girls would benefit from being taught apart, a hurdle also mentioned in Pahlke and colleagues' metastudy. Schools that offer single-sex education often attract a very different public from mixed-sex/coeducational schools, so that comparison is difficult. In the 2014 metastudy, Pahlke et al. took the quality of research designs into account as they categorized studies as uncontrolled (no controls for selection effects, no random assignment) or controlled (random assignment or controls for selection effects). They found that uncontrolled studies showed some modest advantages for single-sex schooling, for both girls and boys, for outcomes such as mathematics performance but not for science performance. Controlled studies, however, showed only trivial differences between students. The researchers also noted a lack of studies on single-sex education among low-income students and ethnic minorities, particularly in the USA.

Kenneth Rowe carried out one of the better studies in this respect. He was given the opportunity to investigate boys and girls from the same school who had been randomly divided into single-sex and coeducational lessons for mathematics. He was unable to establish any cognitive differences, either for boys or for girls. The better pupils seemed to benefit from the mixed classes, irrespective of gender. Boys also seemed to have a personal preference for coeducational classes.

A more recent research study by Fryer and Levitt attempted to look further than the class level, by comparing the results of boys and girls in different countries. They concluded that mixed schools allow the girls to limit the extent to which they lag behind the boys in mathematics.

Finally, we would like to add a nuance of our own. During the discussion of this theme with developmental psychologists we were interested to note that they believe there are valid reasons for arguing in favor of single-sex classes. But this is something we will need to discuss elsewhere: this myth discusses about the effect of separate classes on learning!

Are We Losing Boys from the Education System?

There are some alarming statistics in the 2008 book by Peg Tyre. The writer notes that in that year that boys accounted for less than 43% of those enrolled in college in the USA, and the gap keeps on widening. This book is not the only one claiming we have a boy problem in education. The 2010 PISA report confirmed that this seems to be a general trend in many countries.

But, is this really a boy problem in the sense that all boys are in trouble? Not quite. First of all, it is a good thing, because it means that girls are doing better, as Sara Mead puts it.

If we look at the most recent PISA results, the OECD describes mixed results:

- Girls outperform boys in reading in all countries and economies by the equivalent of one year of school.
- In most countries and economies, girls underperform boys in mathematics; and among the highest achieving students, the gender gap in favor of boys is even wider.

- The gender gap in mathematics performance mirrors the gender gap in students' drive, motivation and self-beliefs.
- Boys and girls tend to benefit equally when they are perseverant and motivated to learn, and have confidence in their abilities to learn mathematics. Consequently, the performance of both boys and girls suffers at the same rate when they lack motivation to learn and confidence in their own abilities.

These results make clear that there are still a lot of boys performing very well, and girls still have work to do to match the highest achieving students.

Even more poignant is what Daniel and Susan Voyer found in a meta-analysis spanning 97 years (1914–2011) encompassing 502 effect sizes drawn from 369 samples from 30 countries, in which 538,710 boys and 595,332 girls in elementary and secondary school took part for mathematics, language, science and social sciences. Of interest here is that they studied scholastic achievement in school (school grades) rather than performance on standardized tests. They reasoned that academic achievement in school "reflect[s] learning in the larger social context of the classroom. School marks also require effort and persistence over long periods of time, whereas performance on standardized tests assesses basic or specialized academic abilities and aptitudes at one point in time without social influences".

They found a small but significant female advantage across the board. Noteworthy findings were that the female advantage was largest for language courses and smallest for mathematics courses. On top of this, the results "showed that the magnitude of the female advantage was not affected by year of publication, thereby contradicting claims of a recent 'boy crisis' in school achievement". They note that "research has shown girls tend to study in order to understand the materials [i.e., school achievement], whereas boys emphasize performance [i.e., on standardized tests], which indicates a focus on the final grades ... Mastery of the subject matter generally produces better marks than performance emphasis, so this could account in part for males' lower marks than females" [comments added].

Voyer and Voyer conclude that the fact that girls generally perform better than boys throughout mandatory schooling seems to be a "well-kept secret considering how little attention it has received as a global phenomenon". So much for the modern-day boy crisis!

How can we improve the situation to provide better education to the boys who need it? Well, the PISA insights already give us a clue. Numerous research studies have been devoted to this subject, but a Dutch report suggests that the best option is simply to concentrate on providing good education for both boys and girls, without taking too much account of gender differences. The researchers looked at schools (academic and vocational) where boys perform relatively well, to see whether these positive results could be attributed to a specific pedagogic and/or didactic approach. The investigated schools seem to opt for a pragmatic approach, in which gender differences in general do not receive specific attention. The recurring elements in the educational philosophy of these schools are: the importance of structure, rules and clarity; the creation of a safe pedagogic climate; adequate personal attention for individual pupils; and a good guidance and care structure for pupils.

Sources

Heemskerk, I., van Eck, E., Kuiper, E., & Volman, M. (2012). *Succesvolle onderwijsaanpak ken voor jongens in het voortgezet onderwijs*. Amsterdam: Kohnstamm Instituut (Rapport 878, Project No. 40534).

Mead, S. (2006). *The truth about boys and girls*. Washington, DC: Education Sector.

OECD (2014). Are boys and girls equally prepared for life? *PISA in Focus*, Retrieved April 26, 2014, from <http://www.oecd.org/pisa/pisaproducts/PIF-2014-gender-international-version.pdf>.

Tyre, P. (2008). *The trouble with boys: A surprising report card on our sons, their problems at school, and what parents and educators must do*. New York: Random House.

Voyer, D., & Voyer, S. D. (2014). Gender differences in scholastic achievement: A meta-analysis. *Psychological Bulletin, 140*(4), 1174−1204.

:-\ Should boys and girls be taught in mixed classes or not? The discussion seems likely to continue, but for the time being there is little to be said in favor of separate classes, as far as the learning effect is concerned.

REFERENCES

Fryer, R. G., & Levitt, S. D. (2010). An empirical analysis of the gender gap in mathematics. *American Economic Journal: Applied Economics, 2*(2), 210−240.

Halpern, D. F., Eliot, L., Bigler, R. S., Fabes, R. A., Hanish, L. D., Hyde, J., et al. (2011). The pseudoscience of single-sex schooling. *Science, 333*(6050), 1706−1707.

Marsh, H. W., & Rowe, K. J. (1996). The effects of single-sex and mixed-sex mathematics classes within a coeducational school: A reanalysis and comment. *Australian Journal of Education, 40*(2), 147−162.

Pahlke, E., Hyde, J. S., & Allison, C. M. (2014). The effects of single-sex compared with coeducational schooling on students' performance and attitudes: A meta-analysis. *Psychological Bulletin, 140*(4), 1042−1072.

Smithers, A., & Robinson, P. (2006). *The paradox of single-sex and co-educational schooling*. Buckingham: Carmichael Press.

MYTH 5

Boys Benefit if They Have Lessons from Men More Regularly

The proportion of female teachers in primary education in the USA was measured at 86.71% in 2011, according to the World Bank. In secondary education it was 61.15%. If we look at the 2013 statistics in Europe, the figures are not all that different. Based on a report by the European Commission in all European countries, women are the majority among primary teachers. Teaching at lower secondary is statistically still female: in approximately half of all European countries, there is a proportion of 70% and above of women teachers. However, female representation decreases markedly at upper secondary level. This is not necessarily the case in the rest of the world. A 2010 UNESCO report describes how globally, the proportion of female teachers of secondary education increased from 48% to 52% between 1990 and 2010. But this growth has been reported in all regions except for sub-Saharan Africa, where the proportion of female teachers has dropped slightly, to 30% (Fiske, 2012).

A Boys' Problem Doesn't Mean the Girls Are There Yet

UNESCO, in its *World atlas of gender equality in education*, warns that we are seeing good progress worldwide for girls, but we are not there yet:

> *Two-thirds of countries have achieved gender parity at the primary level, but access to secondary education remains a challenge for girls in many countries, especially in sub-Saharan Africa and South and West Asia. Those girls who do make the transition to secondary education are more likely than boys to stay in school and pursue their studies. As a result, there has been a significant rise in women's participation in tertiary education, especially in high-income countries where female students outnumber male students. However, these gains do not necessarily translate into better opportunities for women in terms of employment or income.*

One of the important solutions that UNESCO sees is enrolling more women in the profession of teacher.

Source
Fiske, E. B. (2012). *Atlas mundial de la igualdad de género en la educación / World atlas of gender equality in education*. Paris: UNESCO.

We have already seen that we are losing boys out of the education system. Many people are quick to make a connection between this and the proportion of female teachers. In reality, however, it is not quite as simple as that. Fear of the feminization of education is nothing new. Greetje Timmerman and Mineke van Essen showed that this discussion was already raging 150 years ago. Teaching in the USA had already become highly feminized in the late nineteenth century, although scholars disagree about how and why this happened.

Moreover, as with research into the value of separate-sex classes, investigations into the impact of the gender of teachers on pupil learning are far from straightforward. However, the limited number of studies that have been completed all point in the same direction. A 2002 VUB report for the Flemish Government summarized the situation as follows:

> We examined the influence of the gender context of the school on cognitive performance, namely the BIS (Barrett Impulsiveness Scale) behavior and performance in mathematics, and on the attitudes of the pupils. As far as cognitive performance is concerned, neither the gender of the teaching staff nor the gender of the school management had any significant influence. (Siongers, 2002)

It was also apparent that a predominantly female teaching staff had no negative effect on the cognitive performance of boys. This was similarly the case for performance in mathematics. And the same held true for girls: they did not perform better and their attitude towards the subject did not improve simply because they received mathematics lessons from a female teacher.

So, were differences of any kind recorded? Not in terms of cognitive performance, but the researchers did note that there was data evidence to suggest that boys who are given lessons primarily by women have a less traditional view of role models and generally experience a higher level of well-being at school. At the same time, boys in this position have a less strong work ethic, a more negative view of the future and lower self-esteem.

Even so, the consensus based on the majority of reports — many of them from the USA, since this phenomenon became more evident there much earlier than elsewhere — is that the "female peril" has little or no effect on the learning performance of boys at school. Timmermans and van Essen summarize it as follows: "The inventory of the research that has been carried out so far makes plain that there is almost no empirical evidence to support the contention that female teachers have a negative influence on the educational performance of boys".

Boys and ADHD

There has long been a suspicion among the public, seemingly confirmed by research at the Ruhr Universität Bochum and the University of Basel (Bruchmüller, Margraf, & Schneider, 2012), that attention-deficit/hyperactivity disorder (ADHD) has been overdiagnosed. In Germany alone, the number of diagnosed cases increased by 381% between 1989 and 2001. This does not necessarily mean that this trend is bad — perhaps in the past too few cases of ADHD were diagnosed — but it seems that something else is going on, and that boys are once again the victims.

The study showed that with children and adolescents, doctors and psychiatrists too often make their diagnosis on the basis of heuristics and imprecise "rules of thumb", rather than recognized diagnostic criteria. As a result, many wrong diagnoses are made, particularly in cases involving boys. Another striking fact is that male doctors are more inclined to make an ADHD diagnosis than female doctors, which is not perhaps what might be expected.

The findings were based on enquiries made with thousands of doctors and psychiatrists in Germany, 473 of whom eventually took part in the study. The respondents were asked to assess one of four selected cases. Only one of the cases contained the typical characteristics of ADHD; the other three did not. There were also two versions for each case study: a boy version and a girl version. One of the more striking conclusions was that the case with the name Leon (a boy) was more frequently diagnosed as ADHD than the same case with the name Lea (a girl).

The researchers conceded that remarkably little empirical research has been conducted into the diagnosis of ADHD, even though it is a "hot" issue. For the sake of clarity: this does not means that ADHD does not exist. But it does suggest that there may be something wrong with its diagnosis.

Source

Bruchmüller, K., Margraf, J., & Schneider, S. (2012). Is ADHD diagnosed in accord with diagnostic criteria? Overdiagnosis and influence of client gender on diagnosis. *Journal of Consulting and Clinical Psychology, 80*(1), 128−138.

:-\ There is almost no proof that boys do better or worse with male or female teachers.

REFERENCES

Boyle, E. (2004). The feminization of teaching in America. *Program in women's studies, 17* (12), 09.

Fiske, E. B. (2012). *Atlas mundial de la igualdad de género en la educación/World atlas of gender equality in education*. Paris: UNESCO.

Gamazo, A. (2013). EURYDICE (2013): Key data on teachers and school leaders in Europe. 2013 edition Eurydice report (Luxembourg Publications Office of the European Union). *Revista española de educación comparada, 22*, 235—236.

Marsh, H. W., Martin, A. J., & Cheng, J. S. (2008). A multilevel perspective on gender in classroom motivation and climate: Potential benefits of male teachers for boys? *Journal of Educational Psychology, 100*(1), 78—95.

Neugebauer, M., Helbig, M., & Landmann, A. (2011). Unmasking the myth of the same-sex teacher advantage. *European Sociological Review, 27*(5), 669—689.

Siongers, J. (2002). De gevolgen van de feminisering van het leerkrachtenberoep in het secundair onderwijs: Een empirische analyse *[The effects of the feminization of the teacher profession in secondary education: An empirical analysis]*. Brussels: Onderzoeksgroep TOR, Vakgroep Sociologie, VUB.

Timmerman, G., & van Essen, M. (2004). De mythe van het "vrouwengevaar". *Pedagogiek, 24*(1), 57—71.

World Bank (2014). Primary education, teachers (% female). Retrieved April 10, 2014, from <http://data.worldbank.org/indicator/SE.PRM.TCHR.FE.ZS>.

World Bank (2014). Secondary education, teachers (% female). Retrieved April 10, 2014, from <http://data.worldbank.org/indicator/SE.SEC.TCHR.FE.ZS>.

Grade Retention — Being Left Back — Has a Positive Effect on Learning

Pupils being left back — also known as resitting a school year — because their grades are not high enough at the end of the school year is a subject that often invites fierce debate, with fervent supporters and equally fervent opponents. Having said this, the scientific research into the matter is fairly clear: resitting a school year often does not help. Hattie concluded that in some cases it can even have a negative learning effect, resulting in too frequent changes of school and disturbing behavior in class, so that sometimes another resit is necessary.

And, indeed, much of the research does show that the learning of someone who is forced to redo a year actually declines instead of increasing. If there is something you don't understand the first time you hear it, why should it be assumed that you will understand it the second time? As early as 1989, C. T. Holmes wrote that was difficult to imagine anything in education with a more damaging effect on learning than grade retention (as it is known in the USA). The results of a metastudy by Allen and colleagues argue that retention has a negative impact on achievement. More specifically, the researchers claim that if you look at the quality of the research, studies with a low quality show a negative effect, while studies with an average to high quality show a positive effect of 0.04, in fact stating that there is no significant positive effect.

So why does that idea that resitting a year works remain so popular? The teachers involved often notice an initial improvement in pupils required to redo their previous school year, because they are effectively reprocessing the same material. But as soon as they are confronted with new material, this improvement disappears.

This was confirmed in a study carried out in Flanders by the Catholic University of Leuven. The study examined the cases of pupils who had been required to resit the first year of secondary education — the seventh grade in US terms. The researchers concluded that this scarcely had any positive effects at all on the further development of the pupils concerned. On the contrary, if they were compared with pupils who had comparable results but were not required to resit their year, it became apparent that the latter group performed better in both the short term and the long term for mathematics and technical reading.

It must be noted, however, that this does not mean that children who fail to acquire certain insights should automatically be allowed to progress to the next year. The National Association of School Psychologists (NASP) stated in 1998 that "both retention and social promotion are failed practices". Social promotion is promotion of students who do not meet the standards for achievement for their grade. NASP plead instead for early interventions and follow-up strategies. It is crucial that children are given the right specific guidance.

It is often a taboo subject, but accelerated grade progression (skipping a year) for the stronger pupils — usually at the elementary school level — does have a positive learning effect. By "accelerated" we mean allowing pupils, where appropriate, to progress a year ahead of schedule, for some or all of the course content. It is often suggested that such acceleration leads to emotional problems. Hattie has neatly reversed this question, asking whether it is better to risk the emotional problems that may arise if a child finds school boring or insufficiently challenging.

And what about the emotional problems of a child who is told that he has "failed" and is not capable of keeping up with other children in his age group?

Berliner and Glass conclude in their 2014 book that even though retention may work out well for some students, it doesn't work out well for the most of them. The sad thing is that we do not know how to identify those students for whom retention might work and, as Berliner and Glass add, under what conditions. Even sadder is that retention seem to hurt boys more than girls, and poor more than middle-class children.

> :-\ Redoing a year seems to help at first, but for most students in general it quickly has a negative effect. It should only be used in exceptional cases.

REFERENCES

Allen, C. S., Chen, Q., Willson, V. L., & Hughes, J. N. (2009). Quality of research design moderates effects of grade retention on achievement: A meta-analytic, multilevel analysis. *Educational Evaluation and Policy Analysis, 31*(4), 480–499.

Berliner, D. C., & Glass, G. V. (Eds.), (2014). *50 myths and lies that threaten America's public schools: The real crisis in education.* New York: Teachers College Press.

Goos, M., Van Damme, J., Onghena, P., & Petry, K. (2011). *First-grade retention: Effects on children's academic and psychosocial growth throughout primary education* (SSL-rapport nr. SSL/OD1/2011.33). Leuven: Steunpunt "Studieen Schoolloopbanen" (SSL).

Holmes, C. T. (1989). Grade level retention effects: A meta-analysis of research studies. In L. A. Shepard, & M. L. Smith (Eds.), *Flunking grades: Research and policies on retention* (pp. 16—33). London: Falmer Press.

Jimerson, S. R. (2001). Meta-analysis of grade retention research: Implications for practice in the 21st century. *School Psychology Review, 30*, 420—437.

National Association of School Psychologists (1998). *Position statement: Student retention and social promotion.* Silver Spring, MD: Author.

National Association of School Psychologists (2011). Grade retention and social promotion *(Position Statement)* Bethesda, MD: Author.

Picklo, D. M., & Christenson, S. L. (2005). Alternatives to retention and social promotion. The availability of instructional options. *Remedial and Special Education, 26*, 258—268.

Steenbergen-Hu, S., & Moon, S. M. (2011). The effects of acceleration on high-ability learners: A meta-analysis. *Gifted Child Quarterly, 55*(1), 39—53.

MYTH 7

More Money Means Better Education

Cooking costs money. But if you have more money, does this mean that you can cook any better? Yes and no. You can certainly buy more expensive ingredients, but this is no guarantee that your meal will be a success. You can also buy better kitchen tools and equipment, but this too doesn't guarantee a tastier meal. The quality of the dishes (proof of the pudding) is in the eating and will be almost completely determined by the quality of the cook. It is much the same with education. An analysis of the PISA data shows that it is not always the countries that spend most on education that achieve the best results. A 2014 report showed that there has been essentially no correlation between what states have spent on education and their measured academic outcomes. But bearing in mind our earlier comments about comparative pedagogy, this may be because different countries have different needs.

The OECD concluded, based on the PISA data, that greater national wealth or higher expenditure on education does not guarantee better student performance. Among high-income economies, the amount spent on education is less important than how those resources are used. A report by the Dutch Social and Cultural Planning Bureau showed that educational expenditure has risen dramatically in The Netherlands, but that the same cannot be said for the academic return achieved by Dutch pupils. Benedict Clements concluded that about 25% of education spending in the European Union is wasteful relative to the "best practices" observed by the OECD.

Of course, it is important to know what is meant by "academic return". Does it mean cognitive results or does it mean pupil well-being? It could be either or it could be both, depending on the circumstances. The correlation "more money equals better education" is by no means a clear one, and there is a need for further research at the macro level, the level of education policy. It may sound like stating the obvious, but it is important to know that we are investing in the right things, the best things. Spending more money in education can have a great positive impact when used wisely (e.g., when targeted at those students who come to school with the fewest resources).

If we look at some of the myths we have already discussed, the relatively expensive grade retention might be regarded as a bad investment.

Equally, it is not clear whether large schools — with their extensive middle-management structure — are a cost-effective option. At the other end of the spectrum, smaller classes may be a good investment, since the Swedish study referred when discussing class size suggests that this option more than pays for itself over the long term, in the sense that better educated pupils earn more money and therefore pay more taxes. Of course, this is assuming that we can find enough teachers for small classes, and also persuade the politicians to wait 20 years before reaping the rewards of their policy ... .

:-| More money can deliver better education, but it is not the amount of money that counts, it's what you do with it! Money alone cannot buy a good education system. It is essential to believe — and to act on the belief — that all children can succeed in school.

REFERENCES

Berliner, D. C., & Glass, G. V. (Eds.), (2014). *50 myths and lies that threaten America's public schools: The real crisis in education*. New York: Teachers College Press.

Clements, B. (2002). How efficient is education spending in Europe? *European Review of Economics and Finance*, *1*(1), 3−26.

Coulson, A. J. (2014). State education trends, academic performance and spending over the past 40 years. *Policy Analysis*, No. 746.

Darling-Hammond, L. (2010). *The flat world and education: How America's commitment to equity will determine our future*. New York: Teachers College Press.

Fredriksson, P., Öckert, B., & Oosterbeek, H. (2013). Long-term effects of class size. *Quarterly Journal of Economics*, *128*(1), 249−285.

Gupta, S., Verhoeven, M., & Tiongson, E. (1999). Does higher government spending buy better results in education and health care? *International Monetary Fund*, Retrieved from <http://www.imf.org/external/pubs/ft/wp/1999/wp9921.pdf>.

Kuhry, B., & De Kam, F. (2012, January). Waar voor ons belastinggeld? [Value for our taxes?] Sociaal en Cultureel Planbureau. Retrieved July 8, 2012, from <http://www.scp.nl/dsresource?objectid=29580&type=org>.

Organisation for Economic Co-operation and Development. (2012). Does money buy strong performance in PISA? Retrieved January 13, 2011, from <http://www.oecd.org/pisa/pisaproducts/pisainfocus/49685503.pdf>.

Psacharopoulos, G., & Patrinos, H. A. (2004). Returns to investment in education: A further update. *Education Economics*, *12*(2), 111−134.

MYTH 8

Education Never Changes

We no longer ride in a horse and cart, and our cars are already hybrids, soon to be powered by hydrogen or with fully electric motors. We have also progressed from carrier pigeons, to the telegraph, the telephone and digital Internet applications. But school? School is much the same as it was decades ago. Sounds familiar, doesn't it? But is it true?

In one sense it seems to be, at least if you look at the chart in Figure 12, based on work by Larry Cuban, which depicts decades in education. He argues that education is more a question of continuity than of revolution. At the macro level — in other words, the level of regional and national education policy — there are often new and innovative ideas. These filter down to the meso level (i.e., school directors, boards of education, etc.), who try to apply the new theories in practice, but at the micro level — in the classroom — things change very slowly. This slowness is sometimes called the inertia of education.

The chart also makes clear how difficult it is to launch a revolution in the world of education and shows just how hard the job of a head teacher can be.

And before everyone gets irritated: yes, we know that there are plenty of committed teachers who want to move ahead and are keen to initiate real change in the classroom. But we are talking about the big picture, over a much longer period. Viewed in that context, things are not moving all that quickly. We are not saying that this is a good thing or a bad thing; it is simply a neutral observation of the facts as we see them.

Therefore, it should not necessarily be regarded in a pessimistic light; it is simply the statement of a historic pedagogic concept. As such, it is capable of misinterpretation, implying that things in education hardly ever change. In some ways that that is indeed the case, although it actually works very differently from the way you might think. Depaepe, Simon, and van Gorp described how this leads to the paradox of educational

Macro										
Meso										
Micro										

Figure 12 *Decades in education.* Created by Pedro De Bruyckere, based on Cuban, L. (1993). How teachers taught: Constancy and change in American classrooms, 1890–1990. *New York: Teachers College Press.*

renewal: "The many innovations do not change the school. Instead, the school changes the innovations to suit its own needs. It transforms them into its own grammar, its own formal rules for class and school continuity".

In other words, the many innovations do filter down through the educational system, where they are adapted into the practices and procedures that people are used to.

So, is it a myth that education never changes? It depends on the way you look at it. Major revolutions? No, not really. We know of only two real revolutions in education up until now. The first came with the invention of the printing press with movable type (Gutenberg, somewhere between 1440 and 1450). This invention made books less expensive and this meant that the *lector* (lecturer) was not the only one who could afford them. Therefore, teaching was no longer fully dependent on either an oratory by the teacher or a dialog between the student and the teacher (Plato). Now students and learners could also possess books. The second came with the implementation of the slate chalkboard or blackboard (in the first half of the eighteenth century in Europe and 1801 in the USA; 300−350 years after the first revolution), enabling the teacher to present his or her own writing (i.e., notes, demonstrations, etc.) to larger groups of learners. PowerPoint® and even learning management systems are often nothing more than extensions of this principle.

But the lowest level of the Cuban diagram is not an unchanging constant, more a gradual process of change. The insights of experience-oriented education, the use of video, new forms of evaluation, group work: these are all already in use in different forms in our classrooms, so that they may seem old-fashioned, but are much less so than you may imagine. It is difficult to measure this theory quantitatively, but it is based, among other things, on ethnographic research into classroom practice. And if it shows anything, it shows just how hard it is to impose change from above.

:-| Education changes, but slowly!

REFERENCES

Brown, M. (2012). Traditional versus progressive education. In P. Adey, & J. Dillon (Eds.), *Bad education* (pp. 95−110). Maidenhead, UK: Open University Press.
Cuban, L. (1993). *How teachers taught: Constancy and change in American classrooms* New York: Teachers College Press 1890−1990.

Depaepe, M., Simon, F., & van Gorp, A. (2005). Paradoxen van pedagogisering: Handboek pedagogische historiografie *[Paradoxes of pedagogies: Handbook of pedagogical historiography]*. Leuven: Acco.

Masschelein, J., & Simons, M. (2012). *Apologie van de school*. Een publieke zaak *[A school's apology: A public issue]*. Leuven: Acco.

Tyack, D., & Tobin, W. (1994). The "grammar" of schooling: Why has it been so hard to change? *American Educational Research Journal, 31*(3), 453.

CHAPTER 6

Myth Persistence and Myth Busting

Contents

WHY ARE THESE MYTHS SO PERSISTENT?

Having discussed all of these myths, and having shown a great deal of good empirical proof that was and is out there for everyone to see, the question is: Why do these myths persist?

One reason that these and other myths are so persistent relates to the general function of myths in culture and society. Bronisław Kasper Malinowski, one of the twentieth century's premier anthropologists, stated it as follows: "... Myth fulfills in primitive culture an indispensable function: it expresses, enhances, and codifies belief; it safeguards and enforces morality: it vouches for the efficiency of ritual and contain practical rules for the guidance of man. Myth is thus a vital ingredient of human civilization ...".

Also, this persistence of myths (urban legends, folk wisdom, and the like) is a function of information availability. Keith Botelho, writing about *Renaissance earwitnesses*, noted a link between *historia* and *storia* (history and story/rumor), attributing it to the fact that since the introduction of printing with movable type, alternative interpretations of what was going on in society were printed rapidly and widely distributed. He posits that the rise of print culture, combined with increased literacy in Renaissance England, increased our vulnerability to rumor and gossip, concluding that "perhaps this pastiche of voices — an historical and theatrical babel — becomes a more accurate representation of truth than any one particular

© 2015 Elsevier Inc.
All rights reserved.

account". In the book's preface, "Listening in an age of truthnapping", he likens this to our present information society where an overabundance of instant and pervasive information outlets "assault our eyes and ears with spin, which 'aligns more with entertainment than news', and whose success depends upon the audience's failure to engage the content with discerning eyes and ears". And because social media foster tight-knit extensive networks of similar-thinking people, these rumors often circulate widely within certain groups, thus strengthening them through repetition and enhancement before they even meet truth.

This is compounded by what Farhad Manjoo writes about in *True enough: Learning to live in a post-fact society*. Not only can any self-styled expert publish anything he or she wants to, the "experts come at us from all directions, in every medium, through every niche … We consult experts specifically to learn something about which we are ignorant. The transaction is inherently treacherous because ignorance puts us at a disadvantage, too. How can we know whether the 'experts' who dominate the public discourse really are expert?" According to Manjoo, the "real danger of living in the age of Photoshop isn't the proliferation of fake photos. Rather, it's that true photos will be ignored as phonies". In other words, when every picture, every account, every expert, every … is questionable, then all pictures, all accounts, all experts, all … can be dismissed and their "unique power to criticize will decline".

And what about the following research-based reasons?

- *Falsification strengthens a myth*: Norbert Schwarz (Provost Professor at the University of Southern California) and other psychologists have repeatedly shown that denials and clarifications of widely held but incorrect beliefs paradoxically contribute to the resiliency of those beliefs. This means that when we try to refute or repudiate a myth, we may actually be strengthening it by making it more popular.

- *Repetition strengthens a myth*: Kimberlee Weaver (a researcher at Virginia Tech), studying how a "repetitive voice can sound like a chorus", found that when we repeatedly hear the same information, we believe it to be true. Why? Because as we all learned in our Pedagogy 101 course, repetition causes the brain to remember something more effectively (the old adage common to presenters and teachers: I'll tell you what I will present, I present, and then I tell you what I presented). Unfortunately, with respect to myths and urban legends, the human brain is tricked into assuming that the memorized fact is true. Also, hearing something repeatedly deceives the brain into thinking it has heard the information from many different sources (i.e., the repetitive single voice becomes a chorus of voices).

- *We are victims of false and selective memory*: As we saw when discussing the myth about our memory recording exactly what we experience, our memory is very susceptible to misinterpretation and alteration, especially if we receive other — even misleading — information after first experiencing something. Also, when we are given the facts about a myth (see above) we tend to create false memories and believe that the myths are actually the facts.

- *Cultural factors strengthen myths*: A culture is a group of people sharing the same or similar beliefs, values, customs and practices, and this sharing, in turn, further influences the members of that group. If we all do something in a certain way, then we usually see it as being the way to do it and we do not question it, because "that's the way it is done". According to Bo Bennett, who has made it a sport to collect logical fallacies (see his website *Logically fallacious*: http://www.logicallyfallacious.com/), "Using the popularity of a premise or proposition as evidence for its truthfulness . . . is a fallacy which is very difficult to spot because our 'common sense' tells us that if something is popular, it must be good/true/valid".

MORAL PANIC AND EDUCATIONAL MYTHS

In a review of the literature on digital natives, Bennett, Maton, and Kervin wrote that we were experiencing an academic form of *moral panic*. According to Cohen, moral panic occurs when a "condition, episode, person or group of persons emerges to become defined as a threat to societal values and interests" (p. 9). Examples of such moral panics are on the one hand historically harmless ones, such as the "mods and rockers conflict" (Cohen coined the term in 1973 when he examined media coverage of the 1960s' riots in Brighton and other seaside resorts in the UK) or the Dungeons and Dragons panic that allegedly promoted Satanism, witchcraft, suicide, pornography and murder, but on the other hand historically significant ones such as McCarthyism and the Red Scare, which ruined the lives of countless people in the early 1950s, and Adolf Hitler's moral panic that "the Jew will destroy civilization by poisoning us all" if "we do not take steps to preserve the purity of blood".

Bennett et al. describe why such legends catch on so easily and why they are so persistent and hard to eradicate. In essence:

Arguments are often couched in dramatic language, proclaim a profound change in the world, and pronounce stark generational differences ... Such claims coupled with appeals to common sense and recognizable anecdotes are used to declare an emergency situation, and call for urgent and fundamental change ... Another feature of this "academic moral panic" is its structure as a series of strongly bounded divides: between a new generation and all previous generations; between the technically adept and those who are not; and between learners and teachers ... Thus, the language of moral panic and the divides established by commentators serve to close down debate, and in doing so allow unevidenced claims to proliferate.

On the persistence of moral panic, McRobbie and Thornton concluded that (1) the object of the panic (here, the problems with education) receives a lot of free publicity because the assumed and stated negative associations seem to make it newsworthy, and (2) rather than alienating everyone, it actually has the opposite effect, making it attractive to those who either propagate or support the myths to see themselves as alternative and avant-garde. Andrew Noymer, studying the transmission and persistence of urban legends (and whose paper received the 2002 Best Paper Prize from the Mathematical Sociology Section of the American Sociology Association), confirmed what he called a nonlinear model of urban legends, in which

... the most rapid path to endemicity (persistence) occurs when skeptics play an active role in trying to suppress a rumor, a process I label "autocatalysis". This is counterintuitive, since autocatalysis of skepticism should suppress rumors ... When skeptics try to stop a rumor from spreading further, the nature of the dynamics changes from epidemic cycles to endemic transmission; skeptics' actions are at cross-purposes to their intentions. (Noymer, 2001)

In other words, as Anderson and Kellam, in their study of belief perseverance, put it: The beliefs that a person hold persist in the face of data that disproves or even contradicts those beliefs. With this in mind, this book may achieve the opposite of its intention!

WHAT CAN WE DO ABOUT THIS?

The problem facing those who are trying to eradicate these myths is that what we are dealing with here is actually a very attractive, popular and persistent *pseudoscience*. This pseudoscience and its propagation and implementation jeopardize both the quality of our education/educational system and the credibility of the educational sciences as a legitimate science. With respect to the latter, it is not uncommon for people to ask, "What has educational science actually added to making education better?" and "If those educational scientists can't agree with each other, why should we even listen to them?" Even worse, there is a large risk that we are entering into a dangerous downward spiral: The popularity of all of these myths and urban legends paints educational science (and with it the learning sciences as a whole) as a mumbo–jumbo, voodoo science. This has the effect that it becomes increasingly difficult to implement valuable ideas and innovations from the field of educational research into educational practice. The big question is, thus: How can we avoid this downward spiral?

In our view, there is only one answer to this question: The educational sciences must be driven by theories and theory development, not by simple observations and conclusions drawn from them. They must be based on *strong empirical data* gained from experiments set up according to *good research methodologies* (i.e., randomized controlled trials, real control conditions that can be compared to implemented interventions, with respondent populations/samples that are large and representative enough to justify implementation decisions, effect sizes instead of simple significance measurement, and so on) rather than legends, hypes and methodologically unsound research (e.g., Homo zappiens, Web 2.0, brain-based teaching). And then these *evidence-informed* (note that the term evidence-based is not used here: the evidence should inform our choices and decisions) methods need to be slowly but surely tested in ecologically valid, real-life settings where there is a degree of control of extraneous factors and where the constraints on the chosen method are dealt with. Only after that can we think about large-scale implementation.

Evidence-Based: What Is That?

A few words about evidence-based interventions in education. The concept of "evidence-based" comes from the pharmaceutical industry and medical practice. Apart from the question of whether this is ethically permissible in education (i.e., is it ethical to give a child in school a placebo for learning?), let's look at what an evidence-based approach in the pharmaceutical world actually costs. In 2006:

- It cost $359 million per new medicine that was eventually brought to market.

- Five out of every 5000 (0.1%) "aspiring" medicines that are preclinically tested proceed to phase II testing and are tested on people (999 out of every 1000 possibly good ideas are thrown aside before ever reaching this phase).
- Only one of these five is approved (thus only 0.02% of all possible new drugs ever reach the market).
- In 2005, pharmaceutical companies in the USA spent more than $38 billion on research (*New York Times*, January 11, 2006).
- Research and development (R&D) takes up approximately 25% of a company's budget.

Now compare this to how we study new "drugs" for education.

Research should not simply try to find out "what works"; something that one of the authors refers to as Nike® *Just do it* research, but should be aimed at explaining why particular methods help and why others do not help us to reach particular goals in particular types of education under particular conditions. There are no silver bullets, magic potions, one-size-fits-all methods or simple answers in education, or for that matter in any other complex human system, which will work in achieving all goals for all people and under all conditions. The complexity of learning, teaching and education needs to be reflected in its research and theories. The construction of such theories is a long-term endeavor, based on programmed research and the work of many collaborating researchers and practitioners, using a broad variety of research methods ranging from qualitative, explorative studies to large-scale, randomized controlled trials. The step from legend-based education based on pseudoscience to evidence-based education based on science demands a quantum leap. Rather than a quick change in research methodologies or objects of study, it requires a fundamental change in scientific attitude, as Kirschner and van Merriënboer stated.

The Debunking Handbook

According to John Cook and Stephan Lewandowsky, in their pamphlet *The debunking handbook*:

> *Debunking myths is problematic. Unless great care is taken, any effort to debunk misinformation can inadvertently reinforce the very myths one seeks to correct. To avoid these "backfire effects", an effective debunking requires three major elements. First, the refutation must focus on core facts rather than the myth to avoid the misinformation becoming more familiar. Second, any mention of a myth should be preceded by explicit warnings to notify the reader that the upcoming information is*

false. Finally, the refutation should include an alternative explanation that accounts for important qualities in the original misinformation. (p. 1)

Source

Cook, J., & Lewandowsky, S. (2011). *The debunking handbook*. St. Lucia, Australia: University of Queensland <http://www.skepticalscience.com/docs/Debunking _Handbook.pdf>.

HOW CAN I AVOID BELIEVING MYTHS OR PASSING THEM ON TO OTHERS?

It is not always easy to separate fact from opinion, and we are the first to admit that in the past we have been taken in by a number of these fantasy claims. But it is possible to make sure that you are not fooled? Paul Thomas has put together a list of tips that can help you to scan the credibility of the information contained in educational blogs and research findings. We have adjusted these slightly to suit the circumstances of our educational environment.

- *Is there talk of a correlation or a causal connection?* This is an error that occurs time after time. A correlation describes a connection, but the blog or report talks about a causal link. It is not because more ice-cream is sold in the summer that ice-cream leads to more sunburnt shoulders, even though more people do indeed both eat ice-cream and burn their shoulders during the summer (and we assume that all drug addicts drank milk when they were children!).

- *Is the author objective?* Does the writer indicate from what perspective he or she is writing? If the author continues to stress his or her own objectivity, be skeptical. Related to this is the question of whether the author has something to gain, for example the promotion of a book or a teaching or training method.

- *Who is the blog or report actually discussing?* This is another common error. If a certain school has a successful approach, it is immediately asked why all other schools do not adopt this same approach. This far too easily overlooks the fact that education is complex, with many contextual factors that can have an influence. What is the socio-economic status of the pupils? Is the group homogeneous or heterogeneous? Think back to what we wrote about the advisability of comparing countries. It is true that some claims have been examined over a variety of different contexts, but metastudies of this kind seldom make their way into the most popular sources.

- *Is the author honest in describing the opinions of others?* Thomas writes that the education debate in the USA is often polarized. If you dare to oppose the reformers, then you are automatically against innovation in education (even a Luddite). This is a phenomenon that is also becoming more common in other parts of the world. We must confess that during the writing of this book we were also afraid that people would try to categorize us in this or that "camp" (e.g., reformers versus conservatives). In this respect, we are followers of Groucho Marx, who once said that he did not want to belong to any club that would have him as a member!

- *Does the author give evidence, cite research and make connections?* Are there plenty of references and acknowledgements? Does the research, blog or newspaper article make it possible to follow and test all the different steps in the reasoning?

Ritchie, Chudler, and Della suggest the use of the following checklist to assess the validity of a claim. It is not necessary for the claim to comply with all these tests, but the more you can tick off, the more reliable the claim is likely to be.

- *Does the evidence come from a reputable scientific study?* An anecdote is not scientific proof, no matter how interesting it might be, and the plural of anecdote does not constitute data.

- *Is the research published in a peer-reviewed publication?* Peer review, which involves other experts in the field anonymously checking the research before publication, is far from perfect, but it is still the best way to check the quality of the content.

- *Is the test group large enough?* The test group must be representative of the population under consideration; in other words, large enough and randomly chosen.

- *Was a control group used?* This is important, in order to check whether differences may occur naturally rather than as a result of the causes (i.e. an intervention) being specifically investigated. If you only use a test group, you can never be 100% certain on this point.

- *Is it a blind or double-blind experiment?* It is better if neither the research assistants nor the test subjects know whether they are part of the test group or the control group. This helps to limit the placebo effect, the tendency of any medication or treatment, even an inert or ineffective one, to exhibit results simply because the recipient believes that it will work.

- *Was a correct method of statistical analysis used?* Many modern researchers have been shown to use advanced statistical techniques to "massage" causal recommendations from correlational data.
- *Is the effect statistically significant?* John Hattie sees an effect size of 0.4 as being of educational merit. His reasoning — which we paraphrase here — is that maturation (that is, just getting a year older in elementary school) has an effect size of 0.4. Implementing an educational approach that has an effect less than maturation is questionable.
- *Is the experiment based on a widely known theory?* If the research contradicts a generally accepted theory, be skeptical.
- *Is there a conflict of interest?* What do the authors get out of their research? Who is financing the project if the results are positive?
- *Can the experiment be repeated or has it been repeated?* Will different researchers obtain the same results if they repeat the experiment?

INTO THE FUTURE: WHAT ABOUT THE MYTHS TO COME?

As Niels Bohr once said: "It's tough to make predictions, especially about the future". We never dreamed during our academic studies in three different countries that most of these myths would exist, but they now permeate our educational system. How on earth can we predict myths to come? But don't despair! By the time we have eradicated all of the previous myths, new ones will have shot up out of the ground like mushrooms in a forest!

The only thing we can do is try to follow the four steps that Daniel Willingham gives us when confronted with a new claim from a new guru:

1. Strip it and flip it.
2. Trace it.
3. Analyze it.
4. Decide whether to adopt it.

And, all too often: if it sounds too good to be true, it probably isn't.

REFERENCES

Anderson, C. A., & Kellam, K. L. (1992). Belief perseverance, biased assimilation, and covariation detection: The effects of hypothetical social theories and new data. *Personality and Social Psychology Bulletin, 18*, 555—565.

Bennett, B. (2012). *Logically fallacious: The ultimate collection of over 300 logical fallacies (Academic Edition)*. Sudbury, MA: eBookIt.com.

Bennett, S., Maton, K., & Kervin, L. (2008). The "digital natives" debate: A critical review of the evidence. *British Journal of Educational Technology, 39*, 775–786.

Botelho, K. M. (2009). *Renaissance earwitnesses: Rumor and early modern masculinity.* New York: Palgrave Macmillan.

Chatterji, M. (2005). Evidence on "what works": An argument for extended-term mixed-method (ETMM) evaluation designs. *Educational Researcher, 34*(5), 14–24.

Cohen, S. (1973). *Folk devils and moral panics.* St Albans, UK: Paladin.

Cook, J., & Lewandowsky, S. (2011). *The debunking handbook.* St. Lucia, Australia: University of Queensland . November 5. <http://www.skepticalscience.com/docs/Debunking_Handbook.pdf>.

Hattie, J. (2009). *Visible learning: A synthesis of over 800 meta-analyses relating to achievement.* New York: Routledge.

Kirschner, P. A., & van Merriënboer, J. J. G. (2013). Do learners really know best? Urban legends in education. *Educational Psychologist, 48*(3), 1–15.

Lipsey, M. W., & Wilson, D. B. (1993). The efficacy of psychological, educational and behavioral treatment: Confirmation from meta-analysis. *American Psychologist, 48*, 1181–1209.

Malinowski, B. K. (1954). *Magic, science, and religion and other essays.* Garden City, NY: Doubleday Anchor Books.

Manjoo, F. (2008). *True enough: Learning to live in a post-fact society.* Hoboken, NJ: John Wiley & Sons.

McRobbie, A., & Thornton, S. L. (1995). Rethinking "moral panic" for multi-mediated social worlds. *British Journal of Sociology, 46*, 559–574.

Norman, G. (2003). The effectiveness and the effects of effect sizes. *Advances in Health Sciences Education, 8*, 183–187.

Noymer, A. (2001). The transmission and persistence of "urban legends": Sociological application of age-structured epidemic models. *Journal of Mathematical Sociology, 25*, 299–323.

Olsen, D. R. (2004). The triumph of hope over experience in the search for "what works": A response to Slavin. *Educational Researcher, 33*(1), 24–26.

Organisation for Economic Co-operation and Development (2001). *Measuring expenditure on health-related R&D.* Paris: OECD. Available at <http://browse.oecdbookshop.org/oecd/pdfs/free/9201061e.pdf>.

Reinhart, A. L., Haring, S. H., Levin, J. R., Patall, E. A., & Robinson, D. H. (2013). Models of not-so-good behavior: Yet another way to squeeze causality and recommendations for practice out of correlational data. *Journal of Educational Psychology, 105*, 241.

Ritchie, S. J., Chudler, E. H., & Della, S. D. (2012). Don't try this at school: The attraction of "alternative" educational techniques. In S. Della Sala, & M. Anderson (Eds.), *Neuroscience in education* (pp. 222–229). Oxford: Oxford University Press.

Thomas, P. (2011, September 18). Questions to ask when reading research and blogs on school reform and classroom practice. Retrieved from <http://larrycuban.wordpress.com/2011/09/18/questions-to-ask-when-reading-research-and-blogs-paul-thomas/>

Weaver, K., Garcia, S. M., Schwarz, N., & Miller, D. T. (2007). Inferring the popularity of an opinion from its familiarity: A repetitive voice sounds like a chorus. *Journal of Personality and Social Psychology, 92*, 821–833.

Willingham, D. T. (2012). *When can you trust the experts? How to tell good science from bad in education.* San Francisco, CA: Jossey-Bass.

INDEX

Note: page numbers followed by "*b*" and "*f*" refer to boxes and figures, respectively.